The Forgotten Blessing

SWINDOLL
LEADERSHIP
LIBRARY

The Forgotten Blessing

Rediscovering the Transforming Power of Sanctification

HENRY HOLLOMAN

CHARLES R. SWINDOLL, GENERAL EDITOR

ROY B. ZUCK, MANAGING EDITOR

WORD PUBLISHING

NASHVILLE

A Thomas Nelson Company

THE FORGOTTEN BLESSING
Henry Holloman
Swindoll Leadership Library

Published in association with Dallas Theological Seminary (DTS):

General Editor: Charles Swindoll
Managing Editor: Roy B. Zuck

The theological opinions expressed by the author are not necessarily the official
position of Dallas Theological Seminary.

Library of Congress Cataloging-in-Publication Data

Holloman, Henry.
The forgotten blessing : rediscovering the doctrine of sanctification / by Henry
Holloman.
p. cm.—(Swindoll leadership library)
Includes index.

ISBN 0-8499-1375-6

1. Sanctification.   I. Title.   II. Series

BT765.H56   1999   98-26780
234'.8—dc21   CIP

Printed in the United States of America
99 00 01 02 03 04 05 06 BVG 9 8 7 6 5 4 3 2 1

To Shirley,

my beloved wife and

faithful servant of Christ

CONTENTS

List of Tables

# FOREWORD

MY SON'S LITTLE LEAGUE baseball coach used to say, "If you hit a home run, make sure you touch all the bases on your way around or you'll be out!" Well, not only has Dr. Henry Holloman hit a home run, but he's touched all the bases in this book on sanctification.

Most of you who read these lines know as well as I do how difficult that is when writing on the subject of how God grows mature Christians. The biblical teaching of sanctification is not a simple three-step formula; it's a process that takes place in the life of the believer. Neither is it a once-for-all matter occurring quickly; it transpires over a long period of time, superintended by the Holy Spirit.

Using the Scriptures as his authority, Holloman sets out to define sanctification biblically and then applies his definition to practical living. Three values set his work apart from most discussions on this important topic.

First, it is *biblical*. You don't have to read very far before you begin to appreciate Holloman's skill in mining the original intent of the biblical writers and dealing with difficult scriptural passages. Yet his exegesis is uncomplicated enough not to intimidate or overpower the casual reader. In a day when most of what we read on this subject comes across as cursory and popular at best, I find it refreshing to taste the fruits of a diligent man who has done the spade work of "rightly dividing the word of truth." You too will be nourished by his well-prepared servings of truth, baked slowly in the oven of thought.

Second, it is *theological.* Carefully, Holloman takes his findings and crafts them into theological principles that will stand the test of time. There are few things worse, in my mind, than theology void of a relationship with God. Logic alone leaves pastors and lay leaders frustrated and ineffective in their efforts to effect life changes. Holloman maintains the right balance between human understanding and the wisdom of God.

Third, it is *practical.* At last, someone deals practically with such phrases as being "in Christ" and "alive in the Spirit," which, quite frankly, have concerned pastors, teachers, and lay leaders for years. Not until the more recent emphases on small-group ministry and community life have these biblical issues become critical. This book helps us understand the mutually important roles of the Spirit, the Word, and the community of believers in the sanctification process. In addition to that, the book tells how God uses the life of prayer to move believers in a positive direction toward attainable holiness.

Perhaps what I appreciate most about the author's pursuit of this subject is that he writes with compelling passion and conviction. He believes in the power of the Holy Spirit. He believes the Scriptures are "living and active and able." He's convinced that our battles for holiness are not against "flesh and blood but against powers and principalities" which we cannot see. And he concludes correctly that as believers in all these things "we overwhelmingly conquer through Him who loved us." Such refreshing truths!

I heartily recommend this insightful book to anyone—pastor and lay leader alike—who longs to become holy as God is holy. It is my opinion that those who read this volume will join me in applauding this fine scholar who hit a home run. Furthermore we will be grateful that, in touching all the bases, he helped us win, since we are all on the same team.

—CHARLES R. SWINDOLL
General Editor

 ACKNOWLEDGMENTS

WHEN I BECAME A CHRISTIAN over forty years ago, the doctrine of Christian growth, or sanctification, became a major focus of my biblical studies. My training at Dallas Theological Seminary intensified my interest in the spiritual life. I often hoped for the opportunity to share with others the written results of studying and teaching the doctrine of sanctification. God began to fulfill my hope when Dr. Charles R. Swindoll asked me to produce a volume on sanctification for the Swindoll Leadership Library. However, writing this book was not a solo task. Many people helped in many ways to develop my manuscript into publishable form.

Family members and others faithfully prayed that I would have spiritual insight and strength from the Lord during the writing process. I am thankful that through their prayers God ministered to my needs and enabled me to complete this volume.

I am especially grateful to Shirley, my devoted wife and cheerleader. Her constant support and encouragement helped make my "book project" a positive experience.

I wish to thank Mrs. Joan Anderson for cheerfully

performing numerous tasks connected with writing this book in addition to her usual secretarial duties. Thanks also to Miss Joy Mosbarger, who skillfully edited some early drafts of my manuscript.

To all the people officially connected with the production of this book, I express deep appreciation. Dr. Roy B. Zuck, Senior Professor Emeritus of Bible Exposition at Dallas Theological Seminary and managing editor of the series, provided corrections, suggestions, and overall guidance with unusual patience and insight throughout the writing process. Dr. Charles Swindoll, president of Dallas Theological Seminary and general editor of the Swindoll Leadership Library, reviewed my manuscript and wrote the gracious foreword. The editors and staff members of Word Publishing prepared the manuscript for publication with fine technical and creative skill.

I am grateful to the administration, faculty, staff, and students of Talbot School of Theology, a graduate school of Biola University, La Mirada, California, where I am privileged to serve as professor of systematic theology. They provide a helpful context to study, learn, and practice "spiritual formation" or sanctification. Dr. Dennis Dirks and Dr. Michael Wilkins, Talbot's two deans, gave me a reduced teaching load during the spring and fall semesters of 1997 so that I could devote extra time to research and writing. Funding came through a grant from Biola University's Research and Development Committee.

Above all, I thank the Lord Jesus Christ, "who became to us wisdom from God, and righteousness and sanctification, and redemption" (1 Cor. 1:30). Through His grace and power, writing this book was a blessing and not a burden.

CHAPTER ONE

Learning About
Sanctification

THE WORD SANCTIFICATION sounds mysterious, "holier-than-thou," and a little scary. We imagine a sanctified person must have a gloomy face, dress in a long black robe, and avoid an upbeat attitude toward life. Relax. That is not what biblical sanctification is all about.

Sanctification is the greatest work God is doing in the Christian life, the process through which He is making us more Christlike for our good and His glory.

Biblical sanctification is the only way to become more like Jesus. Yet, for many Christians being sanctified, or growing spiritually, is like a forgotten blessing. They have overlooked the thrilling ways by which God can enable us to be victorious over sin and to be deepened in our walk with the Lord. This book will help us discover from Scripture what sanctification is all about and how to apply the biblical principles of Christian growth.

WHAT DOES SANCTIFICATION MEAN?

The birth of our oldest son, Andy, was a momentous event. His birth took thirteen painful hours for my wife, Shirley, to complete. But Shirley and I rejoiced at the safe arrival of our baby boy and our new role as parents. Andy's birth was just a starting point for his growth outside the womb and in the world. His development from a new-born baby to age twenty-one required about 184,000 hours. During this time Andy ate, exercised, trained, socialized, and received nurture from us and many others. This whole process from Andy's birth to his maturity we call growth.

Christians go through a similar process. Through faith in Christ a person is born into God's family and becomes His spiritual child. God has planned that His spiritual infants grow to spiritual maturity, and this requires that they practice biblical principles of spiritual growth and receive spiritual nurture from other Christians. The spiritual growth of Christians is called "progressive sanctification." We are changed dramatically by our spiritual birth (2 Cor. 5:17), but God continues to change us through sanctification.[1]

Spiritual growth, or sanctification, differs from physical growth. Spiritual growth can occur over our whole Christian lifetime, whereas normally a person's physical growth reaches a peak of health and maturity. Then deterioration begins and continues until death. Paul emphasized this contrast between our physical aging and our spiritual renewal: "Therefore we do not lose heart, but though our outer man is decaying, yet our inner man is being renewed day by day" (4:16). So Christians should progress in sanctification toward greater spiritual maturity throughout their earthly life. *Perfect* spiritual maturity is always a goal to gain and never a state we attain before death or Christ's return (Phil. 3:12–14).

Just as a baby's growth to maturity requires eating and training, so sanctification to Christian maturity requires spiritual eating and training (Heb. 5:12–14). We will examine what that process means in more detail in later chapters.

The word *sanctify* in Scripture basically means "to separate or set apart."[2] And the word *sanctified* means the same as *holy*.[3] So progressive sanctification, becoming more holy, and spiritual growth are essentially the same process. This book is about progressive sancitification, and sanctification will be used in this sense unless indicated otherwise.

HOW IS SANCTIFICATION USED IN SCRIPTURE?

Sanctification Usually Applies to People

Sanctification usually refers to people being set apart for God's possession and use.[4] God wants His people to sanctify Him by reverencing Him as their holy God (Lev. 22:32). Jesus taught us to sanctify the heavenly Father's name when we pray (Matt. 6:9). Our prayers then should be both reverent and intimate because God is holy and He is the believer's spiritual Father.

The Father sanctified Jesus, His Son (John 10:36), and the Son sanctified Himself for us (17:19). Our proper response is to sanctify or set apart ourselves from a life centered on self to a life centered on Christ (2 Cor. 5:14–15).

Peter urged Christians to "sanctify Christ as Lord in your hearts" (1 Pet. 3:15). This verse suggests that Christ should have top priority in our hearts, He should control our lives, and we should have intimate fellowship with Him.

In Old Testament times God required that the people of Israel (Lev. 11:44), Israel's priests (Exoc. 19:22; 2 Chron. 5:11), and the firstborn in Israel (including male animals, Num. 8:17) be sanctified or holy. Personal possessions such as a house or a field could also be sanctified (Lev. 27:14, 17). God considers Christians sanctified or holy and that means all we are and have belongs to Him (1 Cor. 1:2; 4:7; 6:19–20). Handing over to the Lord the ownership title to ourselves and our substance is part of sanctified living. This does not necessarily mean that the Lord will dispose of us and our possessions, though He has that right since He owns everything and is sovereign. Rather, God wants us to be faithful stewards of our persons and possessions so that He can bless and use us.

Sanctification Should Have a Godly Purpose

Biblical sanctification is never just an abstract, isolated concept. Sanctification always has a purpose which the biblical context makes clear. In most cases, biblical sanctification means separation *from* ordinary use and *for* God's possession and use (Exod. 19:5–6, 10; 2 Tim. 2:19–21). In a few cases people sanctified themselves or others for an ungodly purpose such as a priest who was "sanctified" or "consecrated" for idol worship (Judg. 17:5, 12). People are warned under the threat of divine punishment not to "separate" themselves from God to commit idolatry (Ezek. 14:7–8; see also Isa. 66:17).[5]

Whenever we read that a person is "sanctified," we need to know if they are sanctified for a godly purpose or for an ungodly purpose. A person may be sanctified from the common and the sinful and *for* God's possession and service. Or a person may be sanctified *from* God and for a sinful purpose (as in the verses above in Ezekiel 14). The direction and the purpose of a person's sanctification makes all the difference. "He who is not with Me," Jesus said, "is against Me" (Matt. 12:30). People have no neutral area or demilitarized spiritual zone to occupy in their relationship to God. Christians should separate themselves from all sin and should commit themselves completely to God as a holy people in order to love, worship, and serve Him wholeheartedly. Otherwise, we can expect firm rebuke from the Lord for partial commitment to Him, Christian mediocrity, and spiritual lukewarmness. Biblical sanctification and spiritual slackers do not go together.

Christian Sanctification is Used in Three Ways

This book is about progressive sanctification, but Scripture also applies sanctification to Christians in two other significant ways: positional sanctification and perfective sanctification.[6]

When I became a Christian, I was immediately interested in understanding the terminology of biblical Christianity. I learned that the doctrine of justification means that God declares the believer in Christ righteous, and the doctrine of regeneration means that the believer is spiritually born of God and given eternal life. I also learned that sanctification means that God sets apart Christians for His possession and use. However, some passages taught that our sanctification is past while other passages taught that it is present or future, and that puzzled me. Once I discovered that there are different types of sanctification, the mental fog began to lift, and I gained a clearer understanding of the biblical doctrine of sanctification.

First, positional sanctification means that believers have a perfect standing in Christ before God, though they are still imperfect in their earthly condition (Acts 26:18; Heb. 10:10, 14). Justification is similar to the doctrine of positional sanctification (1 Cor. 1:30; 6:11). Through our justification by faith we have Christ's righteousness credited to us and a right standing before God (Rom. 3:22–26). Through positional sanctification we have been set apart in Christ to a perfect standing before God (Heb. 10:10, 14). Both justification and positional sanctification are permanent because they are already accomplished for believers "in the name of the Lord Jesus Christ and in the Spirit of our God" (1 Cor. 6:11). So every believer can say, "I have been justified and positionally sanctified in Christ forever."

All Christians are *saints* because of their positional sanctification and regardless of their level of spirituality. Paul taught this truth when he addressed the Christians at Corinth as "those who have been sanctified *[hēgiasmenois]* in Christ Jesus, saints *[hagiois]* by calling" (1:2); However, the Corinthian Christians had willfully remained spiritual infants instead of growing through the Word to spiritual maturity (3:1–3). They needed to grow from spiritual infancy to maturity so that their progressive sanctification would match more closely their positional sanctification.

To apply the *saints* only to certain professed Christians who have been canonized by a religious institution is unbiblical. If a person has faith in Christ, he or she has sainthood. Now the challenge for the believer is to live like a saint, not with a pretty halo, but through practical holiness.

Second, progressive sanctification means that Christians grow in victory over sin and in Christlikeness. Spiritual growth begins with our positional sanctification at the moment of salvation, and it should continue throughout our lives toward greater Christlike maturity (Phil. 3:13–14).

God wants Christians to be progressively sanctified (1 Thess. 4:3), and He continually works to produce it within them. Our sanctification involves a partnership with God, as Paul indicated: "So then, my beloved, just as you have always obeyed, not as in my presence only, but now much more in my absence, work out your salvation with fear and trembling; for it is God who is at work in you, both to will and to work for His good pleasure" (Phil. 2:12–13). We "are being sanctified" by the Lord (Heb. 2:11, marg.), and yet the Lord commands us to pursue sanctification (12:14).

Progressive sanctification is God's way to mature His people. So we should give sanctification high priority in our Christian lives.

Third, perfective sanctification[7] means that Christ will change Christians into His likeness at His return. Paul showed the close connection between perfective sanctification and Christ's return: "Now may the God of peace Himself sanctify you entirely; and may your spirit and soul and body be preserved complete, without blame at the coming of our Lord Jesus Christ" (1 Thess. 5:23). Perfective sanctification is essentially the same as glorification, being fully conformed to the image of God's Son when we reach heaven (Rom. 8:29–30).

Since Christ will make us just like Himself in the future, why should we try to become more Christlike through progressive sanctification now? First, it is God's will or desire (1 Thess. 4:3). Second, God has commanded believers to pursue sanctification (Heb. 12:14). Third, it follows the example of Christ (1 Cor. 11:1). These reasons demolish our excuses for putting the process of sanctification on hold or even slowing down our spiritual growth. Our expectation of Christlike perfection should intensify our pursuit of sanctification (1 John 2:28; 3:1–3).

Table 1 shows how the three types of sanctification relate to each other and to some other key Bible doctrines.

Table 1—Three Types of Sanctification

Positional Sanctification	Progressive Sanctification	Perfective Sanctification
Past point—Spiritual birth	Present process—Spiritual growth	Future point—Spiritual perfection
Salvation from the penalty of sin	Salvation from the power of sin	Salvation from the presence of sin
"I have been saved" (Eph. 2:8–9)	"I am being saved" (James 1:21)	"I will be saved" (1 Thess. 5:9)
Consecration of the body (1 Cor. 6:19–20)	Deterioration of the body (2 Cor. 4:16)	Redemption of the body (Rom. 8:23)
Redemption of the soul commenced	Redemption of the soul continued	Redemption of the soul completed
Justification and regeneration	Sanctification	Glorification
Adoption as God's sons	Maturation as God's sons	Manifestation as God's sons

Positional Sanctification	Progressive Sanctification	Perfective Sanctification
By the Father's will (James 1:18)	In the Father's word (John 17:17)	At the Father's time (Matt. 24:36; Acts 1:6–7)
Through faith in Christ's work of crucifixion and resurrection for us (Acts 16:31; Rom. 3:22–26)	Through Christ's present work of intercession for us and His power in and through us (Heb. 7:25; Eph. 3:17; Phil. 4:13)	Through Christ's future return and transformation of us (Phil. 3:20–21; 1 John 3:1–2)
Of and by the Spirit (John 3:5; Titus 3:5)	From the Spirit 2 Cor. 3:18)	Through the Spirit (Rom. 8:11)

The analytic nature of this chart does not suggest that the Christian life is mechanical or static. The Christian life involves a personal and dynamic relationship to the triune God and His people and compassion for other people. However, the personal, dynamic operation of sanctification needs biblical doctrine to give it structure, just as a dynamic human body needs a skeleton to give it structure. Also biblical doctrine gives our sanctification direction so that we are practicing spiritual growth in God's way and not in just any old way. A train engine is a dynamic machine, but it needs tracks to give it direction. The biblical doctrine of sanctification gives our spiritual growth structure like a skeleton and direction like trian tracks. But in order to grow we must put the doctrine of sanctification into operation. Jesus taught, "If you know these things, you are blessed if you do them" (John 13:17).

Sanctification Is Vital for Spirituality

Spirituality is a relative spiritual condition of a Christian just as health is a relative physical condition of a person. For instance, a Christian may have *some* spirituality and *fair* health but not have *mature* spirituality and *robust* health. Spirituality is determined by how much a Christian has progressed in sanctification. Just as our physical condition normally develops from conception and birth to maturity, so God intends that our spiritual condition develop from spiritual birth to spiritual maturity. A baby is low on the scale of physical growth relative to an adult, and an infant Christian is low on the scale of spirituality relative to a mature Christian. Hebrews 5:12–14 teaches that to become mature Christians with spiritual discernment and ability to make right moral decisions requires time and training in the Word.

A person has no Christian spirituality until he becomes a child of God through faith in Christ (Gal. 3:26). Each Christian experiences spirituality to some degree,[8] but Scripture designates only some Christians as "spiritual."[9]

Christians become spiritual through sufficient progress in sanctification toward Christlike maturity. And Christlike maturity means that a believer imitates Jesus' character, choices, communication, and conduct. (Chapter 8 examines these Christlike qualities and shows how to cultivate them.)

Spiritual growth to maturity is similar in some ways to physical growth to maturity. A child may be growing but still not be grown or mature. In the same way, a Christian may have grown some spiritually but still not be spiritually mature. Baby Christians can have a measure of spirituality (1 Cor. 3:1–3; Heb. 5:13), but they are not yet spiritually mature (1 Cor. 2:6; Heb. 5:12–14).

Wherever you are on God's scale of spirituality, you can and should grow more (Phil. 3:13–14; 1 Pet. 3:18). God places no speed limits on spiritual growth.

WHY STUDY SANCTIFICATION?

Christian sanctification is the only path to true spirituality. "So what? Who needs spirituality anyhow?" This is the cynical reaction of some people. Others frantically search for spiritual experience. And they leave no path untraveled and no stone unturned in their quest for spirituality.

No matter how many paths people may take, the search for true spirituality is futile until they are saved by grace through faith in Christ (Eph. 2:8–9). When we come to faith in Christ, our search for spirituality ends and growth in spirituality begins.

God makes us more spiritual through sanctification, and that is reason enough to study and pursue sanctification passionately. Still, there are other reasons why we should learn about sanctification from the Scriptures.[10]

Study Sanctification to Do God's Will

Most Christians are curious about God's will for their lives, but usually they favor a crystal-ball approach that shows them many nice things happening in their future. God does give us some precious promises for the future (actually enough to take good care of us for now and all eternity). But God keeps enough of the future hidden from us to encourage us to trust Him and to keep us occupied with His presently revealed will. That means practicing sanctification right now, as Paul told the Thessalonian believers: "This is the will of God, your sanctification" (1 Thess. 4:3). Our need to study sanctification then goes far beyond academic reasons and rests mainly on a practical reason—that we should know and do the will of God immediately and eagerly (Eph. 5:17; 1 John 2:17). God's will and sanctification go hand in hand; we must understand and do them together or we disappoint the Lord.

Study Sanctification to Plan Properly for Spiritual Growth

Scripture is our "Guidebook to Spiritual Growth." Therefore learning about sanctification from the Bible is essential for optimum spiritual progress (2 Tim. 3:16–17).

Many Christians can explain how to trust Christ for salvation. They may have "The Romans Road to Salvation" highlighted in their Bibles or know other approaches to personal evangelism. This is commendable, but when these Christians are asked if they have a plan to grow in Christ, they are usually dumbfounded. We need a plan for spiritual growth just as we need a plan to grow in Christ and to help other Christians grow. (Chapter 16 provides guidelines for developing a lifetime plan to maximize your sanctification.)

Study Biblical Sanctification to Evaluate Other Spiritual Teaching

Two dangers confront us in our response to information represented as Christian teaching (or any information for that matter)—gullibility and unreceptiveness. We can be naïve and swallow anything, or we can be too suspicious and refuse even God's truth. Paul commended the Berean

Christians for their balanced approach. "Now these [i.e., Berean Christians] were more noble-minded than those in Thessalonica, for they received the word with great eagerness, examining the Scriptures daily to see whether these things were so" (Acts 17:11). They eagerly received Paul's word, but they checked the Scriptures to be sure what he taught was indeed God's word. We, too, are to "examine everything carefully [and to] hold fast to that which is good" (1 Thess. 5:21).

A firm grasp of biblical truth about sanctification (and other doctrines too) helps us assess current issues of spirituality. Much has been written on the spiritual life. The many books and articles on all phases of Christian living is mind-boggling. The contemporary focus on spirituality, Christian formation, and related subjects presents a barrage of teachings all the way from biblical truth to ideas that are radically unorthodox, cultic, occultic, and even overtly satanic. Yet some Christians are so credulous that they hesitate to evaluate spiritual life teaching because they say, "If it's about the spiritual life, it's bound to be good. Who would ever teach false ideas about spirituality?" Yet, any message must be checked by Scripture, even if it sounds right and seems powerful, because Satan is a notorious counterfeiter and deceiver. Satan can disguise himself, Paul wrote, "as an angel of light" (2 Cor. 11:14).

Errors about "spiritual living" come from many types of media, including bumper stickers, TV talk shows, and even church pulpits. So what is the answer? "Let the word of Christ dwell richly within you" (Col. 3:16). God's Word can enlighten our understanding and enable us to distinguish His way of holiness from false ways of holiness (Ps. 119:130; Acts 17:11; 1 John 2:20, 27). Learning and discerning through the Word can help keep us from becoming confused and easily conned by false teaching about sanctification.

Definitions of spirituality are so varied and conflicting that many people become confused in the morass of religious jargon. Cults and false religions have further complicated the problem by promoting their brands of spirituality. Even among professing Christians the tendency is to understand spirituality, sanctification, and spiritual growth in subjective and innovative ways rather than in a biblical way.

Recently an outsider, chatting with a group of evangelical Christian scholars, asked, "How do they [i.e., Christian scholars] define spirituality?"

Someone offered the facetious but insightful answer, "Just about any way they want to define it." This is a tragic but true answer in a culture with many people hungering to know what spirituality is all about and how to experience it. We need to learn what the Bible teaches about sanctification if we expect to experience true spirituality.

Study and Practice Sanctification to Receive God's Blessings

God delights to bless His people. He gives us these blessings through our growth in Christ:

- We develop Christlike character that expresses godly values and virtues.

- We triumph over sin, the world, the flesh, and the devil.

- We conquer life's inevitable adversities and grow through them.

- We effectively serve the Lord, His people, and others for His glory.

- We can enjoy godliness with contentment.

- We receive God's provisions for our physical needs.

- We have positive spiritual impact on our family, our friends, the church, and the world.

These blessings also benefit our sanctification much as a turbocharger benefits a car. The engine's exhaust powers the turbocharger, and the turbocharger greatly boosts the engine's power. So when you accelerate your sanctification, you boost your blessings, and in turn they boost your sanctification. This win-win cycle between spiritual growth and spiritual blessings should encourage us to grow more in Christ.

CHAPTER TWO

Reflecting God's Character:
God's Purpose through Sanctification

FEW WORDS CAN PLEASE A FATHER as much as hearing a son say, "Dad, I want to be just like you." However, such words may jolt a father because he wonders what kind of role model he is for his son. In some cases a father may frankly admit, "I don't want my son to turn out the way I did."

Our heavenly Father is pleased when we sincerely say, "Father, I want to be like you: holy, loving, kind, and consistent." Unlike some human fathers, our heavenly Father does not have to wonder if He is a good role model for His children because He commands them to be perfect as He is perfect (Matt. 5:48). Paul emphasized that God wants believers to reflect His character: "Be imitators of God, as beloved children" (Eph. 5:1). As we reflect God's character, He sanctifies us.

Our call to imitate the Father does not mean we are to be "little gods," as some cults teach. Rather, God's spiritual children are to imitate the moral character of their Father (5:2–10). Through sanctification we can become increasingly conformed to the image of God (4:24; Col. 3:10).

God created man in His own image and likeness (Gen. 1:26–27). The entrance of sin into humanity through Adam and Eve's transgression has distorted but not destroyed the divine image.[1] Picture the image of God in unfallen Adam and Eve as an encased mirror which perfectly reflected God's moral character and other features of His image. Sin entered and smashed the mirror. The mirror's shattered pieces are still encased, so the mirror gives a detectable—but distorted—reflection of God. This sin of Adam and Eve plunged the entire human race into a devastating fall that affected the divine image in each person, particularly the spiritual and moral functions of the image. Only God through Christ can remedy our ruin in sin and enable us to reflect God's moral character (Rom. 3:22–26).

Some Christians struggle with their need to relate intimately to their heavenly Father and to imitate Him because they feel they lack a proper father figure. This is their typical complaint: "My dad was such a poor father figure and had such a rotten character that I can never have a proper concept of my heavenly Father. I tend to transfer this negative image of my human father to my heavenly Father." In response to this complaint, we need to recognize three key facts.

First, no one has a perfect image from a human father because there have been no perfect human fathers since Adam fell. However, we do have a perfect heavenly Father, and our father figure can be reconstructed to conform to His flawless character.

Second, while it is true that a bad or inadequate father figure can warp our concept of God the Father, we need not be chronic victims of twisted ideas about the Father. We can know the truth about our heavenly Father revealed through His Son and His Word (John 1:18; 17:17). Then the Spirit can use our application of Scripture to help us replace our faulty image of the Father with His true image reflected in Jesus Christ (14:9; 2 Cor. 3:18).

Third, Christians need changes in many other ways besides correcting a faulty father figure. Christian transformation goes beyond repairing damage from the father-child relationship; it includes establishing proper relationships with the Lord and others.

Imitating our heavenly Father and becoming more Christlike actually refer to the same thing. That's because Christ, "the image of the invisible God" (Co. 1:15), perfectly reflects the Father. The Son is "the radiance of His [the Father's] glory and the exact representation of His nature (Heb. 1:3). So the more we grow like the Son, the more we reflect the Father's character.

WHAT GOD IS LIKE

What is God like? This simple question has only four single-syllable words, but no human can completely answer it. Studying the nature and attributes of God can strain the brains of the best theologians.

Should we then dismiss the challenge of knowing about God as too difficult and rather irrelevant anyway? Certainly not! True, no one can know everything about God. God has kept hidden some things about His person and plans. As Moses acknowledged, "The secret things belong to the LORD our God" (Deut. 29:29). And Paul exclaimed, "Oh, the depth of the riches both of the wisdom and knowledge of God! How unsearchable are His judgments and unfathomable His ways!" (Rom. 11:33). Knowledge about God is never complete, but our knowledge of God can be correct and sufficient. We can know God in a personal, saving way through Christ. God has provided for us "everything pertaining to life and godliness" (2 Pet. 1:3), and that includes adequate understanding of God's person and His plan for our sanctification.

The popularity of J. I. Packer's classic book, *Knowing God*,[2] shows that people do thirst to know God better. Packer reminds us that knowing God is more than knowing about God.[3] Still, learning what God is like is essential for developing an intimate, personal knowledge of God. "The highest science, the loftiest speculation, the mightiest philosophy, which can ever engage the attention of a child of God, is the name, the nature, the person, the work, the doings, and the existence of the great God whom he calls Father."[4]

If we expect to reflect God's character through sanctification, we need to learn what God is like. This is true for two reasons. First, we cannot imitate someone we know nothing about. Second, we must know what God is like to be sure we are reflecting His true image and not misrepresenting Him. For example, Christians must learn about God's holy character in order to be holy (1 Pet. 1:15–16).

The best way to learn about God's character is to study His attributes

revealed in Scripture and in His Son. An attribute is an essential characteristic or quality of a person, thing, or group. God's attributes are not
incidental characteristics like a beard, which a man may keep or shave;
they are esssential characteristics, eternal truths about God which describe
Him for us.

The childhood prayer, "God is great; God is good. Let us thank Him
for this food," points up the two major kinds of God's attributes: His greatness and His goodness.[5]

Attributes of God's Greatness

Attributes of God's greatness include His spirituality, personality, life, infinity, self-existence, self-sufficiency, sovereignty, and immutability (or
unchangeableness). God's infinity includes His omnipresence (and the
closely related concept of immensity), His omniscience, His omnipotence,
and His eternity.[6]

Some of God's attributes of greatness are called communicable attributes because they can be shared to some degree by mankind. For
instance, we can know a little about a few things, but God is all-knowing
(omniscient); He knows everything about everything. Some other attributes of God's greatness are called incommunicable attributes because
they cannot be shared at all with finite people.

God's self-sufficiency, an incommunicable attribute, reminds us that
He is totally independent of everyone and everything. Certain people may
be called self-sufficient, but finite humans are always totally dependent
on God for absolutely everything including their next breath (Job 12:10;
Acts 17:25). These incommunicable characteristics are unique to God. So
God does not ask us to possess, develop, imitate, or express His incom-
municable attributes. But He does expect us to grow in knowledge of
Him, which includes learning about His incommunicable attributes.

Though some of God's attributes of greatness are incommunicable,
none of His attributes is impractical. God's attributes help describe Him,
and they are relevant in understanding His relationship to us and our
right relationship to Him. A proper belief about God's attributes can help
us realize that God is sufficient for all our needs. Paul felt insufficient for

the awesome task of ministering the gospel. We should admit that we are insufficient or inadequate in many areas of life. But take courage; like Paul we can find our sufficiency in God.

I recall seeing at a wedding reception a huge banner with the words, "Our Sufficiency Is of God" (2 Cor. 3:5, KJV). The couple claimed this biblical passage for their married life together. Shirley and I had been married for only a few weeks when we attended this wedding, and the message on that banner became a mainstay of our relationship to God and our marriage. Whatever your marital status or need, make the biblical truth of God's sufficiency a deep conviction in your life because you will need it often.

Our all-sufficient God assures us that if we take care of His spiritual purposes such as the pursuit of sanctification (Heb. 12:14), He will provide for all our needs—from daily food and clothes to our deepest feelings of inadequacy (Matt. 6:25–34; Phil. 4:6–7). We gain this conviction through a right belief about God's attributes which undergird His sufficiency for us. Tozer recognized this fact when he wrote, "The man who comes to a right belief about God is relieved of ten thousand temporal problems, for he sees at once that these have to do with matters which at the most cannot concern him for very long."[7]

Attributes of God's Goodness

Attributes of God's goodness are His moral characteristics, and they are communicable or can be shared to some extent with finite human beings. These attributes include His holiness, righteousness, justice, love, grace, mercy, goodness, faithfulness, patience, and truthfulness. These moral attributes are perfect and infinite in God, and they make up His moral character. In Deuteronomy 32:4 Moses highlighted God's moral attributes: "The Rock! His work is perfect, for all His ways are just; a God of faithfulness and without injustice, righteous and upright is He."

We will discuss only the moral attribute of God's holiness because to be holy and to be sanctified are synonymous in Scripture. God's holiness in the ethical sense means He is absolutely separated from all moral evil.[8] John wrote of God's moral holiness: "God is light, and in Him there is no darkness at all" (1 John 1:5). In the symbolism of 1 John, "light" depicts holiness, righteousness, and purity and "darkness" symbolizes sin. God's perfect moral character exemplified in His holiness makes Him totally "allergic to sin and evil," as Erickson put it.[9] God cannot even be tempted to sin (James 1:13). Sin is so intolerable to our holy God that He must eventually judge it (Isa. 13:11; Hab. 1:12–13).

In the presence of the Lord's dazzling and awesome holiness, people are stunned by their own sinfulness (Isa. 6:1–8, Luke 5:8). Here are three practical ways Christians should respond to the moral impact of God's holiness: Separate from all impure and immoral practices (2 Cor. 6:14–7:1; 1 Thess. 4:3, 7); obey Christ (John 14:21) so that He will make you holy as a member of His church (Eph. 5:26–27); and worship, fear, and glorify the Lord, who is holy (Ps. 99:9; Rev. 15:4). As you respond properly to God's holiness, you will become more holy.

HOW GOD BUILDS GODLY CHARACTER

Godly character is a matter of the heart. Jesus spoke of people with "an honest and good heart" (Luke 8:15). In Matthew 12:34–35 He taught a similar truth: "You brood of vipers, how can you, being evil, speak what is good? For the mouth speaks out of that which fills the heart. The good man out of his good treasure brings forth what is good; and the evil man out of his evil treasure brings forth what is evil." The human heart is like a treasure chest composed of values, virtues, and vices (Prov. 4:23; Mark 7:21–23). The Spirit transforms our heart (the source of moral character) at the moment of salvation, and He continues to transform our heart through sanctification.

Responsibility of Believers

Christians are responsible to work with God in developing His moral character in them. This means that we should grow more holy, righteous, just, loving, and godlike so that we increasingly reflect God's character.[10]

What does God want us to do in His "moral character development program"? *First,* learn what godly character looks like by studying God's moral attributes and other moral attributes revealed in Jesus' perfect humanity, such as humility. *Second,* put on these moral characteristics like they were articles of clothing, as Paul exhorted us to do: "So, as those who have been chosen of God, holy and beloved, put on a heart of compassion, kindness, humility, gentleness and patience" (Col. 3:12). *Third,* respond biblically to trials which God uses to build our character. Scripture explains this principle: "We can rejoice, too, when we run into problems and trials, for we know that they are good for us—they help us learn to endure. And endurance develops strength of character in us" (Rom. 5:3–4, NLT). *Fourth,* depend on the Holy Spirit to produce these Christlike characteristics in you. To express godly choices, godly communication, and godly conduct, we must rely on the Holy Spirit's enabling.

Our inward moral character is like a tree's root system. The more the roots hidden under the ground are developed, the more they are expressed visibly above the ground through the tree. And the more we develop our moral character on the inside through sanctification, the more we reflect God's character on the outside. And reflecting God's character shows our spiritual growth.

Teamwork of the Trinity

Sanctification is a major part of God's redemptive plan and it is the primary work He does to develop godly character in His people (Phil. 2:13; 1 Thess. 4:3, 7).[11] Truly, "God . . . is in the holiness business."[12] Each person of the Trinity is at work sanctifying us, but all three persons work together as a team. Table 2 points up the sanctifying work of each person of the Trinity.

Table 2—The Role of Each Person of the Trinity in Sanctification

Father	Son	Holy Spirit
Planned sanctification	Provided sanctification	Performs sanctification
Architect	Administrator	Applier
Ultimate Source of sanctification	Intermediate Agent in sanctification	Direct Agent in sanctification
1 Cor. 8:6; Heb. 10:10	1 Cor. 1:30; 8:6; Eph. 5:26 Heb. 2:11; 10:10, 14	1 Cor. 6:11; 2 Thess. 2:13

WHEN A LOVING FATHER DISCIPLINES US

Disciplining or training His spiritual children is a specific function of God the Father. But how does this relate to holiness? Answer: His discipline helps us to "be holy" (1 Pet. 1:15) because as "He disciplines us for our good, [we] share His holiness" (Heb. 12:10). In other words, His discipline helps us grow spiritually.

Basics about the Father's Discipline

We need to keep in mind three important facts about God's discipline of His own. *First,* all Christians are subject to the Father's discipline. "For those whom the Lord loves He disciplines, and He scourges every son whom He receives" (12:6). His discipline proves His love for us and assures us we are His children. "It is for discipline that you endure; God deals with you as with sons; for what son is there whom his father does not discipline? But if you are without discipline, of which all have become partakers, then you are illegitimate children and not sons" (12:7–8).

God does not discipline the devil's spiritual children (1 John 3:10), just as parents generally do not discipline their neighbors' children. Only believers experience God's discipline; they do not experience His condemnation (John 3:18; Rev. 20:15).

Second, the Father's discipline of believers means "upbringing, training, instruction . . . as it is attained by discipline, correction ."[13] In Hebrews 12:5–11, the emphasis is on "the holy *discipline* of a fatherly God."[14]

Discipline by human parents and discipline by the Father sometimes refers to the whole process of child rearing or training (Eph. 6:4; Heb. 12:11). Or the Father may discipline specifically for the correction of a Christian's unconfessed sin: "But if we judged ourselves rightly, we should not be judged. But when we are judged, we are disciplined by the Lord in order that we will not be condemned along with the world" (1 Cor. 11:31–32). Thus the Father may discipline us to correct wrong living, or He may discipline us (train us) to promote righteous living (Heb. 12:5–11).

Third, God uses different means of discipline to accomplish His purpose for us. He may use various afflictions (Ps. 119:67, 71, 75), physical weakness and sickness (1 Cor. 11:30), sufferings and trials (Heb. 12:7; James 1:2–4; 1 Pet. 1:6–9), sorrowful experiences (Heb. 12:11), and even physical death (Acts 5:1–11; 1 Cor. 11:30; 1 John 5:16–17). These means of discipline may extreme. But God is not a sadist; He does not bring hurt into our lives to see us writhe in agony. The Father has positive purposes in disciplining us, even when our discipline includes severe adversity. Some of the purposes are these:

- to show that the Father accepts believers and treats them as His spiritual children (Heb. 12:5–9)
- to assure His children that the Father loves them (12:6)
- to help His children share their Father's holiness (12:10)
- to produce righteousness in His children (12:11)
- to influence His children to learn and to keep God's Word (Ps. 119:67, 71)
- to keep His children from being "condemned along with the world" (1 Cor. 11:31–32)

Divine discipline is a certainty for Christians. How much we grow through His discipline depends on how well we respond to it.

Right Response to the Father's Discipline

Hebrews 12:5–11 also teaches us how we should respond to the Father's discipline. God has placed every Christian in a lifetime training program to encourage us to increasingly reflect His character. Our Father's purpose in disciplining us is holy and beneficent. If we forget this, we get caught up in the immediate pain and we respond negatively. Proper response to God's discipline includes three things.

First, take the Father's discipline seriously and do not faint from His reproof (12:5). If we take divine discipline lightly and try to shrug it off, God may intensify the discipline until He gets our full attention. The Father disciplines us for helpful purposes, so we should receive His discipline as a friend and not as an enemy.

Second, endure the trials and sorrow involved in discipline (12:7, 11). The word "endurance" in verse 7 is also found in Romans. Because "endurance develops strength of character in us" (5:4, NLT, we can endure tribulation and divine discipline with hope (5:3–5).

Our first response to disciplinary trials is usually to ask God for relief by changing the circumstances or by removing us from the circumstances. Yet God often does neither. Instead, He uses the circumstances to change us. He is more interested in changing our Christian character than in changing our circumstances. When we respond properly to our circumstances, He develops our Christian character more.

Third, respect the Father by submitting to Him. The Father is our all-wise and loving disciplinarian (Heb. 12:9). To "be subject" or "submit" (Greek, *hypotassō*) to God means to arrange ourselves under His authority so that we realize His purpose and His care during our discipline. Hank had two surgical procedures for skin cancer on his forehead. For his physical welfare, Hank chose to submit to the doctor's scalpel and endure the discomfort of these surgeries rather than to rebel, thwart the doctor's purpose, and risk unnecessary harm to himself. In a similar way, our heavenly Father wants us to submit to His spiritual scalpel of loving discipline for our spiritual welfare rather than faint or rebel against Him (12:5).

We also improve our relationship to the Father when we respond biblically to His discipline. Rebellion against His discipline just brings more corrective discipline (1 Cor. 11:31–32).

I learned the importance of right response to discipline through my human father's loving discipline of me. He would strip the leaves from a thin, flexible, willow branch and then apply that branch to the rear of my anatomy where I was most padded. I felt the sting of the willow switch but I was not wounded (so this was not child abuse). My father held me by one hand and my tendency was to run in a circle around him and as far away from him and the switch as possible. But I learned two key lessons in this process. First, I should not pull away from him when he was disciplining me because it gave him more leverage and me more pain. Second, I should draw near to my father and hug him because the discipline was less severe up close to him, and he knew I wanted to restore fellowship with him. Once my discipline was complete, he let me know that He still loved me. And when I confessed my wrong, I knew that I was in fellowship with him once again. That is how our heavenly Father deals with His children.

Right response to divine discipline promotes our sanctification. We become more holy and righteous so that we reflect His character more (Heb. 12:10–11).

It is a fine compliment to a woman when someone says, "You have your father's beautiful eyes." But the greatest compliment is when someone says to a Christian, "You reflect your heavenly Father's character."

CHAPTER THREE

Discovering the New You in Christ:
United with Christ in Sanctification

ONE OF THE MOST POPULAR ACTORS of all time was asked, "How are you?" His reply seemed sarcastic but it was dead serious: "How can I tell you how I am until I know who I am." He clearly admitted that he had a major identity crisis. Most everyone eventually asks, "Who am I?" And most of those who keep searching for their identity never truly discover who they are.

Because God has identified Christians with Christ, they can get a correct answer to the question, "Who am I?" Discovering our true identity in Jesus Christ is crucial for sanctification. "It is critical to discern your position and victory in Christ in order to implement the practices of growth in Him."[1]

BIBLICAL BACKGROUND
OF SPIRITUAL UNION WITH CHRIST

Old Testament Preparation

One of God's main purposes for making humans in His image and likeness was to have intimate fellowship with them (Gen. 1:26–27). The Lord evidently communed regularly with

Adam and Eve before they sinned (3:8), but sin broke this communion (3:9–13, 23). Then in amazing grace God reached out to confront the guilty pair and to reconcile them to Himself. Adam and Eve were restored to fellowship with God, though not to their perfect pre-Fall fellowship.

Very early in Israel's history God revealed that He planned a more intimate relationship with the children of Israel. God described the relationship He desired with His covenant people: "They shall know that I am the LORD their God who brought them out of the land of Egypt, that I might dwell among them; I am the LORD their God" (Exod. 29:46). The outward manifestation of God's presence with His people centered initially on Israel's tabernacle and then on her temple: "Let them construct a sanctuary for Me, that I may dwell among them" (25:8). God promised, "My dwelling place also will be with them; and I will be their God, and they will be My people. And the nations will know that I am the LORD who sanctifies Israel, when My sanctuary is in their midst forever" (Ezek. 37:27–28).

Even under the Old Covenant with its emphasis on the corporate people of God, the Lord still desired intimate fellowship with individual believers For example, David wrote, "When Thou didst say, 'seek My face,' my heart said to Thee, 'Thy face, O LORD, I shall seek'" (Ps. 27:8). The privilege and means of personal fellowship with the Lord is much greater for church-age believers (Heb. 4:14–16; 10:19–22; 1 John 1:3). It is as if the Lord says to us: "Believer, I want to have fellowship with you." Will our response be, "Lord, that's just what I want too—to have intimate fellowship with You"?

God personalized His presence through His Son's incarnation and earthly ministry. "The Word was God," "the Word became flesh, and dwelt among us," and the Word revealed God (John 1:1, 14, 18; 14:9). God in Jesus Christ took a big step toward a more intimate relationship with His people. The Son of Man walked among people as "God with us" in human flesh (Matt. 1:23).

Christ's Promise

Christ was *with* His disciples during His earthly ministry (John 14:25). But the Lord's closest relationship to believers started on the Day of Pentecost when the Spirit descended on the one hundred twenty gathered in an upper room (Acts 2:1–4). At Pentecost the Spirit baptized these believers into Christ's body so that they became "in Christ" (1:5; 1 Cor. 12:12–13). Christ referred to this event when He promised His disciples, "In that day you will know that I am in My Father, and you in Me, and I in you" (John 14:20). "You in Me and I in you" are seven of the greatest words believers can ever hear because they came from the lips of Christ who is truth, and they express our spiritual union with Him (14:6, 20).

Christ's promise that He will indwell believers and that believers will be "in Him" is fulfilled when anyone trusts Christ (2 Cor. 5:17; Col. 1:27). Based on this truth, you can have the most intimate relationship possible with Christ (as well as with the Father and the Spirit). Humans desperately desire interpersonal intimacy, but intimacy outside of Christ is always temporary and conditional and often illusory and sinful. But the intimate relationship between Christians and Christ is eternal, unconditional, genuine, and spiritual.

New Covenant Fulfillment

God's desire to dwell and walk among His people came to fruition in His New Covenant people through their spiritual union with Christ. New Covenant believers can say, "I am 'in Christ' and 'Christ lives in me'" (2 Cor. 5:17; Gal. 2:20). They can even add, "All three persons of the Trinity indwell me" (John 14:23; 1 Cor. 6:19–20; Eph. 4:6).[2] Paul confirmed that God fulfilled to New Covenant believers His promise to indwell His people: "For we are the temple of the living God; just as God said, 'I will dwell in them and walk among them; and I will be their God, and they shall be My people'" (2 Cor. 6:16). Paul went beyond the general promise that God would dwell *among* and *with* His people (Exod. 29:46; Lev. 26:12), for he saw an even more specific fulfillment of God dwelling *in* His people individually.

True, some select individuals in Old Testament times were indwelt by God's Spirit, though his indwelling of them was temporary (Gen. 41:38, RSV; Exod. 31:3; Num. 27:18; Ps. 51:11). However, God's relationship to His Old Covenant people was primarily through His manifested presence among them as a corporate nation. Only under the New Covenant does the Spirit permanently indwell each believer (John 14:16–17).

The Old Testament predicted that God would save believing Gentiles (Hos. 1:10; 2:23) but not that the Messiah (Greek, *Christos*, "Christ") would personally indwell them as Colossians 1:27 teaches: "To whom God willed to make known what is the riches of the glory of this mystery among the Gentiles, which is Christ in you, the hope of glory" (see also Eph. 3:5). So the New Covenant is "prime time" for God's people thus far in earthly redemptive history. In comparison to the Old Covenant, the New Covenant has a superior Mediator in Christ and superior spiritual provisions (Heb. 8:6; 9:15; 12:24). And one of our foremost spiritual provisions under the New Covenant is our position in Christ since it makes all other spiritual blessings available to us (Eph. 1:3).

Sometimes Christians long for "the good old days" of some Old Testament period such as the reign of King David. Others feel they missed out when they read how the disciples walked and talked with Jesus in His physical presence. If you ever feel this kind of religious nostalgia, then realize that "the good old days" are right now in the church age. Christ has come; He has accomplished redemption; and He has given us the New Testament Scriptures through the Holy Spirit. Believers today stand on higher spiritual ground than ever before in redemptive history (1 Cor. 10:11; Heb. 1:1–2). We have something better than Christ physically with us; we are in Him spiritually and He is in us (John 14:20). And some day we will be forever in His personal presence.

BASIC CHARACTERISTICS
OF SPIRITUAL UNION WITH CHRIST

Our identity with Christ is more than just an allegiance to Him; "nor is it a mere moral union, a union of love and sympathy, as between friends."[3] It is a real, spiritual union with Christ. Five characteristics help us understand what our union with Christ means.

Christians Have a Two-way Union with Christ

Christians are united with Christ through two spiritual relationships: they are "in Christ" and Christ indwells them ("you in Me, and I in you," John 14:20).

Our position "in Christ" is permanent and provides numerous spiritual blessings that promote our sanctification. For example, each believer is "a new creation" in Christ, and that enables the believer to lead a transformed life (2 Cor. 5:17, NIV).

The relationship of "Christ in you" indicates His permanent residence in the believer (Col. 1:27). The essence of Christian sanctification is to experience and express Christ's personal presence ("Christ lives in me," Gal. 2:20). Christians can manifest Christ their lives only because He resides in them (Phil. 1:20–21). Sanctification always works "inside out."

Christians Have a "Spiritual" Union with Christ

Our permanent position in Christ is spiritual ("But the one who joins himself to the Lord is one spirit with Him," 1 Cor. 6:17). And Christ's presence in us is obviously of a spiritual nature.

Is this spiritual union with Christ full-blown mysticism so that Christians are absorbed into Christ and lose their personal identity? No, Christians still retain their individual identity and Christ retains His distinct, objective identity just as the Father and Christ are united but each retains His distinct identity. Christians are spiritually fused to Christ and to each other, but their individual personalities are never confused with Christ's or with each other's.

Therefore we should avoid any form of mysticism that goes beyond biblical occupation with Christ and toward individual absorption into Christ. The Jesus of some mystics is not the Jesus of the Bible. Paul cautioned us about people who preach a Jesus other than he preached (2 Cor. 11:4; Gal. 1:2). Our ultimate authority for Christian faith and practice is God's Word, taught by the Spirit, and not our subjective feelings or our experiences detached from Scripture.

Christians Have a Vital Union with Christ

Through our union with Christ, His spiritual life infuses us, fills us, and shows through us ("Christ lives in me," Gal. 2:20; so "that the life of Jesus also may be manifested in our body," 2 Cor. 4:10).

Understanding that we have new life through union with Christ helps us avoid two false notions. First, our spiritual union with Christ is not a dead union like two boards nailed together; instead it is a dynamic union in which Christ's spiritual life flows through us. Christ is like "the Vine" and His life is like the sap that enlivens, invigorates, and nourishes us as His "branches" (John 15:1–8). Second, our spiritual connection with Christ is not a static union but is an active communion that we experience as we abide in Him. By abiding in Christ and drawing on His life, believers have a fruitful, prayerful, and joyful life (15:5, 7, 11).

Christians Have a Union with Christ That Unites Them with Other Members of Christ's Body

Believers are spiritually bonded with Christ and with each other in His spiritual body. This spiritual bond is as real and complete as the union of our physical members with our human body: "So we, who are many, are one body in Christ, and individually members one of another" (Rom. 12:5).

We practice our spiritual union with other believers by interpersonal relationships and ministry to others in the body of Christ.

Christians Have a Secure Union with Christ

We are placed "in Christ" by the permanently indwelling Holy Spirit so that we are forever united with Christ and with other members of His body (John 14:16–17; 1 Cor. 6:19; 12:12–13, 27). Because we are "in Christ" and Christ is in us, nothing can ever separate us from God's love in Christ (Rom. 8:38–39). So our union with Christ through the Spirit gives us "security for eternity."

Eternal security frees Christians from concern about keeping their salvation so that they can fully pursue sanctification and service. We can live for Christ purely from love and gratitude because we have eternal salvation in Him.

These five magnificent features of our union with Christ are the foundation for our sanctification.[4]

SPIRITUAL BLESSINGS "IN CHRIST"

Three truths show the superlative benefits Christians have through their spiritual relationship to Christ. *First,* we have the most spiritual *possessions* available because we are "blessed . . . with every spiritual blessing in the heavenly places in Christ" (Eph. 1:3). *Second,* we have the highest spiritual *position* because God "raised us up with Him, and seated us with Him in the heavenly places in Christ Jesus" (2:6). *Third,* we have the greatest spiritual *privileges* such as confident access "through Him [Christ] . . . in one Spirit to the Father" (2:18).[5]

Some blessings in Christ are for present Christian experience, such as our access to the Father in prayer. Other blessings in Christ are for the future, such as Christ's return, but they have application for present Christian experience (1 Thess. 4:16–17, 1 John 3:2). So we need not wait until heaven to experience our spiritual blessings in Christ. Peter reminded his readers that God has given us great promises for present spiritual living: "For by these He has granted to us His precious and magnificent promises, in order that by them you may become partakers of the divine nature, having escaped the corruption that is in the world by lust" (2 Pet. 1:4).

A NEW CREATURE IN CHRIST

When the Bible states that the believer is a "new creature in Christ," does this mean that our continuity with the past ceases? Or does a Christian's identity stay the same in some ways and change in other ways?

Continuity in the Christian's Identity

A person's name, physique, physical kinships, and basic personality generally do not change when he or she becomes a Christian. We may not need to change our address, vocation, economic status, social status, or tastes simply because of conversion.

Each human has a distinct identity for time and eternity because each person is custom-built by God. There are no "cookie-cutter" humans. All people share the same basic humanity (Acts 14:15), yet each person is unique. God used the same material to make everyone, but someone has suggested that He poured the material into a different mold to make each of us and then threw away the mold. No one ever was, and no one will ever be, just like you. Even if another human was cloned from you, that cloned individual would not share your personal identity even though you would have a common genetic code.

Here are some practical instructions in light of each Christian's God-given identity as a new creature in Christ.

First, accept from God your unique identity in Christ. Believe that God made you as a special person to fulfill His purpose for you. God gave you a special body as part of your unique identity (Ps. 139:13–16), and you cannot jump into another's skin or inhabit a new body during this earthly life. Therefore attitude is everything in this principle. Avoid an attitude about your God-given identity, including your body, that is bitter toward God or envious of others because of your "unfair" lot in life. Rather, have a joyful and thankful attitude in accepting your special identity from God as His best for you. This attitude will help you be content and godly (Phil. 4:11; 1 Tim. 6:6–8).

Second, believe that what counts most is not what other people think of you (1 Sam. 16:7; Luke 16:15) *but what God says about your being in Christ.* Learn and believe God's truth about you from Scripture so that you can evaluate objectively and use appropriately what others say about you. Then you can feel confident about heeding their constructive criticism and rejecting their unjustified negative criticism (Prov. 13:1; 27:6).

Third, recognize that God expresses His creativity and diversity in making people with different personalities. Thus our growth toward spiritual maturity will not cause us to gravitate toward "the same basic Christian personality." Evidently our individual basic personality is as unique as our individual physical body. So we should not take a narrow, egotistical view that says, "If other Christians were like me, they would be completely mature and have the perfectly balanced personality." Also do not try to be exactly like other Christians, but imitate them only insofar as they imitate Christ.

When I was a young Christian growing up in the southern United States, a number of preachers (especially young ones) tried to imitate Billy Graham. Their audience perceived them as unnatural, superficial, and phony, though some of these young preachers mimicked Billy

Graham's voice and gestures remarkably well. These young preachers should have used their own unique God-given styles.

Sometimes Christians use their unique personality to justify their obnoxious, insulting, abrasive, and domineering behavior that is not Christlike. The excuse for such behavior generally is, "Well, that's just me. It's the way God made me, and God accepts me as I am." True, God accepts all true believers, but only because of our perfect position in Christ; otherwise no human could ever find acceptance with the infinitely holy God. However, acceptance in Christ does not mean that God is satisfied with our present condition and practice. God has given us different physiques, but we still need to discipline our bodies as Paul did (1 Cor. 9:24–27). Some of our personality traits may need radical alteration. Put bluntly, we need to replace some vices of the flesh with some virtues of the Spirit (Gal. 5:19–23).

The Spirit is doing surgery on all earthly Christians to change their personality characteristics that do not conform to Christ and His Word. The Spirit's work may be painful, but His work is always spiritually profitable. We need not worry that the Spirit will botch our spiritual surgery. So practice these main means to progress in sanctification: Follow Christ, rely on the Spirit, and obey the Word. These are basic disciplines, but they are like shooting, passing, and dribbling in basketball; you cannot progress in sanctification or in playing basketball without practicing them.

Where our essential personality ends and changeable personality characteristics begin may be difficult to determine. But the distinction remains important because our essential personality evidently has a continuity that changes little after conversion. Still, sinful characteristics should be discarded and replaced by Christlike characteristics. Christians must undergo Spirit-empowered change to put off evil attitudes, communication, and conduct (Eph. 4:22–32; Col. 3:8–9) and to put on godly attitudes, communication, and conduct (3:10–14).

Changes in the Christian's Identity

Before my conversion to Christ, I was familiar with the gospel through my home influence, through preachers such as Billy Graham, through attending a Bible study in a university dormitory, and through my personal Bible reading. But I was nineteen before I trusted Christ as my personal Savior on a Saturday in April, 1956, in Dallas, Texas. I was alone when I trusted Christ. But the next day my roommate, Jim, was present, and he said, "Henry, you are different." Though Jim did not specify in what ways I was different, I knew that God had given me love for Christ, hunger for His Word, desire to talk to God, and inner peace and joy. I also began to experience truth Christian fellowship and desired to share my faith with others. When I returned next month to my home in Memphis, Tennessee, my circle of friends said, "You've changed." My friends and I knew I was different, but I still did not know that God's Word said I was different: "If any man is in Christ, he is a new creature" (2 Cor. 5:17). I later discovered this verse, and the change Christ had made in my life aligned with this biblical truth.

Since you became "a new you" at regeneration without essentially changing your physical and cultural identity, then what distinguishes this new creature in Christ from the old pre-Christian you?

First, Christians are changed in their basic nature through regeneration and they become partakers of the divine nature (1 Pet. 1:3; 2 Pet. 1:3–4). Each believer becomes a spiritual child of God and is permanently indwelt by God the Father, the Son, and the Holy Spirit (John 1:12–13; 14:20, 23; 1 Cor. 6:19–20; Eph. 4:6; Col. 1:27). Instead of being in spiritual darkness and death, Christians receive spiritual light and life through Christ.

Second, Christians are changed because God gives them a new heart (Rom. 6:17; Gal. 4:6). The *heart,* more than any other psychological term in Scripture, indicates the inner personality composed of intellect, will, and emotion. Does the believer's new heart then mean that he also has a new intellect, a new will, and new emotions fully distinct from the old ones? Probably not. But it does mean that our intellect, will, and emotions are being renewed (Rom. 12:2; 2 Cor. 4:16; Eph. 4:23; Col. 3:10). After all, if our new intellect, will, and emotions were brand-new and distinct from the old ones, they would not need renewal.

Third, Christians are changed from inability to receive spiritual things to unlimited potential to receive spiritual things taught by the Spirit (1 Cor. 2:9–16). Instead of being merely natural with no spiritual discernment as in their pre-Christian state, new Christians have some spiritual discernment. Then as they grow to spiritual maturity they increasingly experience "the mind of Christ" (2:16) and "have their senses trained to discern good and evil" (Heb. 5:14).

Fourth, Christians are changed in their perspective because they can see things from a spiritual perspective and not just from a natural perspective. The college I attended had a nominal Christian association but not an evangelical stance. Mature Christians encouraged me as a new Christian to read and memorize Scripture. So I began diligently absorbing biblical truth for spiritual and intellectual growth (John 17:17). My biblical frame of reference developed and helped me evaluate information from my college courses so that I could "examine everything carefully" and "hold fast to that which is good" (1 Thess. 5:21). All believers can develop a Christian worldview and mature spiritual discernment by learning and obeying Scripture through the Spirit's help (Heb. 5:12–14).

Fifth, Christians are changed in their character at conversion, though even a Christian's character still includes some vices. At regeneration Christians are reoriented toward a lifestyle of righteousness in contrast to a lifestyle of sin (1 John 2:29; 3:9–10). Unfortunately, we can retard our reorientation and transformation in character if we choose to remain in spiritual infancy and fleshly behavior.

Ideally, new Christians should develop steadily in their reorientation toward righteous living, in their transformation of character, and in their growth from spiritual infancy to spiritual maturity. All these changes are interrelated and included in the sanctification process. Even when progress in sanctification is rapid after regeneration, more change and greater maturity can be achieved throughout our lives. For example, Christians can always become more like Christ and produce more spiritual fruit (Gal. 5:22–23).

Personal values change for new Christians, and this a necessary part of the growth process. Christians gain a new value system by learning biblical teaching. This biblical value system should cause Christians to refrain from certain attitudes (for example, bitterness and racial prejudice) and practices (for example, stealing and cursing) and to obey other biblical commands taught by explicit precept, by principle, or by example. Also, the biblical value system may cause a Christian to choose a different residence (for example, a residence closer to a local church), to seek a different job (for example, a job not associated with known illegal practices such as dealing drugs), or to rearrange daily priorities (for example, scheduled time alone with God in Bible study and prayer, and time with family members). Many other changes will occur as our growth in Christian values impacts our lifestyle.

Christian values are basic to Christian character because our values determine our choices, communication, and conduct. Hear and watch a person long enough, and you soon discover the main values that propel that person. Their values may center around a vocation, some form of recreation, finances, fame, a cause, or other factors. As we learn and commit to Christ's values revealed in Scripture, those values compose our character and control our choices. Serious Christians seek to change their present values until they completely conform to biblical values.

Sixth, Christians are changed since their "old self" with its sinful, pre-Christian behavior patterns has been "crucified" with Christ (Rom. 6:6) *and "laid aside"* (Col. 3:9). At the same time, Christians have "put on the new self who is being renewed to a true knowledge according to the image of the One who created him" (3:10). We must put into practice this positional truth by continuing to lay aside the old self and to put on the new self. For example, we must shut off our destructive communication and allow only constructive, gracious speech to flow from our mouths (Eph. 4:29; Col. 4:6). No Christian has perfect tongue control, so taming and training the tongue is a lifetime challenge (James 3:1–12). Our challenge is to put off the old self and to put on the new self until none of self and only Christ is manifest in our lives.

Seventh, Christians are changed in their ability to reflect God's image. Before conversion we reflected an image of God deeply distorted by sin. Then at conversion God began to renew that distorted image so that it would increasingly reflect "righteousness and holiness of the truth" (Eph. 4:24).

Eighth, Christians are changed in certain traits or tendencies of their particular temperament (or personality). Packer has observed that each of the four classic categories of temperament (sanguine, phlegmatic, choleric, and melancholic) "has its own strengths and also its weaknesses."[6] Rather than being a victim of their temperaments, Christians should see Christ as their model of holy humanity, which combines "the strengths of all four temperaments without any of the weaknesses."[7] A Christian's weaknesses of temperament may not change immediately at conversion, but they can change gradually through the sanctification process. Our needed temperamental changes occur most rapidly when we are walking in fellowship with the Lord and are obedient to His Word.

Ninth, Christians are changed in their personal relationships. At our conversion our family and friends remain the same folks, but our relationship with them can change drastically. Generally we develop close spiritual bonds with those who are already Christians, and we discover some spiritual tension with those still in unbelief. We should be wise, gentle, gracious, and winsome in relating to non-Christian family members, friends, and other people (Col. 4:5–6). Rely on the Spirit to help you develop these qualities and to witness powerfully for Christ.

The better we understand the areas in which God changes us, the better we can partner with God in the process of sanctification.

Other Spiritual Blessings in Christ

Understanding who you are and what you have "in Christ" will help you discover your true Christian identity and lay a proper foundation for sanctification. We have looked at some points of continuity and some changes in a Christian's personal identity. These other spiritual blessings in Christ will help us discover even more about our Christian identity.

- We have every spiritual blessing in Christ (Eph. 1:3).

- We have redemption in Christ (1:7).

- We have regeneration in Christ (Col. 2:13).

- We have justification in Christ (Rom. 3:24).

- We have reconciliation in Christ (5:10).

- We have spiritual union with Christ, the Head of the body, the church (John 14:20; Col. 1:18).

- We have died to sin through our identity with Christ (Rom. 6:4, 11).

- We have been freed from the sinful nature's passions and desires through our identity with Christ (Gal. 5:24).

- We have been crucified to the world and the world has been crucified to us through our identity with Christ (6:14).

- We have been changed through our identity with Christ (Co. 2:11).

- We have been exalted with Christ (Eph. 2:4–6).

- We are indwelt by each person of the Trinity (John 14:23; 1 Cor. 6:19).

- We have a perfect standing in Christ before the Father (Heb. 10:14).

- We have no condemnation in Christ (Rom. 8:1).

- We have completeness in Christ (Col. 2:10).

- We have been rescued from the domain of darkness through Christ (1:13).

- We have been transferred to Christ's kingdom (1:13).

- We have been called into fellowship with Christ (1 Cor. 1:9).

- We have access to the Father through Christ (Eph. 2:18).

- We have been made members of God's family through Christ (2:19).

- We have been made fellow citizens with the saints in the church age through Christ (2:19).

- We have citizenship in heaven through Christ (Phil. 3:20).

- We have become the Lord's own people through Christ's redemption (Titus 2:13-14).

- We have been made a chosen race, a royal priesthood, and a holy nation in Christ (1 Pet. 2:9).

- We have adoption as adult sons in Christ (Gal. 4:7).

- We have eternal security in Christ (Col. 3:3).

- We have sanctification in Christ (1 Cor. 1:30).

- We have wisdom in Christ (1:30).

- We have unlimited spiritual power in Christ (Phil. 4:13).[8]

- We have spiritual membership in Christ's body, the church, and union with other members of the body (1 Cor. 12:13).

This list is a sampling of our blessings in Christ. For a list of thirty-three items concerning the riches of grace which Christians receive at salvation in Christ, see Lewis Sperry Chafer, *Systematic Theology.*[9] In their book, *The Common Made Holy,* Neil T. Anderson and Robert L. Saucy present another helpful list of biblical truths about the Christian's position in Christ.[10].

Our biggest challenge now is to experience, enjoy, and employ our blessings in Christ. A family may own a grocery store and yet starve to death if they do not take food from the shelves and transfer it to their mouths. And we can neglect our Christian life by leaving these blessings "on the shelf" of heaven. Believers should claim these promised blessings in Christ, and then integrate them into our Christian experience.

I recently heard a Christian educator answer the question of how he experienced God and grew as a Christian. He mentioned that he reads Scripture in the morning and jots down a summary of the truth he discovers. And then he said in effect, "I decide right then to live it." This is a simple but profound principle that shows where many Christians fail. They discover a biblical promise or other truth in Christ, but they decide to leave it rather than live it. The moment you see a promise or other truth in Scripture integrate it into your life. I remember a self-taught preacher urging his audience in homespun language to "take a deep faith-swallow every time you run across a promise in God's Word." Paul would say, "Let the word of Christ richly dwell within you" (Col. 3:16).

Discover your identity in Christ and claim your blessings in Christ. Then watch the impact this will have on your life. We may sink far down in depression if we focus only on who we are and what we have in ourselves ("For I know that nothing good dwells in me, that is, in my flesh," Rom. 7:18). But focusing on the spiritual possessions, position, and privileges we have in Christ gives us a different perspective that can help lift us from depressive thinking and feelings. This is not to deny that depression may also be caused by physiological, mental, emotional, and relational factors, or by a combination of them. Nevertheless by understanding your identity in Christ, you can (a) understand God's truth about yourself and His provisions for you, (b) realize your acceptance before God in Christ, (c) gain a sense of personal well-being and security in Christ, (d) progress steadily in your sanctification, and (e) develop a holistic approach to Christian living and service that considers physiological, mental, emotional, and relational factors. But at the core of all these factors is the spiritual, and that is where we need to begin without neglecting the other factors.

Christians need to believe *who they are* in Christ and *what they have* in Christ in order to grow toward *what God wants them to become in Christ,* namely, mature Christians. Have and live out strong biblical convictions about your identity in Christ. That will put you on a fast track to growth in Christ. If you are on a slow growth track, it is time to discover your identity in Christ and accelerate your growth.

SPIRITUAL BLESSINGS OF "CHRIST IN YOU"

The Christ-in-you relationship began at Pentecost for all believing Jews and Gentiles. Since then Christ has continued to establish personal and permanent spiritual residence in all believers.

Christians can express outward spirituality only if they are experiencing inward spiritual reality. The indwelling Christ was a vital reality for Paul (Gal. 2:20). How can we also experience the spiritual reality of Christ's indwelling presence? First, believe the truth that "Christ lives in me" (2:20). Second, obey Christ's commands because you love Him (John 14:21). If you want Christ to become real to you, become more obedient to Him. "Christ reveals himself to his lovers."[11] Third, maintain intimate fellowship with Christ. Paul prayed that believers would realize a deep personal relationship with Christ in their hearts: "that Christ may dwell in our hearts through faith" (Eph. 3:17). Christ is resident in our lives. Let Him be president. As we do, we can say, "Christ is at home in my heart and has the rule of my life."

CHAPTER FOUR

Conquering Sin and the Flesh through Christ's Victory: Internal Opposition to Sanctification

MOST PEOPLE WANT TO BE IDENTIFIED with a winner. Just ask the avid supporters of the victorious Chicago Bulls basketball team. Some Bulls' fans would be very poor basketball players, but when their team wins they still say, "We won!" Such supporters identify so closely with their team that they share in the team's results—win or lose.

Christians share spiritually with Christ in His death, burial, and resurrection and the results of these events. Romans 6:1–11; and Colossians 2:11–13 teach that Christ won the victory over sin and the flesh through His death, burial, and resurrection. Since Christians are identified with Christ, they can say, "We won the victory over sin and the flesh." But we must by faith claim this victory and apply it to our lives in order to experience victory over sin and the flesh.

CLAIM CHRIST'S VICTORY OVER SIN

The foundation for victory over sin is the Christian's death with Christ to sin. Burial with Christ reemphasizes that we have ended our preconversion life in sin. Resurrection with

Christ introduces the Christian to a new life in righteousness: "Therefore we have been buried with Him through baptism into death, in order that as Christ was raised from the dead through the glory of the Father, so we too might walk in newness of life" (Rom. 6:4).

Death to Sin through Death with Christ

All believers "died to sin" (Rom. 6:2) when they were crucified with Christ at their conversion (6:3–10; Gal. 2:20). Their death to sin was in a judicial and a positional sense. Judicial death to sin means that God declares each Christian dead to sin. Positional death to sin means that God continues to consider each Christian dead to sin. Since God considers Christians dead to it, they are to "consider [themselves] . . . to be dead to sin" (Rom. 6:11). By faith and through God's grace Christians can practice their death to sin by refusing to live in sin. Paul pointed out this truth by asking, "How shall we who died to sin still live in it?" (6:2).

The believer's death to sin with Christ is not an experiential death to sin. If believers were experientially dead to sin, they would not sin. But believers do sin, though sin is never excusable. People who claim to be sinless deceive themselves, disbelieve God, and do not apply God's Word to themselves (1 John 1:8, 10).

Just as death breaks a person's ties with his or her former earthly life, so death to sin for Christians judicially breaks all ties with their preconversion life in sin. Christians still live in their natural bodies and retain certain earthly relationships and responsibilities. They still eat and sleep, walk and talk, and work and rest, but they are judicially freed from their former relationship to sin (Rom. 6:3–22).

Dead people do not sin; they are free from sin in this earthly life (6:7). Even the strongest temptation to sin gets no response from dead people. Alcoholics will never rise in their caskets to take another drink. The mouth filled with blasphemy and profanity utters no sound at all after death. The deceased have perfect victory over sin.[1]

Unlike dead people, Christians are alive and can respond to sin either negatively or positively. But God wants us to respond to sin as if we were dead, to refrain from sin. Ask yourself this practical question: "Am I staying in my casket in relation to sin, or am I walking around like a zombie committing sin?" If the latter is true, reaffirm that you died to sin with Christ. Then by God's grace get back in your casket in relation to sin.

Sometimes Christians tell me they cannot say "no" to certain temptations. But this contradicts 1 Corinthians 10:13, "No temptation has overtaken you but such as is common to man; and God is faithful, who will not allow you to be tempted beyond what you are able, but with the temptation will provide the way of escape also, so that you will be able to endure it." God has made provision for Christians to conquer sin, even sin that may seem imposible to conquer. By faith believers can claim Christ's victory over sin and through God's grace and His Spirit they can resist sin (Rom. 8:13).

Freedom from Bondage to Sin

At conversion a believer dies with Christ to sin and God frees him or her from bondage to sin (Rom. 6:6–7, 17–18, 22). However, this freedom does not mean that a person is free to continue in sin (6:1; Gal. 5:13; 1 Pet. 2:16). We have been freed so that we should no longer be slaves to our old master, sin, but slaves to our new Master, God (Rom. 6:14–20).

Christians become enslaved to their new Master by obeying three commands: Stop letting sin reign in your bodies by obeying its lusts (6:12); Stop presenting yourselves to sin for unrighteous living; and present yourselves to God for righteous living (6:13, 19). The more Christians become enslaved to their new Master by obeying these commands, the more they experience freedom from sin and progress in sanctification. "But now having been freed from sin and enslaved to God, you derive your benefit, resulting in sanctification" (6:22).

Freedom usually has a high price. Ask a veteran wounded in combat, such as Robert R. Ingram, and he will tell you the great cost of fighting for the freedom of a country. Ingram was serving as a twenty-one-year-old Navy corpsman in South Vietnam in 1966. When the platoon he accompanied came under severe attack, he served heroically by helping the wounded, though he himself was critically injured. He survived four wounds, including a bullet through the head, and his vital signs dropped so low that he was tagged "killed in action" and placed in the dead pile. But Ingram survived. And though the paperwork on his war bravery had been lost for about thirty-two years, on July 10, 1998, President Clinton awarded him the Medal of Honor.[2] Robert R. Ingram can testify from personal experience that the cost of freedom is reckoned in human blood.

The redemptive price of freedom from sin's penalty and bondage was at maximum cost—the precious blood of Christ (1 Pet. 1:18–19). We needed spiritual freedom because of our slavery to sin. "Everyone who commits sin is the slave of sin" (John 8:34). We received our spiritual freedom by believing on Jesus Christ (Acts 13:38–39). As Jesus Christ said, "So if the Son sets you free, you will be free indeed" (John 8:36, niv). Keep on obeying Christ and you will experience more freedom from sin's power. Jesus therefore was saying to those Jews who had believed Him, "If you abide in My word, *then* you are truly disciples of Mine." (John 8:31, nasb).

Deathh to Sin but Continued Struggle with Sin

Since Christians are dead to sin, is their struggle with sin over? Indeed not! A major problem remains because Christians retain inherent sin[3] and the indwelling sin principle.

The sin principle functions within each Christian, opposes Holy Spirit, and produces sinful thoughts, attitudes, words, and actions unless counteracted by the Spirit.

I prefer to use the expression "sin principle" rather than "sin nature," "sinful nature," or "old nature." In any case, Christians must sill face their struggle with indwelling sin. But we can conquer sin by claiming Christ's defeat of sin and by relying on the Spirit to counteract our indwelling sin principle.

Buried with Christ but Raised to New Life

The burial of dead people reminds us that all their earthly relationships have ceased. Bill collectors do not go to cemeteries to collect debts owed by the deceased (Other people must take care of the estates of the deceased). People may come to visit the grave of a dead person, but all communication and action are definitely one-way. Death and burial bring final closure to a person's past life. The relationship between a dead person to his or her earthly life is permanently broken. Christians also have a permanently broken relationship to their past life of sin because they died to sin with Christ (Rom. 6:3–11).

A soldier discharged from the army may declare, "It's all over." His former relationship to the army is finished. Since we are dead and buried with Christ, our pre-Christian relationship with sin, the world, the flesh, and the devil is all over. So do not try to revive a romance with your pre-Christian life by fantasizing about the fleshly pleasures of your sinful past. Leave the bridges burned between you and your former life without Christ. Living for self and sin is done. Follow Christ (Luke 9:23), and don't turn back (9:62). Don't even look back (17:32; Phil. 3:13). The worst lies behind you— your old life in sin. The best lies before you—your new life in Christ (3:14).

The moment you trusted Christ you were crucified, buried, and made spiritually alive with Him (Rom. 6:3–4; Eph. 2:5; Col. 2:11–13). You did not even have time to find out how the grave felt. Your burial with Christ closed the door to your past life of sin, but your resurrection with Christ opened up another door to a new life of righteousness.

From a natural viewpoint, death and burial are negative because they mark the end of an earthly life. From the Christian viewpoint, death and burial with Christ are positive because they mark the end of the pre-Christian life centered on self and sin. "Our old self was crucified with Him, in order that our body of sin might be done away with [literally, 'made powerless'] so that we would no longer be slaves to sin" (Rom. 6:6). The "old self" is all the believer's pre-Christian, sinful characteristics produced by the indwelling sin principle (6:6; Eph. 4:22; Col. 3:9).

Sinful self is the core of the pre-Christian life. But the Christian can say, "It is no longer I [the old self] who live" (Gal. 2:20). Christ is the core of the Christian life since "Christ lives in me" (2:20). God does not give us a spiritual resurrection so that we can just try harder in a rerun of the old self-centered life. Instead, we are resurrected with Christ "so we too might walk in newness of life" (Rom. 6:4). Christ's risen life is the Christian's power for newness of life. F. F. Bruce observes, "The resurrection of Christ is presented by Paul as the supreme manifestation of the power of God.

Those who have been raised with Christ have been raised through faith in the divine power which brought Christ back from the dead, and henceforth that power energizes them and maintains the new life with them—the new life which is nothing less than Christ's resurrection life imparted to all the members of His body."[4]

The "old self" is judicially dead and buried. Therefore "lay aside the old self" (Eph. 4:22) and "put on the new self" (4:24). The "new self" is all the Christlike characteristics produced by the indwelling Spirit and conformed to the true image of God. Accordingly, Paul exhorted the Roman Christians to "*lay aside* the deeds of darkness and *put on* the armor of light. Let us behave properly as in the day, not in carousing and drunkenness, not in sexual promiscuity and sensuality, not in strife and jealousy. But *put on* the Lord Jesus Christ, and make no provision for the flesh in regard to its lusts" (Rom. 13:12–14, italics added). Laying aside the old self is like taking off filthy, shameful clothes, and putting on the new self is like reclothing oneself in clean, attractive garments freely provided.

Christians should dress only in the "new self" tailored by God and patterned after Christ (Eph. 4:20–24). You can see if you are spiritually well-dressed by looking in the mirror of God's Word which reveals your inner character as well as your outer characteristics (Heb. 4:12; James 1:22–25). Apply the Word of God, and the Spirit of God will make needed changes in the "clothing" of your character so that you will look more like Christ.

CLAIM CHRIST'S VICTORY OVER THE FLESH

Identification with Christ in His death involves the Christian's death to the sinful "flesh" (or sin principle). The Christian is "not in the flesh but in the Spirit" (Rom. 8:9), and yet the flesh is still in the Christian (7:18; Gal. 5:16–17). So we need to understand Christ's victory over the flesh and claim His victory over it.

Christians Have Crucified Their Flesh with Its Passions and Desires

Christians died to sin and the flesh through crucifixion with Christ at the moment of salvation and not through any efforts at self-crucifixion. We could not crucify ourselves with Christ any more than we could physically crucify ourselves. We might nail both feet and one arm to a cross, but the other arm would be swinging free holding the hammer.

Believers do not crucify themselves, God did this for them through their faith in Christ.[5] This teaching accords with Galatians 5:24, "Now those who belong to Christ Jesus have crucified the flesh with its passions and desires."

Donald Campbell explains Galatians 5:24 this way:

> This [Gal. 5:24] does not refer to self-crucifixion or self-mortification. Rather, it refers to the fact that by means of the baptism of the Holy Spirit, Christians were identified with Christ in His death and resurrection. Paul declared that this had been his experience (cf. [Gal.] 2:20) and that of all believers (cf. Rom. 6:1–6; Col. 2:11; 3:9). While co-crucifixion took place potentially at the cross, it becomes effective for believers when they are converted. This does not mean that their sin nature is then eradicated or even rendered inactive but that it has been judged, a fact believers should reckon to be true (cf. Rom. 6:11–12). So victory over the sinful nature's passions and desires has been provided by Christ in His death. Faith must continually lay hold of this truth or a believer will be tempted to try to secure victory by self-effort.[6]

Self-crucifixion is not needed anyway because each believer can say, "I have been crucified with Christ" (Gal. 2:20), and the results of the Christian's death with Christ are permanent.[7] Though identity with Christ brings a death notice to the "flesh with its passions and desires" (5:24), Christians still have conflict with sinful desires (5:16–17; 1 Pet. 2:11). The flesh relentlessly urges Christians to fulfill its lusts; yet Christians never have to yield to them.

The "sinful flesh" operates like a jack-in-the-box with its suppressed spring. Anytime the spring is not suppressed, the toy figure pops out. And anytime Christians fail to depend on the Spirit to keep the flesh suppressed, the flesh with its sinful deeds pops out. A Christian cannot through self-effort suppress the sin principle anymore than he through self-effort can suppress a physical spring requiring a million pounds of pressure. One of the main purposes of the indwelling Spirit is to do the humanly impossible task for us—to suppress the flesh (Gal. 5:16–21) and to express His fruit (5:22–23).

The flesh in the sense of "sinful flesh" (Rom. 8:3) refers to all the sinful habits developed in and through a person's human nature by the dynamic sin principle. The sinful flesh produces evil thoughts, passions, desires, attitudes, communications, and actions in every area of human life. "Now the deeds of the flesh are evident, which are: immorality, impurity, sensuality, idolatry, sorcery, enmities, strife, jealousy, outbursts of anger, disputes, dissensions, factions, envying, drunkenness, carousing, and things like these" (Gal. 5:19–21). People who fulfill the desires of the flesh manifest the deeds of the flesh.

Believers are said to be "in the Spirit" (Rom. 8:9) and walking "according to the Spirit" (8:4–5). Unbelievers, on the other hand, are "in the flesh" (8:9), walking "according to the flesh" (8:4–5), and having no ability to please the Lord (8:8). Furthermore, "the mind set on the flesh" results in death, is hostile toward God, and does not subject itself to the law of God because it cannot do so (8:6–7).

The sin principle is like a vigorous root that produces a bad tree, and the flesh is like this bad tree. So the flesh is rooted in the sin principle, and the flesh produces its bad fruit called "the deeds of the flesh" (Gal. 5:19). The Spirit opposes the sin principle (Rom. 8:2), the sinful flesh (Gal. 5:16–17), and the deeds of the flesh, which are manifested in and through the human body (Rom. 8:13). Though human nature, including the physical body and its members, is not sinful in itself, human nature influenced and infiltrated by the sin principle constitutes the sinful flesh which is hostile to God.

The flesh does not lie dormant within us like a sleeping enemy that goes into action only when aroused. Scripture teaches and experience confirms that the flesh urges us to carry out its passions, desires, and deeds. Therefore do not leave your bodily members vulnerable because the sinful flesh is a raider who will seize your bodily members and use them as "instruments of unrighteousness" (6:13). Present your body and its members to God as instruments of righteousness so that the Spirit and not the sinful flesh will control them (6:16–19; 8:13; 12:1; Gal. 5:16–17). Each Christian should either affirm or reaffirm this personal decision: "I plan to keep my body and its members committed to God and controlled by His Spirit."

Christians Were Spiritually Circumcised to Remove the Body of the Flesh

Paul's words in Colossians 2:13, "You were dead in your transgressions and the uncircumcision of your flesh," describe the pre-Christian condition. But when a person trusts Christ for salvation, he is "circumcised with a circumcision made without hands, in the removal of the body of the flesh by the circumcision of Christ (2:11). "The circumcision of Christ" is an inner, spiritual change performed by the Spirit, who circumcises the heart or the inner person. This contrasts with the outward, physical circumcision by human hands as it was practiced in Judaism (Rom. 2:28–29). Physical circumcision by itself is an outward action. But spiritual circumcision changes the person's heart and results in genuine love for God and praise from God.

"The body of the flesh" (Col. 2:11) refers to the human body in which the sinful flesh produces all kinds of sins and uses the bodily members to carry out those sins. "Our body of sin" (Rom. 6:6) means we have a "body of the flesh [i.e., sinful flesh]," which results in a "body of death" (7:24).

How do we prevent "the body of the flesh" from manifesting these sins? First, recognize that "the body of the flesh" has been judicially removed "by the circumcision of Christ" (Col. 2:11). This principle aligns with Paul's teaching in Romans 6:6 "that our old self was crucified with Him, in order that our body of sin might be done away with, so that we should no longer be slaves to sin." God has delivered Christians from bondage to sin so that they can conquer sin (6:17–18; 8:13). Second, we are spiritually free to conquer sin by walking according to the Spirit. In this step we build on Christ's judgment of "sin in the flesh" (8:3).

Fighting the sinful flesh with self-effort is as futile as fighting a fire by pouring fuel on it. The more we struggle with the flesh in our own power, the more the flesh seems to overpower us with a vengeance (7:18–25). Only the Spirit can overpower our flesh, so "live according to your new life in the Holy Spirit" (Gal. 5:16, NLT) to counteract "the desire of the flesh" (5:16), "the deeds of the flesh" (5:19–21), and those "deeds of the body" originating from the sinful flesh (Rom. 8:13).

Before salvation the flesh dominated our lives. It brought death, misery, and enmity against God (8:5–8). But in salvation the judicial "removal of the body of the flesh" (Col. 2:11) allows "the Spirit of life in Christ Jesus" to dominate our lives (Rom. 8:2).

RELY ON THE SPIRIT TO EXPERIENCE VICTORY OVER SIN AND THE FLESH

Though Christians are considered dead to sin, sin remains active, attractive, and seductive for Christians. We still feel the pull of sin like the opposite poles of two magnets attracting each other. Just as it takes physical power to keep the magnets apart, so it takes spiritual power—the Spirit's supernatural power—to keep us from yielding to temptation. If we fail to rely on the Spirit, sin becomes more than probable; sin becomes inevitable.

New Christians may be thrilled with the supernatural change in their lives and with their first love for Christ (Rev. 2:4) but shocked that their temptations and tendency to sin still persist from their pre-Christian life. So new Christians (and more mature ones too) wonder, "Where can I find power to resist sin? How can I consistently say no to my sinful desires? Is there a way to win over sin?"

These practical questions remind us that desire for victory over sin may come as a desperate cry from a Christian engaged in a raging conflict with indwelling sin. In Romans 7:14–25 Paul shared in autobiographical form what was evidently his own private war against sin. He explained in this passage that he as a believer tried his best to be sanctified by keeping the Law through self-effort.[8] Did the great apostle Paul emerge as a winner over sin or a loser? Paul admitted that his valiant struggle against indwelling sin ended in total frustration and failure. "For I know that nothing good dwells in me, that is, in my flesh; for the wishing is present in me, but the doing of the good is not. For the good that I wish, I do not do; but I practice the very evil that I do not wish" (7:18–19).

Paul's anguish as a beaten warrior in his battle with sin reached a climax when he said, "Wretched man that I am! Who will set me free from the body of this death?" (7:24). This reminds me of a TV sports program that always showed a ski contestant going out of control and somersaulting over the roof of a building. A verbal caption described the event as "the agony of defeat." A Christian's agony of defeat is when sin inevitably wins over his or her best self-effort to conquer it. Any believer who tries to defeat sin through self-effort will experience spiritual defeat.

Do not think you can do better than Paul did in attempting to conquer sin through human effort. Your best attempt will be like trying to catch poisonous gas in a fish net. It will never work.

God's way to conquer sin works. His Son won the victory over sin and the flesh on the Cross. Because we are identified with Christ the Victor, we can claim His victory as ours.

CHAPTER FIVE

*Overcoming the World through Christ's Victory:
External Opposition to Sanctification*

A MAN, SUCH AS BENEDICT ARNOLD, who changes sides in war, makes a painful discovery. Former friends treat him as a traitor. He becomes an adversary of one-time allies. Changing sides in war suddenly changes his status with his former associates from friend to foe.

Christians have changed sides in spiritual warfare—from the world, the flesh, and the devil's side to the Lord's side. The Father has "delivered us from the domain of darkness [related to Satan's kingdom], and transferred us to the kingdom of His beloved Son" (Col. 1:13).

The world, the flesh, and the devil were never anyone's friends anyway. But at conversion they become the special enemies of the Christian and strongly oppose Christian sanctification. To ignore the world, the flesh, and the devil, and expect them to go away quietly is not God's way to deal with them. Our spiritual opposition is real, but so is Christ's victory over the world, the flesh, and the devil. By faith we can claim Christ's victory as our victory, overcome our spiritual opposition, and progress in sanctification.

This chapter deals with the topic of sanctified living in the world for two reasons. First, Jesus emphasized the believer's relationship to the world. In John 17:13–16, 18 He mentioned "the world" nine times, and in this same context He mentioned the sanctification of believers twice and His own sanctification once (17:17, 19). Thus understanding and practicing sanctification requires understanding and practicing a proper relationship to the world. Second, believers are "not of the world" (17:14), but they are being sanctified only while they are in this world. So this world is the believer's enemy as well as the arena and the battlefield where God sanctifies believers. Sanctification is not a spiritual picnic; it is spiritual warfare in enemy territory! Victory over the world is essential for progress in sanctification.

WHAT THE "WORLD" MEANS IN SCRIPTURE

Self-styled mavericks in society such as Theodore Kaczynski, the "Unabomber," adopt the attitude, "It's us against the world." Christians and the world are against each other too. But the opposition between the Christian and the world differs from the antisocial and rebellious behavior of evildoers. The Christian's pro-God lifestyle based on biblical values automatically opposes the anti-God lifestyle based on the world's values.

In warfare soldiers need to understand the enemy. The same is true of the Christian's warfare with the world. So Christians have an advantage in their warfare with the world if they learn more about the world from Scripture.

Unless indicated otherwise, in this chapter we will use the common New Testament word *world* (Greek, *kosmos*) to mean the evil world system.[1] World in this sense is the temporary system of unsaved humanity spiritually darkened by sin, controlled by Satan, committed to sinful values, and opposed to God's person, plan, and people (Matt. 18:7; John 12:31; Eph. 6:12; James 4:4; 1 John 2:15–17; 5:19).

In biblical usage the evil world system and "this present evil age [*aiōn*]" (Gal. 1:4) are closely related. "This present evil age" emphasizes the period in biblical history when the evil world system stands under Satan's rule (2 Cor. 4:4). The present evil age began with Christ's first coming and will continue until Christ returns to earth and judges Satan and this world (Rev. 11:15; 19:11–20:6). Christ has already pronounced judgment on the world and Satan at the cross. "Now judgment is upon this world;

now the ruler of this world will be cast out" (John 12:31). In biblical teaching "this present evil age" is contrasted with "the age to come" (Mark 10:30), the future period when Christ will bless and reward His people and rule the earth in righteousness.

The evil world system and this present evil age have three noteworthy parallels. First, Christ chose us "out of the world" (John 15:19), and Christ "gave Himself for our sins so that He might deliver us out of this present evil age" (Gal. 1:4). Second, Christians are commanded, "Do not love the world nor the things in the world" (1 John 2:15), and Christians are also commanded, "Do not be conformed to this age [*aiōn*]" (Rom. 12:2, marg.). Third, Satan is called "the ruler of this world" (John 12:31), and "the god of this age [*aiōn*]" (2 Cor. 4:4, marg.); these two titles for Satan evidently involve similar roles.

Though our sanctification occurs in this evil world system and during this present evil age, we should not develop an attitude of pessimism about our situation in enemy territory. Rather, through Christ and His Word we can be optimistic and hopeful. Cheer up! Christ has already rescued us from the condemnation of the present age. And He said, "In the world you have tribulation, but take courage; I have overcome the world" (John 16:33). By God's grace Christians can manifest God's holy character in this evil world system just as a lily can flourish and manifest beauty in a mucky swamp. "For the grace of God has appeared, bringing salvation to all men, instructing us to deny ungodliness and worldly desires and to live sensibly, righteously and godly in the present age" (Titus 2:11–12).

WHY CHRISTIANS HAVE A CHANGED RELATIONSHIP TO THE WORLD

At conversion our relationship to the world is forever changed. This is true for three reasons.

First, Christians have a changed relationship to the world because Christ chose them out of the world (John 15:19). So we are no longer of the world though we are still in it (17:11, 14, 16). Christians have a new allegiance to Christ, and thus the world hates them as it hates Him. Christians also have a new love. They love the Father and the Son and not the world, and they prove their love by obeying God's commands rather than the dictates of the world (14:21, 23; 1 John 2:15–17; 5:2–3).

Second, Christians have a changed relationship to the world through their crucifixion with Christ. "But may it never be that I would boast, except in the cross of our Lord Jesus Christ, through which the world has been crucified to me, and I to the world" (Gal. 6:14). Death with Christ cancels our sinful relationship to the world so that we should no longer love the world or the things of the world. Instead, we are to love God and our neighbors wholeheartedly (Matt. 22:37–40).

Third, Christians have a changed relationship to the world because people of the world lack the Holy Spirit and therefore cannot understand spiritual things or spiritual people (John 14:17; 1 Cor. 2:14). Christians are sometimes surprised that when they share the gospel with unbelieving family members and friends, they do not readily receive it. Jesus' own nation Israel did not receive Him (John 1:11), and even His brothers did not believe Him at first (John 7:5; see also 1 Cor. 15:7). Christ warned His disciples they would be hated and persecuted by the world in the same way the world hated and persecuted Him (John 15:18–25). But we need not get a martyr's complex. Jesus encouraged His disciples to love even their enemies (Matt. 5:44) and to have a positive witness to the world through the Spirit. We too can testify of Christ in the power of the Spirit and show the world love even though the world hates us (John 15:26–27). The Spirit still uses believers as salt and light in the world (Matt. 5:13–14), convicts unbelievers in the world (John 16:7–11), and converts those who believe in Christ (3:5). The world is the Christian's battlefield (16:33), but the world is also the Christian's mission field (Matt. 13:38; 28:19–20).

HOW CHRISTIANS CAN OVERCOME THE WORLD

In order to pursue sanctification in the world, Christians must overcome the external opposition of the world. Christ overcame the world (John 16:33), and Christians can claim His victory over the world by meeting seven requirements.

Be sure you are born of God through faith in Christ (John 1:12–13). Spiritual birth is the Christian's launching pad for victory over the world.

"For whatever is born of God overcomes the world" (1 John 5:4). Until you belong to the Lord by faith in the Lord, you belong to the world and the world will overcome you.

Faith in Christ begins our victory over the world. "And this is the victory that has overcome the world—our faith" (5:4). And the more we live by faith in Christ, the more we continue to overcome the world. Faith is also crucial to meeting these other six requirements.

Believe that through crucifixion with Christ you are dead to the world, released from bondage to the world, and free to live for God (Gal. 6:14). Christians must *believe* they are dead to the world before they can *behave* as dead to the world. To behave as dead to the world means that we, like dead people, refrain from loving the world and living for the things of the world.

The world is also dead to Christians, so the dead world should no longer be attractive to us but rather disgusting and repulsive. Mr. Taylor, a family neighbor during my boyhood, had a fox terrier who loved to chase and kill his chickens. To stop this dog's practice, Mr. Taylor tied a dead chicken to the neck of the fox terrier. Obviously this dog's social life took a sharp nose dive. After several days the dead chicken became thoroughly repulsive to the fox terrier, and then Mr. Taylor detached the chicken's corpse from the dog. From then on the fox terrier avoided all chickens, dead or alive. Likewise, the world should be grossly offensive to us, and we should avoid any sinful response to the world because the world has become like a dead corpse to us through our crucifixion with Christ.

By faith follow Christ and not the ways of the world. Before our changed relationship to the world, we "walked according to the course of this world, according to the prince of the power of the air, of the spirit that is now working in the sons of disobedience" (Eph. 2:2). Unbelievers are numb to the fact that they are controlled by Satan's spirit and the world's spirit. However, Christians "have received, not the spirit of the world, but the Spirit who is from God" (1 Cor. 2:12).

When we rely on God's Spirit and God's Word, we can resist "all that is in the world, the lust of the flesh and the lust of the eyes and the boastful pride of life" (1 John 2:16). Satan used these three sources of temptation from the world to tempt Christ in the wilderness. Christ faced and overcame these temptations because He was filled with the Spirit and knew the Scriptures (Luke 4:1, 4, 8, 12). The Spirit gives us the *power* and Scripture gives us the *principles* to overcome Satan. These biblical principles for victory over the world are like power tools. Power tools work only if we choose to use them and to rely on the power flowing through them. Likewise, we must choose to use biblical principles and to rely on the Spirit's power to overcome the world's temptations, because victory over the world is not automatic.

Walking by the Spirit and in the Word can make a practical difference in how Christians relate to the people and the things of the world. Like Christ, Spirit-filled Christians can love the people of the world and use the things of the world to serve God and people. This sharply contrasts with the way the world uses people and loves things.

By faith avoid worldliness in your character. Worldliness is a person's self-centered attitude of love for the evil world system and earthly things rather than for God and heavenly things. Christians can pretend to avoid worldliness by not living like the world in their outward conduct and yet still love the world and the things of the world in their innermost character.[2] Jesus called this practice hypocritical because it looks like righteous conduct but is inwardly sinful (Matt. 23:28).

Worldliness is basically a character issue. Christians tend to be worldly to the extent that worldly values influence their character. Therefore to overcome the world Christians must build their character with biblical values and virtues and not with the world's values. Again, when Jesus faced Satan's three temptations in the wilderness, He was completely committed to God's values and God's will because Jesus was saturated with God's Word. In Psalm 40:8 the preincarnate Christ expressed His relationship to God's will and God's Word in this way: "I delight to do Thy will, O my God; Thy law is within my heart."

By receiving and obeying God's Word we lay the foundation for God's Spirit to construct biblical values and virtues in our character. The root of a tree determines the fruit of a tree; the source of a well determines the water of the well; and the character of a person determines the outward moral and spiritual characteristics of a person. Therefore the ultimate cure for worldliness in Christians is transformation of their character by the Spirit of God through the Word of God.

A Christian married couple, Jeff and Sarah, have identical Ford Explorers. To Sarah, her car is simply a means of transportation home to work to Little League practice. But Jeff's car is to him a symbol of power; he loves this eight-cylinder, four-wheel-drive Explorer with leather seats in a way that hinders complete love toward God and others. Viewing a car the way this husband does is what John meant by loving the things of the world. Such obsessive love for things is a form of idolatry, which characterizes the unsaved "who set their minds on earthly things" (Phil. 3:19). Christians are warned, "Guard yourselves from idols" (1 John 5:21).

Of course, possessing a car is not wrong in itself, just as owning a donkey or a camel would not have been wrong in Jesus' day. But it is wrong when a car "possesses" a Christian. As Paul wrote, "All things are lawful for me, but I will not be mastered by anything" (1 Cor. 6:12).

A job is a proper means to earn a living, but when someone says, "My job is my life," then that individual has a wrong relationship to God and his job. Owning a home is fine as long as we do not let it own us. My wife and I used to drive by a beautiful two-story house on the way home from church. We noticed that the owners were often working on their home. One day we were shocked to see that in place of that beautiful home, there was only a thin layer of ashes. The local newspaper recorded the homeowners' reaction: "Over the years our home had come to mean everything to us, and now we have lost everything." They lived for things that do not last, and now those things were forever lost. "The world is passing away, and also its lusts; but the one who does the will of God abides forever" (1 John 2:17). When we live for the Lord and other people and not for the evil world system, we live for what lasts.

When anything—such as a home, car, job, money, power, or popularity—or anyone—wife, husband, child, parent—controls us so that the Lord does not have complete control of our lives and our undiminished love, then that is worldliness. Avoid worldliness in your thoughts and attitudes as well as in your conduct. Then your innermost character and also your conduct will be genuine and not hypocritical.

Love God the Father and not the world. "If anyone loves the world, the love of the Father is not in him. For all that is in the world, the lust of the flesh and the lust of the eyes and the boastful pride of life, is not from the

Father, but is from the world" (1 John 2:15–16). We cannot love opposites at the same time just as a physical object cannot travel in opposite directions at the same time. "No one can serve two masters; for either he will hate the one and love the other, or he will hold to one and despise the other. You cannot serve God and mammon" (Matt. 6:24).

The world tempts Christians to reduce their love for the Father. Temptations from the world come through "the lust of the flesh and the lust of the eyes and the boastful pride of life" (1 John 2:16). The world relentlessly tells us, "Obey your thirst. Satisfy your hunger. Fulfill your sexual desires." These legitimate desires can be properly fulfilled in the Father's time and way. But the world implores us, "Love yourself and not the Father. Gratify your desires now in your way." Satan and our fleshly lusts intensify our urge to yield to the world's temptations. The pull of the world is strong, but we can say no to the world by applying the Word and relying on the Spirit. And we can respond in this way because we love the Father (John 14:31).

Distraction from the world requires a positive attraction of love for God. Jesus always obeyed the Father because He loved the Father too much to disobey (John 14:31). The stronger our love for God, the stronger our obedience to God and our resistance to the world. A strong, loving relationship to the Lord is similar to a strong, loving relationship in marriage. A husband is far less likely to be attracted to a woman other than his wife if he already deeply loves his wife and continues growing in his love for her.

One primary way we can grow in our love for God is to appreciate and experience more of His love for us. The more we learn of His love for us and allow His love to flow into us by His Spirit (Rom. 5:5), the more we will love Him. "We love, because He first loved us" (1 John 4:19). Our genuine love for God is really His love rebounding from our hearts and directed back to Him. And growth in love for God lessens our love for the world.

Seek heavenly things and store up heavenly treasures. "If then you have been raised up with Christ, keep seeking the things above, where Christ is, seated at the right hand of God. Set your mind on the things above, not on the things that are on earth" (Col. 3:1–2). The world says, "Do not be so heavenly minded that you are no earthly good." However,

Christians will not be any earthly good if they are not heavenly minded (3:1–11).

Jim Elliot is a prime example of a Christian whose mind and treasures were directed heavenward. Jim was totally committed to God and to his mission to evangelize the unreached Auca Indian tribe of Ecuador. In this endeavor he was martyred by the Aucas on January 8, 1956. His most famous words best describe his heavenward view and values: "He is no fool who gives what he cannot keep to gain what he cannot lose." Later many Aucas became Christians, and Jim's exemplary commitment to Christ and heavenly things has impacted innumerable people.

When our relationship with the Lord cools down, we tend to warm up to the world and to commit spiritual adultery against the Lord (James 4:4). So keep your heart's desire in heaven, and your heart will be less drawn to things on earth. The psalmist wrote, "Whom have I in heaven but Thee? And besides Thee, I desire nothing on earth" (Ps. 73:25). Can you affirm these same words from your heart?

Find your joy in the Lord and not in the world. People naturally seek happiness. And when Christians are not finding their true happiness or inner joy in the Lord, they tend to seek happiness in the world. Lewis Sperry Chafer wrote with keen insight, "The world and 'worldly' Christians turn to so-called 'worldly' things because they discover in them an anesthetic to deaden the pain of an empty heart and life."[3] If we are abiding in Christ and continually filled with the Spirit, we experience true joy in the Lord and need not seek happiness in the world. The psalmist knew where true joy is found. "In Thy presence is fullness of joy; in Thy right hand there are pleasures forever" (Ps. 16:11). "The joy of the LORD is your strength" (Neh. 8:10), but worldly pleasures will weaken your spiritual growth and service.

HOW CHRISTIANS SHOULD RESPOND TO THE PEOPLE OF THE WORLD

We have discussed how to respond to the temptations of the world, but how do we respond to the unbelievers of the world? From Christ's perfect example we can draw some practical guidelines for responding properly to unbelievers.

Maintain moral purity in all relationships to unbelievers (Ps. 1:1). Jesus is described as "holy, innocent, undefiled, separated from sinners and exalted above the heavens" (Heb. 7:26). Though believers can still sin, the New Testament uses the term "sinners" only of unbelievers.[4] Jesus associated with sinners in a social and physical sense, but He was spiritually and morally separated from sinful living. He was "tempted in all things as we are, yet without sin" (4:15). So Jesus did not practice isolation from the sinners of the world by being Pharisaic or monastic. Rather, He mingled with sinners to minister to them, but He was not involved in their sin for He was sinless.

Paul also exemplified sanctified conduct in the world. He reminded the Corinthian Christians "that in holiness and godly sincerity, not in fleshly wisdom but in the grace of God, we have conducted ourselves in the world, and especially toward you" (2 Cor. 1:12).

James taught that Christians should practice Christian social action in the world, yet maintain spiritual purity. "Pure and undefiled religion in the sight of our God and Father, to visit orphans and widows in their distress, and to keep oneself unstained by the world" (James 1:27). We should be in the world serving Christ, without the world being in us. We can properly function in the world like a ship functioning in the water. But when water leaks into the ship or the world enters us, then a serious problem occurs.

Do not compromise biblical values by accommodating the sinful values of the world. Jesus lived for eternal, spiritual values and not for the temporary, material values of this world, for "the world is passing away, and also its lusts" (1 John 2:17).

Have compassion for people. Matthew wrote of Jesus, "Seeing the multitudes, He felt compassion for them, because they were distressed and downcast like sheep without a shepherd" (Matt. 9:36). Jesus' heart went out to the crowds. His compassion was not mushy sentimentalism or self-serving flattery. Jesus' kind of compassion confronted and corrected people in their sin as well as comforted them in their sorrow. So our guideline is to show compassion for people according to truth and with love (Eph. 4:15; 1 John 3:18) the way Jesus did.

As I grow older, I pray that I will show more of Jesus' compassion toward people. In the aging process, we become either more compassionate or more bitter and cynical. Observing that people who show compassionate care are rare, Paul pointed to Timothy as one who exemplified genuine concern for others and their interests (Phil. 2:19–22).

Contact unbelievers and build relationships with them but do not commit their sins. The religious leaders criticized Jesus for being "a friend of tax collectors and sinners" (Matt. 11:19). They said, "This man receives sinners and eats with them" (Luke 15:2). The religious leaders grumbled at Jesus' practice because they could not accept His physical and social contact with sinners even though He maintained spiritual and moral separation from their lifestyle (Heb. 7:26).

Jesus had social contact with Zacchaeus, "a chief tax collector" (Luke 19:2, NIV), and He brought him to salvation (19:8–10). Jesus also allowed a sinful woman to wash His feet with her hair, and she received forgiveness from Him through her faith.

Communicate the gospel to people by the model of your life and the message of your lips (2 Cor. 3:2–3; 4:13). Jesus preached to the multitudes (Matt. 13:2–3), but He also witnessed to individuals such as Nicodemus and the woman at the well. Not all Christians are gifted evangelists, yet God expects each Christian to evangelize (Acts 1:8; 2 Tim. 4:5).

The Gospels record the attentiveness of Jesus' audiences whether He spoke to many people (Matt. 7:28–29) or only one person (Luke 10:39). People wanted to hear what Jesus taught because they sensed He cared for them and lived what He professed to believe. His heart went out to them. Christians should follow Jesus' model by having compassion for people and by communicating the gospel to them clearly, correctly, and relevantly in the Spirit's power (John 15:26–27).

WHEN CHRISTIANS LEAVE THIS WORLD THEY ENTER GLORY WITH CHRIST

Christians are citizens of heaven, Christ's ambassadors to the world (2 Cor. 5:20). The world is enemy territory. The world is enemy territory. But it is also the arena for our sanctification and service until we enter glory with Christ.

God promises that someday Christians will be out of this world and with Christ in heaven (5:8; Phil. 1:23; 3:20–21; 1 Thess. 4:16–17), but this truth should mean more to Christians than just an escape from this troublesome world. Our hope of heaven should invigorate our Christian life and service on earth (1 Cor. 15:58).

Viktor Frankl, a prisoner in Auschwitz and other Nazi prisons, testified from personal experience and observation that humans can endure almost anything if they choose to have hope.[5] Christians have solid hope based on God's sure promise that if we die or if Christ comes for us before our death, we will leave this world and go to be with Christ in heavenly glory. This promise can give us hope in spite of adverse circumstances (1 Pet. 1:3–9), encourage us to persevere in sanctification and service (Phil. 1:20–25), and help us endure suffering, deprivation, imprisonment, and even a martyr's death (2 Tim. 4:6–8).

All Christians share this promise: "When Christ, who is our life, is revealed, then you also will be revealed with Him in glory" (Col. 3:4). Whatever Christians have imagined about the glorified Christ will seem a poor representation compared to the real sight of Christ when He appears

Biblical promises of Christ's coming and our glorification are intended not just to satisfy idle curiosity or to promote sensationalism but to help our spiritual lives. Every New Testament reference to the Lord's coming has practical application for Christian living. Whenever we see a biblical passage about Christ's coming, we should immediately ask, "How should I respond to the truth of Christ's coming according to this biblical passage?" For example, Christians should love Christ's coming (2 Tim. 4:7–8), long for His coming (Rev. 22:20), look for His coming (Titus 2:13). Also, Christians should abide in Him (1 John 2:28) and labor faithfully (1 Cor. 15:58) in view of His coming. Respond to Jesus' coming in these biblical ways and you will enjoy peace and release from worry (John 14:1–3, 27), receive comfort concerning deceased believers in Christ (1 Thess. 4:13–18), and purify your life (1 John 3:1–3).

The fact that God will glorify Christians when Christ returns is so certain that Scripture says, "whom He justified, these He also glorified" (Rom. 8:30). That is, from God's perspective believers are already "glorified" because His purpose cannot fail (8:29). Between justification and glorification God is sanctifying Christians by His Spirit so that they are becoming more like Christ.

Sanctification occurs in the world, but it influences the Christian's experience in heaven. Sanctification requires humility, cross-bearing, and suffering (Matt. 11:29; Luke 9:23; Phil. 1:29). Like Christ, if you humble yourself, you will be exalted. If you bear your cross, you will wear your crown. If you experience earthly suffering, you will experience heavenly glory (Rom. 8:18; 2 Cor. 4:17).

Table 3 show contrasts between Christians' present earthly experience and their future heavenly experience.

Table 3—Two Major Stages of Christian Experience

Stage One—The Present	Stage Two—The Future
In the world	In Christ's presence
Temporary	Eternal
Humility	Exaltation
Cross-bearing	Crown-wearing
Suffering	Glory
Describable	Incomparable
Trials	Triumph

Christ has finished stage one, and He entered stage two at His ascension and exaltation (Eph. 1:19–23; Phil. 2:9–11; Heb. 2:9–10). Christians who die before Christ's return leave stage one and go to be with Christ. Their bodies are dead but their spirits are alive with Christ in heaven (2 Cor. 5:8). This is called the intermediate state.[6] All believers, whether physically dead or alive, enter stage two when they receive a glorified body at Christ's return (Phil. 3:20–21).

Stage one reminds us that sanctification requires humility, cross-bearing, and suffering. Stage two gives hope for the future and encourages us to persevere in the present. "Let us not lose heart in doing good, for in due time we will reap if we do not grow weary" (Gal. 6:9).

Perseverance in stage one brings hope and divine love to our hearts through the Spirit. "Tribulation brings about perseverance; and perseverance, proven character; and proven character hope; and hope does not disappoint, because the love of God has been poured out within our hearts through the Holy Spirit who was given to us" (Rom. 5:3–5).

However difficult your service or intense your suffering for Christ, stage one is still a "momentary, light affliction," and stage two is "an eternal weight of glory far beyond all comparison" (2 Cor. 4:17). Likewise, "The sufferings of this present time are not worthy to be compared with the glory that is to be revealed to us" (Rom. 8:18). When you wonder if your Christian journey through stage one is worth it, consider the victories and glories of stage two and fix your eyes on the Lord Jesus. Then you will gain confidence to run your Christian race so that you finish well (Heb. 12:1–3).

Until Christ returns God has called us to live for Him in the evil world system. Otto C. Keller is an example of a Christian who had great spiritual impact on the world without being of the world. We see this fact in part of W. Phillip Keller's tribute to his father, Otto Keller:

> The net result was that God honored Dad's devotion to his duty as few men have been honored. First of all I give it as my own personal witness that never did I ever see such steady transformation in any person's life as his. The grace of God, the touch of the Master's hand, the gentle influence of God's gracious Spirit were so apparent in his character and conduct that for me as a growing youth it was an ongoing miracle. He was my hero! No one ever moved me more to live only for God and the benediction of my generation.
>
> His was a totally selfless life poured out for others. He gave and gave and gave that others might gain life. This in essence is the very life of God, the love of Christ, demonstrated in the brief, shining life of a common man.
>
> When he died at the comparatively young age of fifty-four, it was the dear Quaker doctor who buried him in the warm soil of the land he loved so well. Dad left behind a legacy of over 500 African pastors and evangelists with uncounted thousands upon thousands of joyous Christians under their care. He had come to Kenya as a common layman in its hour of despair. He left with the honor and majesty of God's mighty presence sweeping across the country.[7]

Through commitment to Christ and God's power, Otto Keller led a holy life and had a significant spiritual impact in a hostile world. So can we.

CHAPTER SIX

Getting to Know the Divine Helper:
The Spirit's Role in Sanctification

DURING THE 1970S our family took a tour through a sawmill next to Payette Lake in McCall, Idaho. We saw how the logs entered the mill from Payette Lake, were processed in the mill, and finally became various sizes of lumber. What impressed me most about the sawmill was the steam engine which powered it. Every function of the sawmill depended on power from that steam engine. No steam engine—no power—no operation of the sawmill. In a similar way Christians are totally dependent on the Holy Spirit's power for the operation of sanctification in their lives.

Every Christian has the Holy Spirit and spiritual power through Him (Rom. 8:9; 2 Cor. 1:22). "Spirit-powered" is the right motto for Christians, yet the motto is practically meaningless unless we understand and use the Spirit's power to sanctify us.

Some Christians sense their need for the Spirit's power but then live as if He did not exist. Someone has suggested that Christians function about 90 percent of the time with no concern about the Holy Spirit. If this figure is correct, then many Christians are definitely not experiencing the Spirit's available power in their sanctification and service.

The problem of powerless Christians is not caused by the divine Spirit. The Spirit is all-powerful and perfectly willing to help us. But if we expect to tap His power, we must understand His role in our lives and then we must respond properly to Him.[1]

THE HOLY SPIRIT IS A DIVINE PERSON

Recognize That the Spirit Is a Divine Person

"I believe in the deity and personality of the Holy Spirit." This statement represents the belief of orthodox Christians throughout church history. As the third person of the Trinity, the Holy Spirit shares the same divine essence as the Father and the Son (Matt. 28:19; John 14:16–17; Acts 5:3–4).[2] The deity and personality of the Spirit require that we reject all concepts of the Spirit that consider Him less than full deity or only an impersonal "it" or "force."

Relate to the Spirit as a Divine Person

Since the Spirit is a divine person who lives in each Christian, our relationship to Him should be personal, reverent, obedient, and intimate.

Jesus Christ emphasized that the Spirit is a divine person and that believers can have an intimate relationship with Him (John 14:16–17, 26; 15:26–27; 16:7–8, 13–15). Christ taught that the world does not know the Spirit, but He told His disciples, "You know Him because He abides with you and will be in you" (14:17). In this verse the Greek word translated "you know" (*ginōskete*) generally goes beyond factual knowledge (which the world can have about the Spirit) to include experiential knowledge.

A personal, intimate knowledge of the Spirit begins with a personal, saving knowledge of Christ. When a person trusts Christ, he or she immediately becomes God's spiritual child, and God becomes that person's heavenly Father. The Lord Jesus says, in essence, to a new believer, "I want you to meet your spiritual Father in heaven and to recognize that the Holy Spirit now dwells in you."

Since the disciples already knew Christ as God's Son and their Savior, they also knew the Father and the Spirit.[3] Christ promised the disciples further teaching to help them develop a closer relationship with the Father and the Spirit as well as with Him (1423; 16:12–15).

Believers can experience "the fellowship [koinōnia] of the Holy Spirit"[4] (2 Cor. 13:14) which means "association, communion, fellowship, close relationship."[5] Thus believers should avoid the kind of impersonal, mechanical relationship to the Spirit that some illustrations imply. Two gears smoothly meshing instead of clashing together illustrates a proper "relationship," but two gears cannot respond to each other in voluntary, intelligent, effective, and creative communication as two persons can. Individuals and their relationships change in ways not possible with inanimate objects. Think of the many interpersonal dimensions in marriage and the potential for growth or for deterioration in a married couple's relationship. We relate to the Spirit as a divine person and not as an inanimate object or an abstract concept.

God the Spirit is unchangeable in His divine being and attributes, but this does not mean His relationship to believers is rigid or mechanical. Rather, God intends that believers have a dynamic and personal relationship to the Spirit (Rom. 8:16, Gal. 5:16). The interface between believers and the Spirit can be even more intimate and multidimensional than any relationship involving only human persons. Of course, the imperfection and consequent room for growth in the relationship between us and the Spirit is totally on our side. As our relationship to the Spirit grows, so our Christian life grows.

Respond to the Spirit in Balance with Response to the Father and the Son

The persons of the triune Godhead exist and work together in perfect harmony, and Scripture teaches that Christians can have fellowship with the Father, the Son, and the Spirit (1 Cor. 1:9; 2 Cor. 13:14; 1 John 1:3). Therefore growth in our relationship to one person of the Trinity enhances our relationship to the other two.

Scripture also teaches that each person of the Godhead has distinct roles. For instance, in prayer we recognize the Father as the main Addressee of our prayers (Matt. 6:9; 18:19), the Son as the Mediator of our prayers (Eph. 2:18; 1 Tim. 2:5), and the Spirit as the Helper in our prayers (Rom. 8:26–27). So the general formula for prayer in the New Testament is to the Father, through the Son (or in the name of the Son), and in the Spirit.

Respond to the Spirit and to Your Feelings within Biblical Boundaries

Our response to the Spirit and our expectations of His activity should function within biblical boundaries. Otherwise we will get out of step with the Spirit and hinder our relationship to Him and His purpose for us.

Within biblical parameters Christians can properly relate their human experiences and feelings to the Spirit's person and work. For instance, Christians experience the Spirit's ministry as He "bears witness with our spirit that we are children of God" (Rom. 8:16). Christians can feel grief about their sin, just as the Spirit feels grief about their sin (Eph. 4:30).

Without a biblical framework human experience can be misinterpreted and lead to false doctrine. Human feelings can mislead Christians, especially when Christians confuse their feelings with the Spirit's leading. Four guidelines can help us relate our experiences and feelings to the Spirit and His ministries.

- *Beware of judging your relationship to the Spirit by your physical, emotional, or even "spiritual" feelings.* Christians may feel an awesome exhilaration either in solitude or in a huge crowd of other Christians. Such feelings, however, do not necessarily mean one is in close communion with the Spirit. We can mistake good feelings in pleasant circumstances for divine approval of our spiritual condition. Christians can appear carefree, happy, and very expressive to God and others and yet have a wrong relationship to the Spirit through some hidden sin.

- *Recognize that your feelings can change almost instantly while your relationship to the Spirit may remain the same.* Over the telephone someone tells you your father just died. Or you receive news that one of your children has been in an accident and is in a life-threatening condition. I have personally experienced both situations. Did my sudden change of emotions because of these announcements mean that my spiritual condition went from good to bad or from bad to good because my feelings went from joy to sorrow and from carefree to deep concern? Trying to see reality only through one's momentary feelings is like looking through a kaleidoscope and rotating it before each view. Each view is different and so one's feelings may change in short intervals. But underneath our variable feelings we can respond biblically to the Spirit and develop a deep, intimate, stable relationship with Him. So remember to judge your spiritual condition by God's unchanging Word and not by your changeable feelings.

• *Cultivate your spiritual and emotional health by acknowledging your true feelings completely to yourself and God and selectively to appropriate humans* . A few months before my father died, he reminded me, "Henry, you can share anything with me." He meant it; and I cherished that privilege. Thankfully, I have that same open communication with my wife, Shirley. We all need a family member or friend with whom we can share openly and confidentially.

More importantly, we can share everything with our heavenly Father, with Jesus our Savior, and with the Holy Spirit, our divine Helper. People operate under pressure the same way containers do. Even the strongest containers will burst under enough pressure, so they need relief valves for safety. For your spiritual, mental, emotional, social, and physical welfare, use your relief valve—share honestly and totally with God, as Asaph the psalmist did (Psalm 73). Holding in all your feelings neglects God's provision for your relief and can endanger yourself and others.

• *Recognize that biblical response to the Spirit can produce a sense of spiritual well-being despite unpleasant emotional, relational, and physical feelings* (2 Cor. 6:10). Christians in a right relationship to the Spirit experience God's love and presence, inner peace and joy, and other fruit of the Spirit (Gal. 5:22–23).

• *Let Scripture control your thinking, feelings, and relationship to the Spirit.* Then you can exercise freedom of experience and expression within biblical boundaries and avoid an "anything goes" approach that can lead to doctrinal aberration and bizarre behavior.

THE HOLY SPIRIT SANCTIFIES CHRISTIANS

The Spirit is the Christian's divine "Helper" (*paraklētos*; John 14:16, 26; 15:26; 16:7). We need to know how the Spirit sanctifies us so that we can cooperate with Him and fully benefit from His sanctifying work.

The Spirit Sanctifies Christians through a Lifelong Process

Sanctification is a lifetime spiritual journey that requires human effort and God's empowerment. We may have crises and dramatic turning points in our spiritual pilgrimage that can accelerate our sanctification. Yet there is no experience in this life that can make Christians perfect so that they no longer need progress in sanctification. *Perfect* Christlike maturity always lies before us as the goal of sanctification. Paul recognized this truth in his own experience: "Not that I have already obtained it, or have already become perfect, but I press on in order that I may lay hold of that for which also I was laid hold of by Christ Jesus" (Phil. 3:12).[6]

Progress in sanctification requires steadfastness and a fixed focus on the goal just as a lengthy footrace does. Therefore "let us run with endurance the race that is set before us, fixing our eyes on Jesus" (Heb. 12:1–2).

New Christians should grow rapidly toward spiritual maturity rather than lagging in spiritual infancy for several years as did the Corinthian Christians (1 Cor. 3:1–3) and also the Christians addressed in Hebrews (5:12–14).[7] Even Christians who reach spiritual maturity soon can always progress more in sanctification and reach higher levels of Christlike maturity (Phil. 3:12–14).

Instead of believing that sanctification is a lifelong process or that spiritual maturity requires "time" (Heb. 5:12) and "practice" (5:14), some Christians try shortcuts to spiritual maturity; current thinking promotes a quick-fix approach. Modern advertising has trained people to want everything their way and immediately. Virtues of self-control and patience to delay gratification in order to achieve a higher purpose or a greater value are hardly considered options in present thought. Quick-fix methods to attain spiritual maturity are ineffective and inevitably disappointing. Dallas Willard correctly observes, "But the one lesson we learn from all available sources is that there is no quick fix for the human condition. The approach to wholeness is for humankind a process of great length and difficulty that engages all our own powers to their fullest extent over a long course of experience. But we don't like to hear this. We are somewhat misled by the reports of experiences by many great spiritual leaders, and we assign their greatness to these great moments they were given, neglecting the years of slow progress they endured before them."[8]

Instant methods to attain Christlike maturity will surely fail us just as crash diets may bring quick weight loss but fail to achieve permanent results. Conscientious dieters need to follow a proper plan of eating and exercise that can help achieve lasting weight loss and good health. And Christians need to follow the biblical plan of empowerment from the Spirit, spiritual nourishment from the Word, and practice of biblical disciplines to attain Christlike maturity (Heb. 5:12–6:1).

Christians have tried many shortcuts to achieve instant spiritual maturity, but we will examine only two.

First, some Christian speakers and writers give the impression that through an unconditional surrender to God, Christians will immediately reach a high level of spirituality, love, peace, joy, and Christian victory with reduced spiritual conflict. Scripture does command us to present ourselves to God so that we will progress in sanctification and realize His will (Rom. 6:13, 16, 19; 8:6; 12:1). Though decisive dedication to God prepares us for greater spiritual growth, it cannot bring instant spiritual maturity or relieve our conflict with sin, the world, the flesh, and the devil in this earthly life.

Commitment to God is like a foundation for a building. The foundation of a building is indispensable, but the rest of the building will not go up instantly. Laying a solid foundation is prerequisite to the long, arduous task of erecting the building's superstructure. Christians should first lay the foundation of dedication to God[9] and then build on their dedication a superstructure of spiritual growth (Phil. 3:12–14).

Second, some Christians expect to grow quickly through an alleged "secret" to spirituality. Some believe the secret to spirituality is for earthly Christians to experience total sanctification and eradication of all their sin, but such teaching is unbiblical and deceptive.[10] As John wrote, "If we say that we have no sin, we are deceiving ourselves, and the truth is not in us" (1 John 1:8).

What if the alleged spiritual secret is biblically neutral because it is neither supported nor condemned by Scripture? For example, some Christians find journaling very helpful. We may recommend journaling to others, not as a biblical command, but as a practical means that may help promote spiritual growth. Christians who write a daily spiritual journal but neglect the Spirit, the Word, and other means of sanctification will greatly limit their spiritual growth.

If a supposed secret to spirituality is taught either explicitly or implicitly in Scripture, then it is not a secret. During most periods in church history certain biblical teachings were neglected while others were overemphasized. Teachings neglected for a time would seem like well-kept secrets when they became prominent again. This was certainly the case when the Reformers began to articulate justification by faith. And certain doctrines about Christian living such as the spiritual disciplines may suffer neglect and then receive their appropriate place in current Christian teaching. But neglected doctrines are not really secrets if they are truly biblical, for God has already revealed them in His Word.

Whenever we encounter an alleged secret of sanctification, we should first determine if it is biblical. If it is taught in Scripture, then it is not really a secret. If it is not taught in Scripture, then it cannot be the key to spiritual living since Jesus indicated that the main means of sanctification are revealed in God's truthful Word. "Sanctify them in the truth; Thy word is truth" (John 17:17).

Individuals, groups, churches, or movements that teach and practice unbiblical methods of sanctification mislead and victimize others in the worst way—in their spiritual life. Wrong ways to sanctification produce only disappointment, hypocrisy, and spiritual retardation in Christian living instead of Christlike maturity.

Christians can avoid becoming victims of spiritual fraud by focusing on biblical methods of sanctification and by using biblical truth to evaluate all teaching about sanctification or any other alleged Christian teaching (John 17:17). Then we can discern God's truth from false teaching and maximize spiritual growth.

The Spirit Sanctifies Christians toward Christlike Maturity

God intends to conform every Christian to His Son's image (Rom. 8:29), and the Spirit is sanctifying Christians toward that goal.[11] Paul elaborated on this process: "But we all, with unveiled face beholding as in a mirror the glory of the Lord, are being transformed into the same image from glory to glory, just as from the Lord, the Spirit" (2 Cor. 3:18). Scripture is the primary means to reveal "the glory of the Lord" to Christians, and the Spirit is transforming Christians "into the same image [i.e., the Lord's image] from glory to glory."[12] The New International Version translates the expression "from glory to glory" as "ever-increasing glory." Here "glory" is the radiant manifestation of Christ's perfect character most fully revealed in the New Testament.

God's sanctification process reminds me of Mount Rushmore National Memorial. Mount Rushmore was just another granite cliff. But Gutzon Borglum, the designer and supervisor of this memorial, could envision within this chosen granite cliff the facial sculptures of four United States presidents: George Washington, Thomas Jefferson, Theodore Roosevelt, and Abraham Lincoln. These potential sculptures visualized by Borglum became actual through his and his son's work.

Likewise, God envisions the potential of each believer to bear His Son's image (Rom. 8:29). And God is actualizing His vision by sculpting us into Christ's likeness through His Spirit. Mount Rushmore furnished the material for these presidents' sculptures, but believers do more than furnish the material for their transformation through sanctification; God requires believers to participate in the process (Phil. 2:12–13).

Examine your participation in your sanctification with this question: Am I learning more of Christ from Scripture, applying more Scripture to my life, and depending more on the Spirit to make me more like Christ? When you can consistently answer yes to these questions, you are experiencing the essence of sanctification because you are becoming what God envisioned you to be —Christlike.

The Spirit Sanctifies Christians Primarily through God's Word

God's Spirit is the personal change-agent in sanctification, and God's Word is His instrumental change-agent. "The sword of the Spirit . . . is the word of God" (Eph. 6:17). Normally the Spirit uses Scripture and not a mystical experience to sanctify Christians. The Spirit produced Scripture (2 Pet. 1: 21), and He teaches therein that scriptural truth is essential for spiritual growth (John 17:17; 2 Tim. 3:15–17; 1 Pet. 2:2). Knowing that the Spirit sanctifies us through the Word does not automatically sanctify us. The Spirit sanctifies us as we learn and apply the Word by His help.

Proper response to both the Spirit and the Word is crucial for spiritual growth and for balance in Christian living. God never intends that we choose between the Spirit and Scripture anymore than we would choose which hand to clap with. In each case we need both. When you give the Spirit and the Word proper place in your spiritual life, you help protect yourself from one of Satan's main tactics in spiritual warfare—imbalanced Christianity. Physical and spiritual falls both happen most easily when people are off balance.

Christians need Scripture to reveal God's will and the Spirit to help them understand and do God's will (Eph. 5:17–18; Col. 3:16–17). Knowing and doing God's will according to Scripture puts us on the right path to pursue sanctification (Ps. 119:133; Heb. 12:14). Otherwise our personal senses and the whims of other people control us so that we become confused about the right path to take and the right decisions to make in Christian living. Jeremiah recognized the inability of humans to guide their own lives when he said, "I know, O LORD, that a man's way is not in himself, nor is it in a man who walks to direct his steps" (Jer. 10:23). God's Word is our map (Ps. 119:105), and God's Spirit is our Guide (Rom. 8:14) to keep us following Christ instead of floundering in the Christian life.

Scripture provides objective criteria to help us evaluate our experiences, feelings, thoughts, and intentions in relation to the Spirit's ministries and private promptings (Phil. 4:8). When our experiences, feelings, thoughts, or intentions are contrary to Scripture, then we know that they are not from the Spirit, but when they fall within the boundaries of Scripture, then they could be the Spirit's means to prompt and lead us in God's will. Christians should not conclude that all their feelings and impressions are Spirit-produced. But each Christian should seek to discern through a of combination Scripture, prayer, wise counsel, peace of heart, and sensitivity to the Lord when personal impressions and promptings are from the Spirit.[13]

Professed experiences "in the Spirit" without biblical and rational control can lead to confusion, uncontrolled emotionalism, and even fanaticism both in the local church and in individual Christians. Someone may claim, "I glowed 'in the Spirit' like a bright light during an evening of solitude in the desert." If no witnesses were present when this event allegedly happened, then it is difficult to prove that it did or did not occur. Even if it did occur, this does not prove that it was right according to God's prescribed will. An experience may be real but not right. Adam and Eve's original transgression was very real to them—maybe the most poignant event in their lifetime—but it definitely was not right.

Certain Christians make animal-like noises in the presence of others and claim that their practice is "in the Spirit." However, the Spirit-produced Word encourages ministry that edifies other Christians and not just oneself (1 Cor. 14:5, 12, 17). Making animal-like noises is not prescribed in the Word of God, and it is difficult to see how this practice edifies others and promotes peace and orderliness (14:1–40). Christians may mean well when they claim to have spectacular "in-the-Spirit" experiences such as glowing in the dark or making noises like animals. However, such experiences and practices can divert us from a Christ-centered, Scripture-based, and Spirit-filled Christian life. If we seek to understand and do God's will revealed in His Word, God's Spirit will surely empower us to perform God's prescribed will.

What if Scripture is emphasized without the Spirit? Then we may conform to the letter of Scripture in a cold, perfunctory way that paralyzes our spirituality. This approach characterized the legalistic Pharisaism of Jesus' time. He denounced this empty form of religion and pronounced judgment on its practitioners (Matt. 23:13–36). Christians who neglect the Spirit may end up living like the hypocritical, legalistic Pharisees (see Gal. 3:1–5).

Our Lord aimed several criticisms at Pharisaic legalists: They emphasized minor biblical details and neglected major biblical commandments (Matt. 23:23); they sometimes displaced biblical truth with human tradition (Mark 7:1–13, esp. v. 13); and they were guilty of hypocrisy (Matt. 23:13–15, 23, 25, 27–29). We must avoid Pharisaic legalism which emphasizes (a) the letter of the law without the life of the Spirit, (b) the head and its factual knowledge without the heart and its personal relationships, and

(c) outward conduct without inner character. Such an approach leaves no practical place for the Spirit's work in the inner person. Christians who give proper place to both the Spirit and Scripture find that He gives them spiritual reality, liberty, and vitality (Rom. 8:2; 2 Cor. 3:17) in place of hypocrisy, legalism, and lifeless religion.

Christians can agree that they need the Spirit's power for their spiritual life to function just as they need an engine for their car to function. But often *knowledge* about the Spirit and His power is substituted for *appropriation* of the Spirit and His power. This subtle substitution may account for the moral failure of many Christians through scandalous sin. So Paul's warning is always timely for all Christians, "Therefore let him who thinks he stands take heed lest he fall" (1 Cor. 10:12). The more intensely we pursue sanctification by obeying God's Word and relying on God's Spirit the less liable we are to fall into sin.

CHAPTER SEVEN

Responding Biblically to the Spirit:
The Spirit's Role in Sanctification (Continued)

KNOWING HOW TO RESPOND to different people can be difficult. If we face a tax audit, we want to respond properly to the tax auditor's questions. If we have a job interview, we hope our responses will favorably impress the interviewer. And if we do not personally know the tax auditor or the interviewer and the exact questions they may ask, then knowing how to respond to them may be difficult.

Right response to the Spirit is much more important than right response to tax auditors and job interviewers (though good preparation and prayer for God's help in these human relations is certainly appropriate). And if responding properly to other humans can be difficult, then you would expect that proper response to God's Spirit is much more difficult if not impossible. Thankfully, just the opposite is true. Believers can know the Spirit personally (John 14:17), though He is an infinite, divine person. Furthermore, believers can know from Scripture exactly how they should respond to the Spirit. The Spirit is unchangeable in His being and characteristics. So the right response to Him never changes, whereas the right response to other humans often does change with the situation. Christians can and must respond properly to the Spirit to have a right relationship to Him and to promote their sanctification.

In our response to the Spirit we should follow four biblical commands. Two are negative—"Do not grieve the Holy Spirit of God" (Eph. 4:30) and "Do not quench the Spirit" (1 Thess. 5:19), and two are positive— "Be filled with the Spirit" (Eph. 4:18) and "Walk by the Spirit" (Gal. 5:16).

DO NOT GRIEVE THE HOLY SPIRIT

Any sin grieves the Holy Spirit because sin opposes the Spirit's perfect holiness. The context surrounding Ephesians 4:30 reveals some specific sins that grieve the Spirit.

Sinful Actions Grieve the Spirit

Stealing is an example of sinful actions that grieve the Spirit (Eph. 4:28, see Exod. 20:15). Christians may think of stealing only as robbing a bank, embezzling money from an organization, or breaking into a house and taking valuable property. But stealing can be as subtle as giving your employer fewer hours of work than you agreed to perform for certain wages. A skilled worker at a manufacturing company was asked, " How many people work at your place of employment?" He replied, "About half of them." And the other half, composed of slackers, included some Christians.

A Christian organization allowed some of its employees to have a private code number for personal use of a copier at a reasonable cost per copy. But the practice had to be stopped because some of these Christians would not pay for their copies. That is stealing, and it grieves the Spirit, even if those employees thought the organization somehow owed them the copies without charge.

When Paul reminded Christians not to steal, he added a positive practice. "Let him who steals steal no longer; but rather let him labor, performing with his own hands what is good, in order that he may have something to share with him who has need" (Eph. 4:28, NASB). In addition to refraining from stealing, Christians should earn their living by legitimate labor and then go the extra mile by sharing with those in need (Acts 18:3; 2 Thess. 3:7–12).

Sinful Language Grieves the Spirit

"Let no unwholesome [literally, 'rotten'] word proceed from your mouth" because foul and destructive speech pains the Spirit (4:29). "Slander" is an example of sinful speech (4:31). Anyone who maligns another aligns with "the devil," whose name means "the slanderer" (1 Pet. 5:8; see Rev. 12:10). Scripture regards slander as verbal cannibalism because it damages and can destroy the reputation of others. "But if you bite and devour one another, take care lest you be consumed by one another" (Gal. 5:15).

Yet many people still believe this saying: "Sticks and stones may break my bones, but words can never hurt me." This quote is a half-truth because the first part is true, but the second part is plainly false. Wrong words do hurt, and they stick in victims like barbed hooks. Verbal abuse is often the most serious hurt that people inflict and suffer, and we know it by experience, observation, or both.

To avoid grieving the Spirit and hurting other humans, we must practice tongue-control. No one can tame the tongue through mere human power. But Christians can yield to the Spirit and gain tongue-control through *His* power. And Christians who gain control of their tongue show that they have progressed in sanctification to become a "perfect" (Greek, *teleios*, "mature") Christian (James 3:2).

Christians may gain control of their tongues but not necessarily of their thoughts. Christians with an uncontrolled thought life are still immature. Admittedly people do not speak everything they think, and wisely so. We can hide our thoughts from people more easily than we can hide our speech. Still, the contents of the heart and the communication of the mouth are closely connected. As Jesus said, "For the mouth speaks out of that which fills the heart" (Matt. 12:34). People often have wrong thoughts that they never plan to reveal. Then in an unguarded moment they impulsively push the "play" button of their mouth and the hidden tape in their heart begins to roll. The mouth does eventually expose the hidden things of the heart. In order to control our mouth and its words, we must let the Spirit control the source of our words, our heart. Only then do we avoid thoughts and talk that grieve the Spirit.

Christians should stop grieving the Spirit with sinful speech. They should also replace destructive words that harm others with constructive words that communicate God's grace so that they edify other believers and evangelize unbelievers (Col. 4:5–6).

Sinful Attitudes Grieve the Spirit

Christians grieve the Spirit through sinful attitudes as well as through sinful actions and words. "Let all bitterness and wrath and anger and clamor and slander be put away from you, along with all malice" (Eph. 4:31). In contrast to these sinful attitudes which generally lead to sinful words and actions, God commands Christians to "be kind to one another, tenderhearted, forgiving each other" (4:32). Our first step is to stop grieving the Spirit with our sin, but then we need to take a second step and replace our sinful attitudes with right attitudes.

When Christians do not grieve the Holy Spirit with their sins, the Spirit can fill them and produce His fruit in and through them. Then we have the Christlike character and power to be kind and tenderhearted toward others and to forgive them when they hurt us with wrong attitudes, words, and actions.

If Christians have buried feelings of bitterness and anger, these feelings will keep springing up despite attempts to keep them suppressed. Denial of these destructive feelings only intensifies and prolongs their harm, and they can keep the stomach agitated and the head aching. Christians need to deal with an unforgiving spirit saturated with anger and bitterness, though they may believe that their sinful feelings are justified. These sinful feelings are like an anchor dragging behind a boat that cause one's spiritual growth to slow, stop, or even go downward. Feelings of bitterness and anger and an unforgiving attitude severely grieve the Spirit and hinder His sanctifying work within us.

If you have these negative emotions, you can find release from them by taking these steps: (a) confess to God that you have these sinful feelings and by faith claim God's forgiveness (1 John 1:9); (b) forgive anyone who has sinned against you (Eph. 4:32); (c) confront your victimizers in love and share with them your concerns; and (d) replace your sinful attitudes with right attitudes (4:32). Christians who take these steps lay a firm foundation for emotional health and spiritual vigor. Otherwise, a Christian's public life may look fine, but in his or her private life sin is seething and the Spirit is grieved.

How do we know when we have grieved the Spirit?

Disobedience to God's Word is the surest signal that we have grieved the Spirit. Since Scripture originates from the Spirit and expresses His perfect will, anything contrary to Scripture is contrary to the Spirit. The Spirit is pleased when we obey Scripture and pained when we disobey it.

Also our feelings may indicate that we have grieved the Spirit. To interpret correctly our physical, emotional, and relational feelings can be difficult. We already discussed the danger of gauging and guiding our spiritual life by feelings and without biblical input. Christians should evaluate their lives within a biblical framework but also carefully consider their feelings.

Just as people can usually detect through their feelings a wrong relationship with another human, so Christians generally sense through their feelings when they have a wrong relationship with the Spirit. When we have a lingering and deep conviction that we have grieved the Spirit and find confirmation in Scripture, then our feelings have pointed us in the right direction.[1] We can find help in understanding how the Spirit relates to our feelings by reading chapter 8, "The Spirit and Our Emotions," in Charles Swindoll's book, *Flying Closer to the Flame*.

A believer's emotional sensitivity when he or she grieves the Spirit can be even greater than in human relations because Christians can have a much more intimate relationship to the Spirit than to any human. And strained, bad, or broken relationships are usually the major source of grief for individuals. So Christians probably know better than they wish to admit when they grieve the Spirit. Our sin hurts the Spirit and us too.

You can stop grieving and hindering the Spirit by practicing four principles: (a) Recognize that your disobedience hurts and hinders the Spirit. (b) Confess and forsake all sin. (c) Claim God's promise of forgiveness and cleansing so that the Spirit can freely change you and work through you. (d) Obey Scripture through the Spirit's power to prevent sin. By following these four principles you can allow the Spirit freedom to fill them and sanctify you.

DO NOT QUENCH THE SPIRIT

Christians are commanded, "Do not quench the Spirit" (1 Thess. 5:19). What does it mean to quench the Spirit? Some teach that quenching the Spirit is a wrong response to the Spirit's ministry within oneself.[2] However, the next verse, "Do not despise prophetic utterances" (5:20), infers that quenching the Spirit means hindering the Spirit's manifestation through others rather than through oneself.

Lang says the command is Paul's "warning against a deliberate suppression of the extraordinary operations of the Spirit in the congregation."[3] Hogg and Vine also note, "the figure latent in the verb ['quench'] here is that of Matt. 3:11, Acts 2.3, and . . . the meaning seems to be 'do not prevent or obstruct the manifestations of the Holy Spirit's power in others.'"[4] For instance, if a Christian exercises the gift of exhortation within biblical guidelines (Rom. 12:8), we quench the Spirit if we try to squelch this Christian's exhortation.

When we quench the Spirit's ministry through other Christians, we grieve the Spirit within us and hinder their ministry to us. Ministry to one another helps Christians grow. Therefore when interpersonal ministry in the body is hindered, the whole body is hindered in its corporate growth toward Christlikeness. Instead of quenching the Spirit, permit and receive the Spirit's ministry through other Christians to you and to other members of Christ's body (1 Thess. 5:19).

BE FILLED WITH THE SPIRIT

God expects all Christians to be filled with the Spirit. Paul wrote, "And do not get drunk with wine, for that is dissipation, but be filled with the Spirit" (Eph. 5:18). The Greek verb for "be filled" (*plērousthe*)[5] indicates that the Spirit does the filling and that believers should be Spirit-filled continually. Four practical questions need to be considered about the Spirit-filled life.

What Does It Mean to Be Spirit-Filled?

Two main lines of evidence support the conclusion that to be Spirit-filled means to be Spirit-controlled.[6]

First, when we examine representative contexts in which the Greek verbs for "fill"[7] and the Greek adjective for "full"[8] occur in relation to the Spirit and to other things, we find that whatever fills people takes control of their attitudes and actions. For example, people filled with the Spirit bless, praise, and thank the Lord, boldly proclaim the Word of the Lord, give to others, and experience joy (Luke 1:67; Acts 4:31–35; 13:52). But people "filled with rage" at Jesus tried to destroy Him (Luke 4:28–29; 6:11), and the religious leaders "filled with jealousy," imprisoned the apostles (Acts 5:17–18).

Second, the comparison between "drunk with wine" and "filled with the Spirit" in Ephesians 5:18 indicates that the Spirit controls a Spirit-filled Christian just as wine controls a wine-filled person. However, the results of being Spirit-controlled are in contrast to the results of being wine-controlled. Spirit-controlled Christians live according to the will of God in their character, choices, communication, and conduct. Wine-controlled persons live contrary to the will of God and according to their flesh in their character, choices, communication, and conduct.

Why Do Christians Need to Be Spirit-Filled?

Christians need to be Spirit-filled because God commands it. Christians are not commanded to be regenerated by the Spirit, indwelt by the Spirit, baptized by the Spirit, or sealed by the Spirit because all these ministries of the Spirit occur once for all at the time of salvation. But believers may be filled with the Spirit repeatedly, and they may lack the Spirit's filling and thereby grieve the Spirit through their disobedience.

Sometimes Christians view God's command to be Spirit-filled as an option rather than an obligation. They may feel unworthy to be Spirit-filled and believe that the Spirit-filled life is reserved for an elite class of Christians. Yet God requires all Christians to be Spirit-filled, and Christians who are not Spirit-filled disobey God's command and miss the spiritual blessings of a Spirit-filled life.

"Be filled with the Spirit" is just as much a divine command as "Do not get drunk with wine." Suppose an evangelical church member were found drunk in a congregational meeting of his church. The other church members would expect the church leaders to take biblical steps to deal with this Christian's drunkenness (Gal. 6:1) because Scripture prohibits drunkenness (Rom. 13:13; Eph. 5:18). We would hold the drunken Christian accountable for flagrantly disobeying Scripture. But do we hold Christians accountable for not being Spirit-filled? Probably not. This is inconsistent practice, and it will continue until the church body and individual Christians take seriously God's command regarding the filling of the Spirit.

Christians need to be Spirit-filled to know and do God's will (Eph. 5:17–18). The filling of the Spirit in every New Testament occurrence "signifies the empowering presence of the Spirit of God, enabling the individual to accomplish the will of God."[9] God's will for believers includes and emphasizes their sanctification. "For this is the will of God, your sanctification" (1 Thess. 4:3). The Spirit-filled life that fulfills God's will and pursues sanctification is not for "super" Christians only; it is the kind of life God expects from each Christian (Heb. 12:14).

How Can Christians Be Spirit-Filled?

Christians can be Spirit-filled by meeting five basic requirements. These are not complex, mysterious, austere, and burdensome stipulations. Rather they are basic Christian practices that are interrelated, included in Christian obedience, and intended to bring spiritual liberty and blessing. Also, meeting these requirements is not just "following a formula" or "complying with regulations." Instead these requirements are ways by which we can rightly relate to the Holy Spirit. Practice these requirements, and you will enjoy them and their result—the Spirit-filled life.

- *First, to be Spirit-filled, Christians must confess and forsake their sins* (Prov. 28:13; 1 John 1:9). All sin counters the Holy Spirit's perfect purity and hinders His ministry through Christians. The Spirit's desire to fill and use our human lives shows His great condescension, and His desire to fill and use clean lives shows our need for confession and cleansing of all our sin (see Ps. 139:23–24).

86

The Spirit is the divine Sanctifier, and the close connection between sanctification and cleansing from sin is taught in 2 Corinthians 7:1. "Therefore, having these promises, beloved, let us cleanse ourselves from all defilement of flesh and spirit, perfecting holiness in the fear of God." Cleansing ourselves from sin (Ps. 119:9, 11), helps us conform to the Spirit's character and experience His control. And Spirit-controlled Christians always advance in sanctification.

- *Second, to be Spirit-filled, Christians must present (yield or offer) themselves to God* (Rom. 6:13, 16, 19; 12:1). Paul commanded believers, "Put yourselves at God's disposal" (Rom. 6:13).[10] When you do this, the Spirit takes control, works God's will through you, and sanctifies you (1 Thess. 4:3).

We grieve the Spirit when we hold back anything from God because "the Holy Spirit, whom God has placed within us, jealously longs for us to be faithful" (James 4:5, NLT). Anything we withhold from God, we leave at the disposal of the world, the flesh, and the devil. The devil is not timid about stepping in and taking control of unyielded areas of our lives. Therefore yield all to God so that you "do not give the devil an opportunity" (Eph. 4:27).

- *Third, to be Spirit-filled, Christians must maintain a life focused on Christ* (Col. 3:16–17).[11] The Spirit's ministry is focused on Christ, for the Spirit testifies of Him (John 15:26–27), teaches about Him (16:12–15), glorifies Him (16:14), and transforms believers into His image (2 Cor. 3:18). Therefore to align with the person and purpose of the Spirit, we must focus on Christ and obey Christ. Scripture calls us to keep our lives Christ-centered instead of self-centered (5:14–15). When we are Christ-centered, our lives are Spirit-filled.

- *Fourth, to be Spirit-filled, believers must be obedient to God's Word.* A comparison of Ephesians 5:18–20 and Colossians 3:16–17 shows that being Spirit-filled and obeying Scripture are closely connected. Both passages begin with a command: "Be filled with the Spirit"

(Eph. 5:18), and "Let the word of Christ richly dwell within you" (Col. 3:16). Obedience to each command yields the same results— a ministry of singing, praise, and thanksgiving to one another and to God (Eph. 5:19–20; Col. 3:16–17).[12]

The place we give the Word in our lives measures our willingness to let the Spirit fill us. We can expect the Spirit to fill us when we let Christ's Word richly indwell us. And the more we are Spirit-filled, the more we can receive, understand, and obey Christ's Word. The Spirit and the Word work together as supportive partners, so we need to let them both fill our lives.

- *Fifth, to be Spirit-filled, Christians must live by faith.* Believing God is as essential to Christian living as breathing oxygen is to physical living. "Without faith it is impossible to please Him" (Heb. 11:6). "And whatever is not from faith is sin" (Rom. 14:23).

Christians have been saved by faith (Acts 16:31; Eph. 2:8–9), and they should go on living by faith (Col. 2:6). As Paul wrote, "The righteous man shall live by faith" (Rom. 1:17), and "I live by faith in the Son of God" (Gal. 2:20).

Faith is more than a requirement to be Spirit-filled. Faith is the principle that underlies the four previous requirements and activates them. By faith we confess and forsake our sins; by faith we present ourselves to God; by faith we keep our lives Christ-centered; and by faith we obey God's Word. Once we meet the requirements for being Spirit-filled, we are to believe that God will fill us with His Spirit.

A Christian can memorize these five requirements and still miss the Spirit-filled life. Does this mean the formula failed? No, the requirements are biblically based, and if any Christian meets the requirements, he or she will be Spirit-filled. But knowledge without action is like a dead battery; it accomplishes nothing. If you truly hunger and thirst for the Spirit-filled life (Matt. 5:6; John 7:37–39), you will learn and do the requirements, and the Spirit will fill you. The spiritually hungry heart says, "I love God and want to obey His command to be Spirit-filled. I want what God wants for me at any cost."[13]

Some may think these requirements for the Spirit-filled life are like mechanical and legalistic steps that stifle the spiritual life. This is a legitimate concern, but these requirements are dynamic and liberating biblical truths (John 8:31–32; 1 John 5:3) and not legalistic or burdensome.

Should Christians pray to be Spirit-filled? General practice of prayer is certainly included in the requirement to obey the Word in order to be Spirit-filled. Still, Christians can also pray specifically for the Spirit's filling according to these purposes: (a) to express genuine desire to be Spirit-filled, (b) to ask for God's help to meet the requirements to be Spirit-filled, and (c) to express trust that you will be Spirit-filled as you meet the requirements through God's power. This kind of prayer for the Spirit's filling is biblical so long as it comes from an obedient life and conforms to God's will. Also, if Christians are indifferent about being Spirit-filled, they can pray appropriately that God will change their indifferent attitude into a spiritual passion for a Spirit-filled life.

Here is a fitting prayer for the Spirit's filling:

> Thank you, heavenly Father, for your holiness, love, and sovereign plan. I want to worship you in spirit and in truth and to do your will. I praise you for your Son, Jesus Christ, who died for me, saved me, and gave me a holy position in Himself. I am grateful for your indwelling Spirit and His purpose and power to make me holy because You are holy. I confess my sins of
> _____ [name your specific sins here] and claim your promise to forgive me and to cleanse me from all unrighteousness. Lord, I desire to be a Spirit-filled Christian. Help me to meet the requirements for the Spirit's filling so that I will obey you, become more like your Son, serve your people, and witness for You. Lord, I believe that You will fill me with your Spirit as I obey You. Glorify Yourself through me, O Lord! I pray in Jesus Christ's name Amen.

What Are the Main Results of Being Spirit-Filled?

The Spirit-filled Christians can expect these wonderful results.

- Spirit-filled believers manifest Christlike character (Gal. 5:22–2).

- Spirit-filled believers overcome sin, the world, the flesh, and the devil (Gal. 5:16–18; Eph. 6:10–18).

- Spirit-filled believers can pray "in the Spirit" and according to God's will (Eph. 6:18; Jude 20).

- Spirit-filled believers can fulfill their biblical responsibilities in their personal, interpersonal, marital, family, and vocational relationships (Eph. 5:18–6:9).

- Spirit-filled believers have power for bold and effective evangelism (Acts 4:31).

Some of the results of the Spirit-filled life overlap the requirements of the Spirit-filled life. For instance, a major requirement for the Spirit-filled life is obedience to God's Word (John 14:21; Col. 3:16–17), yet we listed obedience to biblical responsibilities in human relationships as a major result of the Spirit's filling. If some requirements to be Spirit-filled are virtually the same as the results, how can we first get the results to meet the requirements? It is like asking how to get an egg without a hen.

This question can be answered by viewing the Spirit-filled life in three stages: (a) When Christians initiate obedience to meet the requirements for the Spirit's filling, God empowers them to obey. (b) Consequently they become Spirit-filled and produce the results of the Spirit-filled life. (c) Then through the results of the Spirit's filling they can express more obedience and become more Spirit-filled.[13] This cycle repeats itself as long as Christians increasingly obey the requirements for the Spirit's filling. So each stage in the cycle of the Spirit-filled life enhances the other stages. In other words, the Spirit-filled life produces sanctification, and sanctification promotes the Spirit-filled life. These results should motivate us to give high priority to the Spirit-filled life because the Spirit's filling is "the source of anctification as well as all spiritual fruitfulness."[14]

WALK BY THE SPIRIT

God commands Christians to "walk by the Spirit," and if you obey this command, "you will not carry out the desire of the flesh" (Gal. 5:16). Walking is used in both the Old Testament and New Testaments to represent a person's way of life, manner of conduct, or lifestyle (Gen. 17:1; Ps. 1:1; Eph. 2:2; 1 John 1:7). Walking by the Spirit means that we function under the

Spirit's control in every activity legitimate for Christians. So we must "be filled with the Spirit" (Eph. 5:18) before we can "walk by the Spirit."

A Spirit-controlled Christian is comparable to an airplane on the runway that is pilot-controlled, empowered, and ready for takeoff. The airplane taking off and flying under the pilot's control depicts a Christian functioning under the Spirit's control or walking by the Spirit. If our life is Spirit-filled, we can walk by the Spirit, and then all our choices, communication, and conduct can be controlled by Him.

Our responsibility to walk by the Spirit correlates with the principle that Christians "walk by faith, not by sight" (2 Cor. 5:7). Walking *by faith* means we continually and consciously rely on God and His provision for all our needs. Walking *by the Spirit* means we continually and consciously rely on the Spirit's control to prevent sin and to progress in Christlikeness. Thus walking by faith and walking by the Spirit are two essential principles in the Christian life that enhance each other.

How much the Spirit controls and changes your life depends on how much you respond to these commands. Christians serious about sanctification will obey these commands immediately and consistently.

CHAPTER EIGHT

Aiming for Christlikeness:
God's Goal for Sanctification

THE BOYS AND GIRLS in the commercial say, "I want to be like Mike," that is, Michael Jordan, the famous Chicago Bulls basketball star. Older people are reminded that they still can be creative and productive like Grandma Moses, who took up painting when she was seventy-six years old and became an acclaimed artist. Almost everyone from toddlers to senior citizens looks for role models to follow.

Christians also look for role models, but who should their role models be? The only perfect model for Christians is Jesus Christ, and God's goal for Christians is conformity to Christ's perfect humanity. A believer can imitate other believers but only insofar as they are Christlike (1 Cor. 11:1; 1 Thess. 1:6–7). Christians commit idolatry when they give godlike status and worship to mere humans or to angels (1 John 5:21; Rev. 22:8–9). But Christians can rightly worship and imitate Christ because He is fully God and also perfect man (Matt. 14:33; John 5:23; Heb. 1:6).

Even unbelievers can show traits that the Lord commends to His people (Luke 16:8). Jesus recognized the wisdom of people who count the cost before they commit themselves to a building project or to warfare, and He taught that likewise people should count the cost before they commit themselves to follow Him as disciples (9:28–33).

This chapter emphasizes that Christlikeness is God's goal for Christians and that sanctification is His way for believers to become more like Christ.

SCRIPTURE SHOWS THAT CHRISTLIKENESS IS THE GOAL OF SANCTIFICATION

"Hitch your wagon to a star." "Aim for the top." "Be the best you can be." These mottoes urge us to pursue lofty ambition. But is ambition right or wrong for Christians?[1] Ambition is wrong when our goal is self-exaltation, since God warns us not to seek great things for ourselves (Jer. 45:5; Matt. 23:12). But ambition is right when our goal is to become like Christ for God's glory. Four key biblical points support this goal for sanctification.

First, God has predestined His people to "become conformed to the image of His Son" (Rom. 8:29), and God is accomplishing this goal in His people through sanctification (2 Cor. 3:18).

Second, the Spirit transforms Christians into Christ's image, and this transformation is the essence of sanctification.

Third, Paul aimed to "present every man complete [Greek, *teleion*, 'full-grown' or 'mature'] in Christ" (Col. 1:28). He intensely desired to see Christ's character developed and displayed in each believer. Paul expressed this passion in Galatians 4:19, "My children, with whom I am again in labor until Christ is formed in you." Christlike maturity then is the goal of spiritual development.

Fourth, the objective of the church, the corporate body of believers, is Christlikeness according to Ephesians 4:13: "until we all attain to the unity of the faith, and of the knowledge of the Son of God, to a mature man, to the measure of the stature which belongs to the fullness of Christ." In this context "a mature man" does not refer to individual believers but to the maturity of the body of Christ. The reference in verse 12 to "the building up of the body of Christ" supports this interpretation. However, "we" is used distributively of individual believers in verse 15, "we are to grow up in all aspects unto Him who is the head, even Christ."[2] The biblical concept of the body of Christ assumes that the body consists of individual members and that the body grows more Christlike only as the individual members grow more Christlike through ministry to each other (4:12). According to 4:13–15, "Christ then is the Source of a believer's growth and also the Aim and Goal of his growth."[3]

Other more general teaching of the New Testament also reveals that Christlikeness is the pattern and goal for Christian sanctification.

Teaching of Christ

Jesus commanded His followers to learn from Him and to imitate His example: "Take My yoke upon you, and learn from Me, for I am gentle and humble in heart" (Matt. 11:29). Followers of the Master become like Him, just as trainees show the influence of their trainer. "A pupil is not above his teacher; but everyone, after he has been fully trained, will be like his teacher" (Luke 6:40). Some surveys show that the example of a Christian teacher's life is rated higher by the students as a major means of Christian nurture than a teacher's lectures about Christian nurture. True, communicating biblical truth in understandable ways is essential if others are to grow, but the impact of biblical truth is reinforced by the truth lived in a human example. Thus the model of our Christian life may impact people more than the message of our lips, especially if we are a role model of Christlikeness as Paul was.

Jesus impacted His followers through His doing as well as through His teaching (Acts 1:1). He practiced humble service when He washed His disciples' feet (John 13:5–14), and then He told them, "I gave you an example that you also should do as I did to you" (13:15). None of the disciples would ever forget the Lord of glory on hands and knees washing their feet and the lesson in humble service they learned from Christ's action (see 1 Pet. 5:5).

Through His works and words Jesus provided a flawless example for Christians to imitate. And He commands all who claim Him as Lord to obey Him, follow Him, and live like Him (Luke 6:46; 9:23; John 13:15).[4]

Teaching of Paul

Christ was Paul's spiritual model, and Paul challenged Christians to "be imitators of me, just as I also am of Christ" (1 Cor. 11:1; see 1 Thess. 1:6).

Imitation of Christ is not a way of salvation since no one can perfectly follow His example (Rom. 3:23). Christ is the ultimate model of godly living for the saved, but they must remember that any genuine imitation of Christ works "inside out." Believers can manifest genuine Christlikeness only because Christ dwells in them and reproduces His character through them. The flesh can imitate but not duplicate Christlike characteristics. Imitation of Christlike characteristics by the flesh is like imitation fruit; it looks like the real thing but it is fake. A wax apple may look real, but tasting it is very different from tasting an actual apple. Fleshly imitations of Christlikeness always fail because God always distinguishes the artificial from the authentic.

Paul taught some practical guidelines for imitating Christ:

- Manifest Jesus Christ through your life.

- "Put on the Lord Jesus Christ" (Rom. 13:14) by developing and displaying Jesus' virtues through the Spirit's power.

- Live as Christ did for the benefit of others and not for self (Rom. 15:1–3).

- Represent Christ as His living letter so that people can learn about Jesus by observing your life (2 Cor. 3:3).

- Love sacrificially as Christ did by giving yourself to serve others (Eph. 5:2, 25).

- Have the humble attitude of Jesus with confidence that God will exalt you in His time (1 Pet. 5:6).

- Testify to unbelievers as Christ did with Spirit-filled boldness and winsomeness (1 Tim. 6:13).

Paul aimed for some specific objectives in His pursuit to know and experience Christ more, and he stated these objectives in Philippians 3:10: "that I may know Him and the power of His resurrection and the fellowship of His sufferings, being conformed to His death." The apostle admitted that he had not yet attained perfect maturity in Christ (3:12). So we should not picture Paul standing on the elevated ledge of perfection and telling other Christians journeying upward that he had attained absolute perfection whereas they hadn't. He was still running intensely in the Christian race toward the goal of perfect Christlikeness. He was definitely a "front runner" (probably *the* "front runner") who kept pressing on to finish as a winner for Christ (1 Cor. 9:24–27; Phil. 3:13–14; 2 Tim. 4:7–8).

Teaching of the Writer to the Hebrews

In Hebrews Christ is most prominent as our Great High Priest who mediates the New Covenant, redeems His people, and represents them in heaven (Heb. 4:14; 5:9; 9:15). Christ our High Priest also sympathizes with our weaknesses and exemplifies victory over every type of temptation because He "has been tempted in all things as we are, yet without sin" (4:15). Someone rightly said, "Jesus has walked in everyone's shoes apart from sin."

Jesus came to earth in human flesh (2:14, 17–18), lived in perfect holiness among humans (4:15; 7:26), and left us a flawless example to follow (12:2–3). And Hebrews reveals some practical ways to follow His example: overcome temptation (4:15), learn obedience through suffering (5:8), practice holy living (7:26), and endure undeserved opposition (12:1–3).

Teaching of James

James is the "wisdom book" of the New Testament. The author emphasizes divine wisdom received through prayer (James 1:5–8), based on God's "word of truth" (1:18), and contrasted with earthly wisdom (3:13–18). The wisdom of the Word sanctifies us when we receive and practice it (1:21–25). And the fruit of wisdom from the Word is "Christlikeness— peace, and humility and love (James 3:17)."[5]

Teaching of Peter

Peter told suffering Christians, "Christ also suffered for you, leaving you an example for you to follow in His steps" (1 Pet. 2:21). Christians need to know that through God's grace they can endure suffering in a Christlike way (5:10, 12).

Peter commanded Christians to "grow in the grace and knowledge of our Lord and Savior Jesus Christ" (2 Pet. 3:18). Rejecting sin and receiving the Word are requirements to grow more Christlike (1 Pet. 2:1–2). Peter listed spiritual qualities beginning with "faith" (2 Pet. 1:5) and ending with "love" (1:7) which believers should cultivate and thereby reflect "true knowledge of our Lord Jesus Christ" and imitation of His character (1:8).

Teaching of John

John taught that Christians should back up their claim of abiding in Christ by conducting themselves like Christ (1 John 2:6). When Christ comes we will be exactly "like Him" (3:2). In the meantime, Christians should "abide in Him, so that when He appears, we may have confidence and not shrink away from Him in shame at His coming" (2:28). We also purify ourselves "just as He [Christ] is pure" by focusing our hope on His coming (3:3).

In Revelation John showed that Christ is our example of overcoming all earthly opposition (Rev. 11:15; 17:14; 19:15–20:15). Christians overcome all earthly opposition through faith in Christ (John 16:33), and they will share with Him in judging and ruling the world (1 Cor. 6:2–3; 1 John 5:4–5; Rev. 3:21; 5:10).

CHRISTIANS GLORIFY GOD BY BECOMING CHRISTLIKE THROUGH SANCTIFICATION

How can the goal of our sanctification be Christlikeness? Is not the chief end of man to glorify God and to enjoy Him forever? The goal of Christlikeness and the goal of glorifying God do not conflict when we see how they relate to each other. Christlikeness is the *immediate* goal of our sanctification. And Christlikeness is also our main means of glorifying God, our *ultimate* goal (1 Cor. 10:31). In other words, progress in sanctification makes us more Christlike, and the more Christlike we become the more we glorify God.

CHRISTIANS MUST CHANGE TO BECOME CHRISTLIKE

Commit to Spiritual Change in Your Life

To grow more like Christ, Christians need radical changes in their living just as some persons need radical surgery to become more healthy. Sometimes the only way to gain in holiness, as in physical health, is through pain. God used a painful trial in the apostle Paul's life to develop more Christlike characteristics in him (2 Cor. 12:7–9). And God often uses pain in our lives to make us more like Christ. The spiritual gain is always worth the pain that God permits us to suffer.

You may agree mentally with the preceding paragraph, but do not underestimate your inclination to resist change, especially when change is painful. Our human nature balks at change even when we know that the change is for our spiritual benefit. Some Christians regard personal change the same way the comic regarded his impending death: "I really don't mind dying; I just don't want to be there when it happens." And our real feeling is, "I don't mind change so long as it doesn't affect me."

We resist change for many reasons. Change may disturb our desire to "sleep in" when we need to get up to spend vital time with the Lord. Change can bring extra burdens into our lives when we turn from a self-centered life to a life centered on others and their needs. Change can cause persecution for Christians who go public with their biblical convictions in opposition to popular opinion. We resist change for countless other reasons, and such resistance can slow and even stop sanctification, whereas receptivity to change accelerates it. So if you want unhindered sanctification, then be ready to make and accept the drastic changes God reveals in His Word and plans for your life, and God's Spirit will accomplish those changes.

Use God's Means for Spiritual Change in Your Life

In addition to the work of the Father, Son, and Spirit in sanctification (as discussed in chapters 2–7), God provides Scripture, prayer, discipleship, and spiritual disciplines, circumstances, and other Christians to transform us into His image.[6] We will consider each of these in more detail in later chapters.

We need to keep each means of sanctification in balance with the others so that we avoid a lopsided approach to our spiritual growth. We will neither neglect nor overemphasize any biblical means of sanctification if we give each means the same relative emphasis that Scripture does.

Some Christians prayer, especially for pressing physical needs, more than learning and obeying God's Word or having ministering to God's people. This unbalanced approach produces warped believers, lopsided Christian living, and limited spiritual growth.

By aiming for holistic Christian living and growth through a biblically balanced approach to sanctification, we avoid following the latest novel, radical, or faddish ideas about spirituality. Taking a radical approach to spiritual growth just to be controversial, outrageous, or noticed is actually self-centered rather than Christ-centered.

CHRISTIANS CAN MANIFEST CHRISTLIKENESS

To get a clearer picture of a Christlike Christian, we need to look at some specific characteristics of Christ as revealed in Scripture. Then we will see some specific ways to manifest Christlikeness through our Christian humanity.[7]

Christlike Christians Manifest the Fruit of the Spirit

We see Jesus' character beautifully portrayed in the Spirit's fruit of "love, joy, peace, patience, kindness, goodness, faithfulness, gentleness, self-control" (Gal. 5:22–23).[8] Jesus perfectly expressed these nine virtues because He was completely and continually Spirit-filled (Luke 4:1). We too must be Spirit-filled to manifest Christlike character through the fruit of the Spirit (Eph. 5:18), and thereby glorify the Father and the Son (John 15:8; 16:14).

Christlike Christians Love God and Their Neighbor

Christ showed perfect love for His Father by His obedience to death on the cross (John 14:31; Phil. 2:8). And by His sacrificial death, Jesus also showed His great love for people who are described as "helpless," "ungodly," "sinners," and "enemies" in their unsaved condition (Rom. 5:6–10).

Paul prayed that Christians might understand more of the inexhaustible knowledge of Christ's love (Eph. 3:18–19), But Christlike believers take a step further by loving God and other humans as Christ does (Matt. 22:37–39; John 13:34–35; 1 John 3:16).

We need more than mere human power to love the way Jesus loves. God met our need by giving us the Spirit to produce His kind of love in and through us (Rom. 5:5). Spirit-filled Christians are empowered to love God, fellow Christians, and other humans, including even their enemies, with supernatural love (Gal. 5:22).

Loving other Christians requires our accepting them just as Jesus has accepted us as spiritual children of God and fellow members of Christ's body. Unbelievers or sinners are still our neighbors, and therefore we are to love them also (Matt. 22:39). Loving unbelievers or sinners as Christ did our receiving them but not their sin or sinful lifestyle. We should not use the qualification, "but not their sin or sinful lifestyle," as a hypocritical cover-up for an attitudinal rejection of sinners. Jesus' love and acceptance of others was genuine in action and attitude.

Despised sinners, social and religious rejects, and oppressed groups were drawn to Jesus. For instance Luke 15:1–2 states, "Now all the tax gatherers and the sinners were coming near Him to listen to Him. And both the Pharisees and the scribes began to grumble, saying, 'This man receives sinners and eats with them.'" While Jesus was morally "separated from sinners" (Heb. 7:26),[9] He had physical contact with them and socialized with them, and Israel's religious leaders condemned Jesus' relationship with "sinners" (7:36–39, esp. v. 39; 15:2). And Christ condemned the hypocritical practices of these religious leaders (Matt. 23:13–36).

Women and children felt that Jesus accepted and cared for them. He treated women as equal in value to men and showed them personal attention. A group of women faithfully followed Jesus, ministered to Him, and observed His final suffering (Matt. 27:55–56), and some women were associated with His burial and His resurrection (27:61; 28:1–10). These women were deeply devoted to Him because they knew He genuinely cared for them (see 1 John 4:19). A Christian man shows Christlikeness more by how he treats women and children than by how he treats his "good old buddies."

In Jesus' life we see perfect love expressed toward God and people. And the Spirit can radiate that love through us. When we have Spirit-produced love, we take seriously the two great commandments (Matt. 22:37–40), we reflect Christlike character (Gal. 5:22), we show people we are Christ's followers (John 13:34–35), and we have proper motivation to serve others (Gal. 5:13).

Christlike Christians Do the Father's Will

Doing the Father's will was Christ's driving passion: "My food is to do the will of Him who sent Me, and to accomplish His work" (John 4:34). All that Jesus thought, said, and did was in God's will, and therefore He could say, "I always do the things that are pleasing to Him" (8:29). Christians can imitate Christ's response to the Father's will in four main ways.[10]

First, in His preincarnate state Christ declared His desire to do God's will: "I delight to do Thy will, O my God" (Ps. 40:8). Doing God's will was His pleasure and not an irksome task or even something He did simply from duty. The more Christlike we become, the more we desire and delight to do God's will.

Second, Christ came into the world to do God's will, and He knew that God's will included severe suffering for sinners (John 6:38; Heb. 10:5–10).[11] Though Christ was perfect and deserved to be appreciated, He came not to be appreciated but to accomplish His Father's will. And doing His Father's will led to rejection (John 1:11) and death by crucifixion (Matt. 26:42). The main purpose of Christlike Christians is not to receive appreciation or to please people but to accomplish the Father's will at any cost (Rom. 12:1–2).

Third, Jesus gave the Father's will priority over His own will and personal needs (John 4:31–34; 6:38). For Christlike Christians, doing the Father's will is at the top of their "to do" list, and no personal sacrifice is too great and no task is too difficult to achieve the Father's will. God expects and enables His people to know and do His will, and God promises us wonderful benefits for doing His will.

Fourth, Christ persevered in God's will. Even when facing crucifixion for the sins of the world, Jesus said to the Father, "Not My will, but Thine be done" (Luke 22:42). Jesus was on a mission, and He would return to heaven only when His mission was accomplished on earth (John 17:4; 19:30). Christlike Christians seek to follow God's will and to allow nothing to distract or derail them from doing His will.

How we answer the three following questions will help us gauge how Christlike our response to God's will is: Are we committed to doing the Father's will, nothing more, nothing less, and nothing else? Do we have a deep desire, delight, and determination to do the Father's will so that His will takes priority over our will and even our personal needs? Do we include the pursuit of sanctification as an essential part of persevering in God's will for our life?

Christlike Christians Serve Others

When Christians have Spirit-produced love, they care for others and serve them as Jesus did. Jesus came to serve sacrificially and not to be served (Matt. 20:28). Though He was the disciples' Lord, Leader, and Teacher, He told them, "I am among you as the one who serves" (Luke 22:27). Picture the Lord of glory stooping down to wash His disciples' dirty feet (John 13:3–17). He took the role of the lowest household servant and presented a show-and-tell lesson in humbly serving others. The disciples could see, hear, and feel Jesus' ministry to them, and they never forgot it. Christ applied His teaching about humble service to His followers in their cultural context. "If I then, the Lord and the Teacher, washed your feet, you also ought to wash one another's feet. For I gave you an example that you also should do as I did to you" (13:14–15). The transcultural principle to be drawn from Jesus' teaching is summarized in Paul's command, "through love serve one another" (Gal. 5:13).

The vivid memory of Jesus serving others was deeply embedded in Peter's mind. Over thirty years after this foot-washing event, Peter exhorted Christians to "clothe yourselves with humility toward one another" (1 Pet. 5:5). The Greek word rendered "clothe yourselves" is a rare word that refers to a slave putting on an apron before serving. So Christians are to imitate their Lord, who girded himself and served (John 13:4–17).[12]

No external pressure or impure motive moved Jesus to perform the ultimate service of dying for us (John 10:17–18). Love for His Father (14:31), for His own (13:1; Eph. 5:25), and for the world (John 3:16) was why He went to the cross and paid the price with His very life. The same love for God and humans must motivate our service for others. Otherwise even the most sacrificial service profits nothing (1 Cor. 13:2–3).

People often remember the simplest acts of service done for them, especially by those who serve out of love for Christ and expect nothing in return for their service. I have observed at the funerals of Christians that the most prominent memories of a person are whether he or she was Christlike in character and faithful in service. And that is what counts most before the Lord because He commends and rewards the "good and faithful servant" (Matt. 25:21, NIV).

How do you know if you are rendering Christlike service produced by the Spirit? If you can truly say, "I would be content if only the Lord and I knew about my service to others," then probably your service comes from the pure motive of Spirit-produced love. And Christians can have confidence that Jesus does perfectly remember and reward even their simplest acts of service done in His name (10:42). Consider the promise of Hebrews 6:10, "For God is not unjust so as to forget your work and the love which you have shown toward His name, in having ministered and in still ministering to the saints."

The more Christians become like Christ through sanctification, the more they can serve Him. This does not mean that only "super Christians" can serve the Lord. New Christians as well as mature Christians can serve the Lord in appropriate ways. Still, spiritual growth to greater Christlikeness does enhance our Christian service.

Christlike Christians Evangelize Unbelievers

The more Christlike we become, the more we share Lord's compassion for people and their needs. His compassion included the needs of the whole person, but He focused on the spiritual needs of people (Mark

2:1–12; 14:7). His passion was for lost people to be saved and then trained as disciples. "For the Son of Man has come to seek and to save that which was lost" (Luke 19:10). Presenting the gospel with Spirit-empowered love is a primary way we show Christlike compassion.

Christlike evangelism should produce new coverts, who then need to grow spiritually. And Christlike maturity should produce Christlike evangelism, which again produces new converts. And as these new converts grow and evangelize others, the cycle starts over again. The Lord used this cyclical pattern when He trained His disciples so that they could make new disciples, and these new disciples could make still other disciples (Matt. 28:19–20; see 2 Tim. 2:2).[13]

Manifesting Christlike qualities is the measure of a believer's sanctification. Asking, "How much have I progressed in sanctification?" is the same as asking, "How Christlike am I?" So the measure of our progress in sanctification and the measure of our personal growth in Christlikeness read the same on God's scale.

CHAPTER NINE

Growing in Grace:
God's Sufficiency for Sanctification

GRACE IS ONE OF THE SWEETEST sounding words in the English language. We compliment someone when we say, "You are a gracious person." However, the biblical concept of divine grace is more than a sweet-sounding abstraction or a complimentary term applied to God. Grace so characterizes God that He is called "the God of all grace" (1 Pet. 5:10), and Jesus was "full of grace and truth" (John 1:14).

Divine grace has enjoyed some public favor, as shown by the popularity of John Newton's great hymn, "Amazing Grace." However, I am convinced that few people understand the biblical doctrine of grace, fewer yet have received God's saving grace, and evidently only a small percentage of those saved by grace truly live by grace.

Few people truly grasp the biblical concept of God's grace because it is so different from the way people normally think and operate. The biblical teaching that salvation is a gift of God's grace and that grace can motivate and empower Christians to live successfully for God is foreign to the way people have learned to function. Grace is particularly strange to Americans with their self-sufficiency and our attitude that hard work can get us anything and take us anywhere, even to heaven.

Since people do not naturally understand and receive God's saving grace through faith in Christ, each new generation needs a clear and correct communication of the gospel of the grace of God.[1] Genuine Christians know from Scripture and by experience that salvation is by grace through faith, but not all Christians realize that sanctification is also by grace through faith .

I was blessed to have a caring earthly parents who spent time with me and communicated their love to me. One of my father's greatest contributions to me was his emphasis on the biblical doctrine of grace. Ephesians 2:8–9 was one of his favorite Bible passages because it so plainly teaches that we are saved by grace: "For by grace you have been saved through faith; and that not of yourselves, it is the gift of God; not as a result of works, so that no one may boast." My father often spoke of God's wondrous grace and mercy toward undeserving sinners. Even before I became a Christian, he helped me begin to grasp God's grace in Christ. I am forever grateful for my grace-oriented heritage. We make an immeasurably valuable contribution to people by helping them understand and receive God's grace and live by it.

This chapter examines the biblical concept of grace and then discusses how God's grace operates in our sanctification.

THE BIBLICAL CONCEPT OF GRACE

The term *grace* in both the Old and New Testaments,[2] usually indicates God's free and unmerited favor toward people, particularly His redeemed people (Ps. 84:11; Rom. 3:24–26; 2 Cor. 9:8). Vine describes grace bestowed by God as "the friendly disposition from which the kindly acts proceed, graciousness, lovingkindness, goodwill generally, e.g., Acts 7:10; . . . in this respect there is stress on its freeness and universality, its spontaneous character, as in the case of God's redemptive mercy, and the pleasure or joy He designs for the recipient; thus it is set in contrast with debt, Rom. 4:4, 16, with works, 11:6, and with law, John 1:17; see also, e.g., Rom. 6:14, 15; Gal. 5:4."[3]

Thus biblical grace includes both God's attitude and His actions of undeserved favor toward imperfect people (Num. 6:25; 2 Cor. 9:8). Grace comes from the Father (1:12; 1 Tim. 1:2), the Son (John 1:16; Gal. 1:6;

1 Tim. 1:2), and the Holy Spirit (who is called "the Spirit of grace," Zech. 12:10; Heb. 10:29).

The biblical concept of God's grace is epitomized in "His great love" manifested through the saving work of Christ (Eph. 2:4; see also vv. 5–7). God will forever display the magnificence of His grace toward His people, as Paul noted in 2:7: "in order that in the ages to come He might show the surpassing riches of His grace in kindness toward us in Christ Jesus." Each Christian can rightly say, "I am an eternal trophy of God's grace."

THE BIBLICAL REVELATION OF GRACE

The revelation of God's grace occurs in three major stages in redemptive history.

First, the Old Testament begins to reveal God's grace and prepares for the fuller revelation of grace through Christ (Gen. 6:8; Exod. 33:19; Num. 6:25; Neh. 9:17; Ps. 45:2; 119:58; Zech. 4:7; 12:10). Grace underlies God's saving and sanctifying work in the Old Testament (e.g., Gen. 15:1–6 [see Rom. 4:1–5]; Ps. 32:1–2 [see Rom. 4:6–8]; Ps. 84:11). For example, God's grace was displayed in saving Noah and his family through the Flood (Gen. 6:8–8:22), in justifying Abraham (15:6) and David (Ps. 32:1–2), in His gracious blessing of Israel (Num. 6:24–27; Neh. 9:17), in providing good things for the upright (Ps. 84:11), and in the rebuilding of Israel's restoration temple (Zech. 4:7). Still, the Old Covenant emphasizes law while the New Covenant emphasizes grace. "For the Law was given through Moses; grace and truth came through Jesus Christ" (John 1:17, NIV). The Old Testament then is mainly a period of preparation for the full revelation of grace in Christ (1:14, 16; 1 Pet. 1:10–12).

Second, the Gospels record the full revelation and ministration of God's saving and sanctifying grace through the person, words, and works of Jesus Christ (John 1:14, 16–17; 2 Cor. 8:9; 1 Pet. 1:10–12). We see Christ's grace most clearly demonstrated through His sacrifice on the cross. "For you know the grace of our Lord Jesus Christ, that though He was rich, yet for your sake He became poor, that you through His poverty might become rich" (2 Cor. 8:9).

Third, the rest of the New Testament after the Gospels is a reflection of the grace revealed and provided through Christ. The biblical writers from Acts through Revelation consider Christ's person and work the basis for the believer's justification and sanctification by God's grace (Rom. 3:22–26; 6:1–2, 14). Because of Christ's full revelation and ministration of God's grace, New Covenant believers can experience more of God's grace than anyone ever before in redemptive history.

THE VARIOUS OPERATIONS OF BIBLICAL GRACE

When Peter mentioned "the manifold grace of God" (1 Pet. 4:10), he meant that God's multifaceted grace has many different functions for many different purposes. For Christians the primary operation of God's grace begins with initial salvation, includes sanctification and other aspects of Christian living, and climaxes in glorification.

Some Christians do not recognize the various operations of divine grace in Christian living. They think God's grace is restricted to initial salvation and that if God spoke audibly to each new Christian, He would say something like this: "My spiritual child, I have saved you by My grace and now you are on your own. Give your Christian life and service your best effort. I will send My Son for you someday, and He will judge you to see how well you lived and worked for Me." If you think that something is missing here, you are right, because God's grace is missing in this explanation of postsalvation living.

Grace is certainly not missing, however, in the biblical plan for Christian living. Grace is an essential factor in sanctification, and therefore Christians can never be, do, or become what God has planned for them without His grace. Paul taught this truth when He testified, "But by the grace of God I am what I am, and His grace toward me did not prove vain; but I labored even more than all of them, yet not I, but the grace of God with me" (1 Cor. 15:10).

Grace in Salvation

God is gracious to grant and preserve any human life, since every individual is born spiritually dead in sins (Eph. 2:1). By His grace God

110

continues His providential care of all creation and particularly of humans (Matt. 5:45). Yet the greatest blessing of God's grace is personal salvation received through faith in Christ (Acts 16:31; Eph. 2:8–9).

God does not stop the flow of grace to His people after their salvation. He keeps the floodgates of grace open so that grace can abound to us and flow out to others through us (2 Cor. 9:8; 1 Pet. 4:10).

Grace in Sanctification

In Roman's, Paul's emphasis in this letter changes from the doctrine of justification in 3:21–5:21 to the doctrine of sanctification in 6:1–8:17. Specific terms for "sanctification" (6:19, 22; Greek, *hagiosmos*, "sanctification" or "holiness") occur in Romans 6, and the concept of sanctification pervades this chapter. Likewise, specific terms for "grace" (6:1, 14, 15) occur in Romans 6, and the concept of grace also pervades this chapter. Practical victory over indwelling sin is an aspect of sanctification, and it is combined with "grace" in 6:14, "For sin shall not be master over you, for you are not under law but under grace."

Grace in Service

Like salvation and sanctification, Christian service, too, is by God's grace. "And God is able to make all grace abound to you, so that always having all sufficiency in everything, you may have an abundance for every good deed" (2 Cor. 9:8). Paul zealously served by grace as 1 Corinthians 15:10 indicates: "I labored even more than all of them [that is, the rest of the apostles], yet not I, but the grace of God with me." Zealous Christian service always includes some suffering and other difficulties. Still, God's strengthening grace can make Christian service a joyful, dynamic activity rather than dull drudgery.

God's grace is also closely connected to spiritual gifts. God gives each believer at the moment of salvation at least one spiritual gift, which is an ability to serve other Christians for the edifying of the church, the spiritual body of Christ (Rom. 12:6; 1 Cor. 12:11, 28–31; Eph. 4:7–8, 11). The Greek term *charismata* (literally "grace-things" or "grace-gifts") suggests that we have these spiritual gifts through God's grace.[4] The Spirit empowers Christians to use these spiritual gifts so that the corporate body of

Christ and its individual members grow toward Christlikeness (1 Cor. 12:4, 7–11; Eph. 4:11–16; 1 Pet. 4:10). The ultimate purpose of exercising spiritual gifts is to glorify God (4:11).

Grace in Suffering

The Christian life includes suffering for Christ's sake as well as normal human suffering in a fallen world (Phil. 1:29).

Just as God's grace is greater than any human sin (Rom. 5:20), so His grace is greater than any human suffering. The Lord's answer for Paul's suffering is the same as His answer for our suffering: "My grace is sufficient for you" (2 Cor. 12:9).

Grace enables us to endure suffering and to reap positive benefits from suffering. God uses our suffering to humble us and empower us (12:7), to build our character and hope (Rom. 5:3–5), and to mature us (James 1:2–4). These positive benefits of suffering also promote holy and righteous living in God's children.

Grace in Christian Communication

Christ perfectly exemplified verbal communication characterized by grace. Christ's hearers noted "the gracious words which were falling from His lips" (Luke 4:22), and Psalm 45:2, NLT says of the Messiah, "Gracious words stream from your lips." We follow Christ's example when we obey Colossians 4:6, "Let your speech always be with grace, seasoned, as it were, with salt, so that you may know how you should respond to each person." Communication with grace is characterized by wisdom (Matt. 13:54; Luke 21:15; Col. 4:5) and by genuine concern for people.

Grace in Any Situation

The measure of God's grace is limitless as He is limitless. John 1:16 says, "For of His [Christ's] fullness we have all received, and grace upon grace." The expression "grace upon grace" means that one provision of grace supersedes another. Thus Christ gives us greater supplies of grace when continuing needs grow greater and He gives us new supplies of grace for new needs that arise. Our needs are never greater than Christ's grace, and He is never late with His provision. "Let us therefore draw near with confidence to the throne of grace, so that we may receive mercy and may find grace to help in time of need" (Heb. 4:16).

If we come to God through Christ, with faith, and in humility we can have confidence that we will receive sufficient grace for whatever our need.

My wife, Shirley, and I have experienced this practical truth. While I was attending seminary, Shirley did child care in our home and I worked part-time. We sought to handle our finances faithfully and to avoid any overdue bills. But unexpected medical expenses brought a financial crisis. We had only several dollars and insufficient income to cover both living expenses and the medical bill. God's Word reminded us that we could approach God's throne through Jesus Christ and "find grace to help in time of need" (Heb. 4:16). After several days we received the exact amount of the medical bill from an anonymous source. Even greater than God's specific provision for our medical bill was the assurance that our Lord is always there for us with sufficient grace.

All Christians will face crises, whether in financial, physical, spiritual, mental, emotional, or relational areas. These inevitable problems offer us two choices. We can choose to go to pieces. Or we can choose to go to God and receive grace for whatever and whenever we have a need.

Grace at the Second Coming of Christ

All the operations of grace presented so far pertain to this life. But more grace is to come. Peter told Christians, "Fix your hope completely on the grace to be brought to you at the revelation of Jesus Christ" (1 Pet. 1:13). This will be God's climactic operation of grace for Christians, the final phase of salvation when Christ returns and transforms all believers into His perfect likeness (Phil. 3:20–21; 1 John 3:2). By His grace we will enjoy eternity in Christ's presence.

OTHER FUNCTIONS OF GRACE IN SANCTIFICATION

Christians Can Conquer Sin by Grace

One of the reasons God has placed Christians "under grace" is so that we can master sin instead of sin mastering us. However, some see grace as a problem rather than a solution for the Christian's relationship to sin. These skeptics about the Christian's proper use of grace think that emphasizing grace will cause believers to use grace as a license to sin instead of a means for victory over sin. In Romans 6 Paul expected and answered two questions based on this misunderstanding of grace.

The first question is, "Are we to continue in sin so that grace might increase?" (6:1). The question probably arose from two of Paul's earlier conclusions: (a) that justification is by grace through faith and not by works of the Law (3:21–28) and (b) that where sin abounds grace abounds even more for God's greater glory (5:20). Thus some recipients of Paul's teaching might reason this way: "Let's sin more so that God can display more grace and get more glory."

Paul answered this wrong reasoning with an emphatic negative and a rhetorical question: "May it never be! How shall we who died to sin still live in it?" (6:2). Since the end does not justify the means, we are not justified in sinning more so that God can display more grace and get more glory. Also, by God's grace we "died to sin" (6:2) through our spiritual identification with Christ (6:3–4). God's grace calls us to walk in newness of life and righteousness and not in the old life of sin (6:2–13).

The second question is, "Shall we sin because we are not under law but under grace?" (6:15). Paul assumed that this question would arise based on his previous statement: "For sin shall not be master over you, for you are not under law, but under grace" (6:14). Some might think that this teaching would allow them to be lawless and at liberty to sin without blame.

Paul first answered this faulty thinking with another emphatic negative, "May it never be!" (6:15). Then he explained that grace frees us from sin so that we can become slaves of obedience unto righteousness (6:16–18). Moreover, grace encourages and empowers believers to present their bodily members as "slaves to righteousness" (6:19; see also v. 22). Grace then does not give us freedom to sin (6:1; Gal. 5:13; 1 Pet. 2:16). Grace is our great liberator from sin and not our license to sin.

Christ said, "Everyone who commits sin is the slave of sin" (John 8:34). He showed the error of thinking that committing sin is liberating. Participation in sin is like an animal struggling in a net. The more the animal struggles, the more it becomes entangled in the net. And the more people sin, the more they become enslaved to sin. Sin is a bondage-maker; grace is a bondage-breaker (Rom. 6:14; 7:14). By grace we can conquer sin and progress in sanctification.

Christians Can Learn Holy Living from Grace

Grace can conquer our sin (6:14), and grace can also teach us "to deny ungodliness and worldly desires and to live sensibly, righteously and godly in the present age" (Titus 2:12). Grace teaches us holy living through the Scriptures. In fact, Scripture is so closely connected with God's grace that twice it is called "the word of His [God's] grace" (Acts 14:3; 20:32).

"The true grace of God" is a major subject of Peter's first letter (1 Pet. 5:12). Peter's "grace" teaching emphasizes holy and righteous living, especially in the midst of suffering.

THE NEED TO LIVE BY GRACE

The entire Christian life from spiritual birth and throughout eternity is an operation of God's grace (Eph. 2:1–10). Christians start with salvation by grace through faith (2:8–9), and God does not switch them to some other means of sanctification such as the "flesh" (Gal. 3:3). Just as we received new life in Christ by grace, so we continue our new life in Christ by grace (Rom. 5:17; 6:14; 1 Cor. 15:10). Paul taught that God's grace carries over from salvation to godly living (Titus 2:11–12).

A grace-oriented approach to sanctification is essential because any substitute for grace will surely fail us. We should continue to appreciate God's grace, to resist legalism which opposes God's grace, and to grow in grace.

Appreciate God's Grace

One of my mentors used to say, "It's hard to overestimate the sinfulness of man." Probably the only thing more difficult to overestimate is the greatness of God's grace, for Paul observed, "Where sin increased, grace abounded all the more" (Rom. 5:20). Grace is greater than all human sin, and therefore God's grace can save the worst of sinners (5:21; Heb. 7:25).

Christians should continually appreciate God's grace manifested in their initial salvation and in their Christian life, as Paul did (1 Cor. 15:10; 1 Tim. 1:12–16). So thoughts of God's grace should occupy our hearts, and gratitude for grace should flow from our lips.

Another way we can show appreciation for God's grace is by participating in the communion service (also called the Lord's Supper, breaking of bread, remembrance meeting, or Eucharist). Remembering Christ and His death by partaking of the bread and the cup highlights God's greatest act of grace in sacrificing His Son on the cross for us (Matt. 26:26–28; 1 Cor. 10:16; 11:23–26). Thus each time we participate in the Communion service we can gain a renewed appreciation for Christ's great love and a stronger grip on God's grace.

Resist Legalism, Which Opposes Grace

Scripture teaches that believers are to live under grace and not under the Law. "For sin shall not be master over you, for you are not under law but under grace" (Rom. 6:14). This does not mean that Christians are to be antinomians (those against law) or libertines (those free from law or restraint in behavior). Paul described his Christian relationship to law as "not being myself under the Law" (1 Cor. 9:20), "though not being without the law of God but under the law of Christ" (9:21).[5] Paul was not under the Old Covenant Law, but he was not lawless; instead he was under "the law of Christ."

"The law of Christ" is basically Christ's command (Matt. 28:19–20; John 13:34–35; 14:21) revealed through the New Testament writers (John 16:12–13; Gal. 6:2; James 1:25; 2:8, 12) and intended for church-age believers (1 Cor. 9:21; Gal. 5:6, 18; 6:2; Heb. 8:10). Six additional facts help clarify the biblical concept of "the law of Christ":

- It is intended to function in a context of grace (John 1:17; Rom. 6:14).

- It includes the two great commands concerning love for God and for one's neighbor (Matt. 22:37–40).

- It is a law of love expressed by obeying Christ's commandments (John 14:21, Gal. 6:2).

- It is described as "the perfect law, the law of liberty" (James 1:25) and "the royal law" (2:8).

- It is properly obeyed by believers through Spirit-produced love (John 14:21; Gal. 5:6, 13, 22–23).

- It is liberating rather than weighty ("His commands are not burdensome," 1 John 5:3; see also Matt. 11:30).

Christ frees Christians from the Old Covenant Law (Rom. 6:14; 7:1–6; Gal. 3:13–14; 5:1; Col. 2:14; Heb. 8:13), and Paul warned believers to maintain their freedom in Christ: "Keep standing firm and do not be subject again to a yoke of slavery [that is, the Mosaic Law]" (Gal. 5:1). Therefore we need to guard against leaving our freedom in Christ and our life under grace and becoming enslaved to legalism.

Legalism in Christian living may appear in two different forms, though often legalistic Christians practice both forms together.

In the first form of legalism Christians pursue sanctification by trying to keep the Law through self-effort. This legalistic approach to sanctification opposes the principle of grace, neglects the power of the spirit, and leads to spiritual frustration and failure in attempting to conquer the sinful flesh.

Christians experience freedom from bondage to legalism and victory over sin when they live by grace, rely on the Spirit, and obey Scripture through the power of Spirit-produced love.

A second form of legalism imposes on Christians a code of human regulations about external observances and deeds. This form of legalism requires outward conformity to certain human regulations as a measure of religious achievement; does not properly consider one's inner character, motivation, power, and goals as essential factors in biblical spirituality; and appeals to fleshly performance and human pride. Paul evidently had this form of legalism in mind when he referred to Christians who submit to regulations "in accordance with the commandments and teachings of men" (Col. 2:22). Paul warned the Colossian Christians that their legalistic regulations were contrary to their identity with Christ. "If you have died with Christ to the elementary principles of the world, why, as if you were living in the world, do you submit yourself to decrees, such as, 'Do not handle, do not taste, do not touch!'" (2:20–21). Submission to these ascetic prohibitions is supposed to produce spiritual victory over the flesh. Instead, legalistic asceticism has two serious problems: It is the practice of "self-made religion" (2:23), and it does not sanctify (2:16–23), for it is of "no value against fleshly indulgence" (2:23).

Victory over sin is not achieved by refraining from legitimate satisfaction of bodily appetites such as self-controlled eating (1 Cor 9:24–27; 10:31), sexual expression within marriage (7:1–5), and enjoyment of God-given material riches while trusting God instead of wealth (1 Tim. 6:17). Christians who obey the Word and rely on the Spirit can enjoy right satisfaction of human appetites and refrain from satisfying wrong appetites, which involves such practices as gluttony, immorality, and worldliness (1 Cor. 6:13, 18; Phil. 3:19; 1 John 2:15–17).

Both forms of legalism involve a fleshly self-effort to conform to an outward code instead of an inward willingness to obey God from a Spirit-filled heart. In Richard Henry Dana's classic work, *Two Years before the Mast*, a certain Captain Thompson became so oppressive that his crew lost their desire to do their duties willingly, cooperatively, and joyfully. Captain Thompson's oppressed and frustrated crew was in sharp contrast to another ship's crew who served with happiness and vigor because they had a fair, caring, and gracious captain. Similar to this second crew, Christians serve a God of grace and have "the Spirit of grace" within (Zech. 12:10) so that they can willingly, vigorously, and joyfully live for their gracious God. Serving God by grace and with freedom in Christ is quite different from serving in bondage to an oppressive, deadening, and joyless legalism.

Attempting sanctification through legalism and experiencing sanctification under grace and by the Spirit are mutually exclusive principles. "But if you are led by the Spirit, you are not under the Law" (Gal. 5:18).

Christians practicing legalism are operating by works instead of faith and by the flesh instead of the Spirit.

Table 4 summarizes contrasts between legalism and grace as they relate to salvation and sanctification.

Table 4—Main Contrasts between Legalism and Grace

Legalism	*Grace*
Operates through the flesh (Rom. 8:3)	Operates through faith (Rom. 4:16; Eph. 2:8)
Cannot save or sanctify (Rom. 3:20; 7:14–25; 8:3; Gal. 2:16, 21; 3:1–5)	Can save and sanctify (Rom. 3:24–26; 6:14; Eph. 2:8; Titus 2:11–12)
Depends on human power power (Rom. 7:18–25; 8:8; Gal. 3:3)	Depends on divine (Rom. 6:14; 1 Cor. 15:10; Eph. 2:8–9)
Produces works of the Law by the flesh (Rom. 3:20; Gal. 3:2, 5)	Produces good works by faith (Eph. 2:8–10; Titus 3:8)
Emphasizes the flesh and the works of the flesh (Rom. 7:18; 8:2–3; Gal. 5:19–21)	Emphasizes the Spirit and the fruit of the Spirit (Rom. 8:4, 13; Gal. 5:16–18, 22–23)
Cannot conquer "fleshly indulgence" (Col. 2:23; see Rom. 7:18–19)	Can conquer sin (Rom. 6:14; 8:13) and "the desire of the flesh" by the Spirit (Gal. 5:16)
Brings spiritual bondage and wretchedness (Rom. 6:14; 7:1–6, 24; Gal. 3:23–25; 4:3, 9; 5:1)	Brings spiritual freedom, life, and peace (John 8:31–32, 36; Rom. 6:14; 7:1–6; 8:6; 1 Cor. 9:20; Gal. 3:24–25; 4:7, 21–31; 5:1, 18)
Causes frustration (Rom. 7:18–19)	Promotes progress (Rom 8:13; 1 Cor. 15:10; 2 Cor. 3:18; Phil. 3:13–14; 2 Pet. 3:18)
Fails (Rom. 7:18–25)	Succeeds (Rom. 5:20; 6:14; 8:1-4, 13; 1 Cor. 15:10; Gal. 5:16)

As this table reveals, legalism is not a minor matter or a negotiable difference in belief and practice between Christians. Legalism is a major barrier to successful sanctification. All Christians enslaved to legalism need to be liberated from legalism into grace, taught to live by grace, and helped to remain spiritually free under grace.

Sally was a Christian in bondage to legalism through a religious organization that wrapped her in a straitjacket of unchristian regulations.[6] Her religion required her to observe Old Testament dietary and sabbatical laws. She shared with me her deep concern about her Christian experience. Clearly her Christian life was burdensome, and she lacked spiritual vitality, liberty, and joy.

Sally was very attentive as we discussed her legalism in light of Paul's teaching in Romans and Galatians about grace and Christian liberty. She discovered from Scripture her freedom in Christ . She no longer needed to struggle for God's favor under an oppressive, hopeless, and joyless legalism. By God's grace Sally had overcome the spiritual paralysis of legalism. Now she could depend on God's grace to keep her free and growing in Christ.

Grow in Grace

Believers have been introduced into God's grace and they "stand" in this grace (Rom. 5: 2). But God expects His people to do more than stand in grace; He commands them to "grow in the grace and knowledge of our Lord and Savior Jesus Christ" (2 Pet. 3:18).

We enter and appropriate God's grace for our sanctification and other needs by practicing five key requirements: (a) by humble instead of proud before the God of grace (James 4:6); (b) abide in Christ who provides His fullness of grace (John 15:1–7); (c) receive and obey God's Word of grace (Acts 20:32); (d) be filled with the "Spirit of grace" (Eph. 5:18); and (e) go continually and confidently to God's throne of grace (Heb. 4:16).

The more we appropriate God's grace, the more we progress in sanctification by grace.

Many Christians wonder, "How can I experience spiritual liberty, victory, vitality, and abundance in my Christian life?" The biblical answer is: "Learn to live and grow in grace."

CHAPTER TEN

Living by the Word:
Scripture's Role in Sanctification

SUPPOSE SOMEONE TOLD a physical health expert, "I will do anything reasonable for health except eat right and exercise." You need little imagination to guess how the health expert would probably respond: "Forget about consulting me. I can't help you if you won't eat right and exercise, because they are essential to good health!"

Receiving and obeying God's Word are just as essential to sanctification as proper eating and exercising are for good physical health. Yet many Christians neglect to learn and obey Scripture, and consequently they hinder their spiritual growth. God offers no alternatives to His method of sanctification through His Word (John 17:17).

SANCTIFICATION REQUIRES PROPER RESPONSE TO GOD'S WORD

The sanctifying work of the Word is not automatic because Christians can know and hear the Word and still not respond to it (John 13:17; James 1:22). The following are four ways Christians must respond to God's Word for significant progress in sanctification.

Learn God's Word

Learning involves listening, reading, observing, analyzing, synthesizing, comparing, questioning, retaining, and many other activities. Doing all these activities to learn Scripture is not as difficult as it may seem. People already automatically practice many of these requirements for understanding Scripture. You can begin to practice the other needed activities and continue to upgrade all your Bible reading and study skills. To increase your efficiency in Bible reading or any type of reading, consult *How to Read a Book*, by Mortimer J. Adler and Charles Van Doren.[1] For thorough and practical help in personal Bible study use *Living by the Book* by Howard G. Hendricks and William Hendricks.[2]

The two most basic ways to gain general knowledge of biblical content are repeated reading and memorization of Scripture. A more detailed knowledge of Scripture requires use of Bible study methods and tools, skillful interpretation of Scripture (ideally in the original languages), and development of a doctrinal system. However, Christians can learn the major principles of sanctification through careful reading and study of the Bible in their native language. You will benefit by using several committee translations,[3] a complete concordance for at least one of the translations, and an up-to-date evangelical Bible dictionary or encyclopedia. Some current committee translations in English are the *New American Standard Bible* (1995 edition), the *New International Version*, the *New King James Version*, and the *New Revised Standard Version*. The recent *New Living Translation* presents an outstanding thought-for-thought rendering of Scripture produced by a large number of reputable evangelical scholars.

Some people prefer to use a ready-made calendar schedule for reading the whole Bible one or more times annually. Others have the same goal but devise their own plan. Success in Bible reading requires discipline to follow a chosen plan. A "hit-or-miss" approach to Bible reading usually has mostly misses, and consequently people following this method usually have a patchy knowledge of Scripture.

Initial enthusiasm for reading and studying the Bible may help us start well, but enthusiasm tends to wane. Then we need discipline by God's grace to continue studying and growing through God's Word. Many Christians confess, "I don't get very much from my Bible reading. I'm too busy to focus on the words and meaning of Scripture. And the message of Scripture seems dull and irrelevant. Some preachers and Bible teachers make God's Word come alive to me, but that doesn't happen when I read and study the Word."

Why do Christians often feel defeated in their attempt to read and study the Bible when this practice should be a spiritual highlight in their Christian life? Four main obstacles cause Christians to fail in personal Bible study:

- Poor concentration on Scripture

- Undisciplined approaches to reading and studying Scripture

- Unprepared hearts

- Satanic opposition.

If you read Scripture but retain very little of it, here are some suggestions to help you concentrate on the Word and to get the Word into your heart where it can transform your life.

- Make a "to do" list on a daily calendar record so that distracting responsibilities do not hinder your focus on reading and understanding God's Word. For example, your list can remind you to pay bills, attend a meeting, get gas for your car, pick up clothes at the cleaners, and other such items. The moment a distracting item enters your mind, note it so that it will no longer disturb your concentration.

- Note key words and ideas, logical connections, summary principles, investigative questions, and practical applications in your Bible or in a notebook. For instance, when you read Ezra 7:10 you should note that Ezra devoted himself to "study," "practice," and "teach" God's Word. Then immediately commit yourself to do the same. Making notations helps you to read the Bible with purpose and to enjoy personal discovery of spiritual truth.

- Mark or record key verses for summarization, memorization, meditation, and application. Alert Bible students will note that the principal point of the story about Zacchaeus in Luke 19:1–10 is summarized in verse 10, "For the Son of Man has come to seek and to save that which was lost." Marking or recording while you are reading Scripture helps you concentrate and recall what you have learned.

- Search Scripture with the intent to discover and do God's truth. The more willing we are to obey God's Word, the more God helps us know and practice spiritual truth (John 7:17). Since the Bible is a unified body of truth, the separate truths fit together harmoniously. Therefore the biblical truths we learn by studying Scripture can form a pattern in our minds like the pieces of a jigsaw puzzle fitting together.

Using these guidelines can help us find spiritual delight and benefit in our Bible study instead of dullness, frustration, and disappointment.

We need discipline to overcome laziness and to study Scripture properly and diligently (2 Tim. 2:15). Christians struggle with the human tendency to be lazy, even in their attempt at serious Bible study and spiritual progress. Donald Grey Barnhouse, one of the great Bible expositors of the twentieth century, admitted that he was naturally lazy. Yet he took decisive action to conquer his laziness and to master the Bible, and he ministered the Word with amazing authority. We, too, can take decisive action to learn, practice, and teach Scripture, and God's grace will help us overcome our lethargy and accomplish our purpose.

Also, we need to prepare our hearts to receive and obey God's truth. Ezra is a prime example of practicing this principle: "Ezra had set his heart to study the law of the LORD, and to practice it, and to teach His statutes and ordinances in Israel" (Ezra 7:10). Christians with prepared hearts eagerly receive God's message and go beyond thinking and talking about biblical truth; they practice the truth (John 13:17; James 1:22).

We can overcome Satan's resistance to Bible study by relying on God's Spirit and by following the list of proper responses to the Word given in this chapter. (Chapter 14, "Winning in Spiritual Warfare," considers more principles for victory over Satan.)

Memorize God's Word

The Bible teaches by command and by personal examples that we should memorize Scripture. God commanded Israel to "impress these words of mine on your heart and on your soul" (Deut. 11:18). The psalmist said that he memorized the Word to prevent sin in his life: "Thy word I have treasured in my heart, that I may not sin against Thee" (Ps. 119:11). Jesus used memorized Scripture to resist Satan's temptations in the wilderness (Luke 4:1–12). He did not respond to the approach of Satan by saying, "Uh-oh, here comes the devil; I'd better start a crash Bible memory program." Having already stored God's Word in His heart, Jesus effectively employed the Word as "the sword of the Spirit" to vanquish His archenemy (Eph. 6:17).

Several excellent programs are available to give structure, guidelines, and selected passages for memorizing Scripture.[4]

Some Christians have other Christians hold them accountable for their Scripture memory work by listening to them recite memorized verses. Others successfully memorize Scripture through their personal discipline alone.

I have found that it helps to start memorizing Bible verses that are already somewhat familiar, even if you must begin memorizing only one familiar verse such as John 3:16 or one familiar passage such as Psalm 23. Verses that are already somewhat familiar and verses that are especially meaningful give us stronger motivation to memorize them. The key to Scripture memorization is review—and to review each day.

I recall the late Dr. Wilbur Smith mentioning that if he could live his life over again he would practice more personal holiness, more personal evangelism, and more memorization of Scripture.

Scripture memorization has been one of the most helpful spiritual disciplines in my own personal spiritual growth. I hope that you are or will become involved in an effective program of Scripture memorization.

Meditate on God's Word

Do you think of Christian meditation as a pleasant pastime for retirees or other people with a leisurely schedule? Do you think it is a nonessential for successful spiritual living? If so, think of what God told Joshua about meditating: "This book of the law shall not depart from your mouth, but you shall meditate on it day and night, so that you may be careful to do according to all that is written in it; for then you will make your way prosperous, and then you will have success" (Josh. 1:8). Meditation in the Word is a noteworthy mark of the godly person according to Psalm 1:2: "But his delight is in the law of the LORD, and in His law he meditates day and night."

Both Joshua 1:8 and Psalm 1:2 teach continual meditation. Start meditating when you awake in the morning and keep on meditating until you go to bed. Then sleep on your meditative thoughts from the Word and they will likely be your first thoughts when you awake in the morning (Pss. 4:4; 63:6; 77:6; 139:17–18). Biblical meditation keeps God, His works, and His Word uppermost in our thoughts throughout the day. As we meditate on the Word and apply it, the Spirit can use it in sanctifying us.

The following three principles can help us be more effective in biblical meditation.

- *Christian meditation requires biblical knowledge.* Christian meditation assumes that biblical knowledge is held in memory or retrieved from some type of storage. The more Scripture we have memorized, the greater scope of God's truth we have available for meditation.

Regularly reading and memorizing Scripture is one of the first habits that new Christians should develop. Reading the entire Bible and memorizing key verses from various parts of the Scriptures help familiarize us with "the whole purpose of God" (Acts 20:27). Then with verses stored in our memory, we can meditate anytime and anywhere even without Scripture in printed or other recorded form. Someday some Christians may have only the Scriptures they have memorized!

- *Christian meditation means to reflect on, ponder, or consider a scriptural word, phrase, clause, or portion, particularly concerning God, His character, His works, and our relationship to Him.* As the psalmist Asaph wrote, "I will meditate on all Thy work and must on Thy deeds" (Ps. 77:12). Meditation is an activity of the heart, and in Hebrew thought the heart generally refers to one's personality, including the intellect, will, and emotions (4:4; 19:14; 77:6). Thus biblical meditation should involve and influence our thoughts, decisions, and affections.

Stimulate your meditation on biblical truth by asking these three questions: What does it mean? How does it relate to other biblical truth? How does it apply to my relationship to God and to my personal, family, church, vocational, and social life?

- *Christians are to meditate by filling their minds and hearts with thoughts about the triune God, His attributes, His works, His Word, and whatever accords with His character.* Thus Christian meditation differs significantly from Eastern meditation since the latter is an attempt to empty the mind.

When we meditate on God's Word and obey it, He promises us a fruitful spiritual life (Josh. 1:8–9; Ps. 1:2–3). Meditating on God's Word helps us grow in our relationship to the Lord (63:6–8), helps us receive guidance from Him, gives us "perfect peace" (Isa. 26:3), and fills us with praise and thanks to God.

Obey God's Word

Our most basic responsibility in sanctification is to obey God's Word. We should obey His Word completely, at any cost (Luke 14:26–33), and out of love for God and others (Matt. 22:37–40; John 14:21). In addition to these key qualifications of biblical obedience, we should consider four principles that can help us better understand and practice biblical obedience.

(1) Obedience to God's Word is emphasized in both the Old and New Testaments (Exod. 19:5–6; Matt. 28:20). Christ reflected this emphasis on obeying the Word when He said, "My mother and My brothers are these who hear the word of God and do it" (Luke 8:21). James wrote his letter from a profound understanding of the Old Testament, and he told His readers, "But prove yourselves doers of the word, and not merely hearers who delude themselves" (James 1:22). The New Testament repeatedly uses such verbs as *obey, do, observe,* and *keep* in relation to the Word of God.[5] These dynamic verbs challenge us to act on our biblical knowledge.

(2) Of course, if we are to obey His Word, we must know it. "If you *know* these things," Jesus said, "you are blessed if you *do* them" (John 13:17, italics added).[6] The condition, "if you know these things," is a Greek grammatical form that assumes knowledge of "these things."[7] Therefore Christians must *have* biblical truth before they can practice it, just as Christ taught that we must have His commandments before we can keep them (14:21). So God's order is always to learn Christian truth from Scripture and then live it.

Failure to practice known biblical truth is sin. "Therefore, to one who knows the right thing to do, and does not do it, to him it is sin" (James 4:17). The choice to do the truth or to disobey it has serious consequences for Christians (1 Cor. 11:31–32; James 1:22–25).

(3) Obeying God's Word brings blessing. As already noted, Christ taught, that we are blessed if we follow His Word (John 13:17). The Greek adjective *makarios* means "blessed " or "happy." People can be blessed because of health, wealth, or other physical and material benefits. However, Jesus called "blessed" or "happy" all those "who hear the word of God and observe it" (Luke 11:28). *Makarios* is also used in the beatitudes (Matt. 5:3–12), which provide some specific ways to obey Christ and some specific blessings for obedience. The song is correct: "Trust and obey, for there's no other way to be happy in Jesus, but to trust and obey."

(4) To obey the Scriptures we must reject sin. This principle is emphasized in James 1:21, "Therefore, putting aside all filthiness and all that remains of wickedness, in humility receive the word implanted, which is able to save your souls." The first part of this verse commands believers to forsake any sin still left in their lives, and this action builds on their dramatic break from sin at regeneration.

Christians may refrain from overt sinful actions (murder, adultery, theft, impure speech, or an uncontrolled temper) and yet still struggle with subtle covert sins (covetous thoughts, evil motives, or lustful looks). Whether our sin is outward or inward, in action or attitude, in thought, word or deed, we must confess and forsake it (Prov. 28:13).

Christ expects us to deal seriously with sin in our lives. He said, "If your right eye makes you stumble, tear it out and throw it from you. . . . If your right hand makes you stumble, cut it off and throw it from you (Matt. 5:29–30). The Lord is not requiring physical mutilation as a way of stopping personal sin; otherwise many sincere people would have only a left eye and a left hand. Instead His point was that we should reject personal sin specifically, immediately, rigorously, and thoroughly.[8] Most Christians know that the longer they wait to deal with their persistent sin, the more difficult it is to overcome them as those sins become deeply ingrained in their lives through habitual practice.

Therefore believers need to remove any sin still persisting in their lives, in accord with the exhortation in 2 Corinthians 7:1, "Let us cleanse ourselves from all defilement of flesh and spirit, perfecting holiness in the fear of God." This requires confession of sins committed, and forsaking the practice of those sins (Prov. 28:13). "Let everyone who names the name of the Lord abstain from wickedness" (2 Tim. 2:19). We also stay spiritually clean from sin by storing the Word in our hearts and then using it when faced with temptation (Ps. 119:9, 11).

The need for Christians to receive the Word is presented in the second part of James 1:21, "In humility receive the word implanted, which is able to save your souls" (1:21).[9] The expression "to save your souls" refers to present salvation from the power of sin which is based on the past salvation or regeneration mentioned in 1:18. So 1:21 relates to the working of the Word in progressive sanctification. When we receive God's Word and rely on the Spirit, He helps us conquer sin and become more like the Lord Jesus.

The more we reject sin, the more we can receive the Word, and the more we receive the Word, the more sin we will see to reject. When we receive the Word, its spiritual light exposes our sins (Ps. 119:130; 1 John 1:5–9), even "the thoughts and intentions of the heart" (Heb. 4:12). And as we confess and forsake any known sins, our hearts are prepared to receive more from God's Word.

If we fail to reject sin and receive the Word, we put ourselves into a spiritual tailspin. An airplane left in a tailspin will reach its maximum downward speed, so that recovery from its tailspin is most difficult. Christians in a spiritual tailspin need to admit it and recover immediately. God has a wonderful recovery program for those in such a tailspin, and it operates when we confess our sins, forsake our sins, and begin to respond positively to God and His Word. Only then can we start to soar to new heights of spiritual growth.

God graciously forgives Christians and restores them from their sin when they turn to Him in genuine confession. However, Christians should not presume on God's gracious "recovery program" by continuing in a pattern of sin that takes them further away from God and brings more discipline from Him (Heb. 12:5–11). Airplanes in a tailspin that do not recover in time will crash. And Christians who sin severely enough can go beyond recovery in this life and suffer premature death, though not with loss of their salvation (Acts 5:1–11; 1 Cor. 5:1–11; 11:30–32; see also John 5:16–17). So Christians should not see how long they can stay in a spiritual tailspin before they deal with sin. If you are persisting in known sin, then admit it and recommit yourself to the Lord so that He can restore you.

SANCTIFICATION REQUIRES CONTINUAL RESPONSE TO GOD'S WORD

Scripture is God's menu for healthy, balanced, and rapid spiritual growth. Paul reminded Timothy that following "the words of the faith and of the sound doctrine" can nourish God's servants (1 Tim. 4:6). The "milk" of the Word is for spiritual infants or baby Christians and the "solid food" of the Word is for spiritual adults or mature Christians (1 Cor. 3:1–3; Heb. 5:12–14).

Both spiritual infants and mature Christians must keep feeding on the Word to keep growing. The challenge for spiritual infants is to progress from elementary teaching to more advanced teaching of Scripture. The challenge for the spiritually mature is to progress from advanced biblical teaching to even more advanced teaching available through the inexhaustible breadth and depth of Scripture.

Some who have been Christians for many years may think, "I'm already a fairly mature Christian, and so I don't need to receive more of God's Word. I know enough Scripture and have sufficient spiritual experience to get along quite well in the Christian life." This is definitely a wrong approach for even the most mature Christian for two main reasons.

First, when Christians diminish their intake and application of Scripture, they slow or stop their progress in sanctification and can even regress in spiritual living. Then the Father disciplines them to encourage them to pursue sanctification again (Heb. 12:5–11, 14). God wants our entire spiritual journey to be marked by continued growth in Christ. And our rate of spiritual growth depends primarily on how rapidly we learn and obey the Word.

Second, even the most mature Christians still need spiritual food to maintain spiritual health and to grow even more mature. Normal people reach their limits of physical maturity but keep eating to maintain physical health.

However, Christians can always become more spiritually mature, and they must continue receiving spiritual food to sustain spiritual growth. Accordingly, Peter commanded all Christians to "grow in the grace and knowledge of our Lord and Savior Jesus Christ" (2 Pet. 3:18). Learning basic Bible teaching usually comes easily for new believers. But then progress from "the elementary principles" or "milk" of Scripture to the advanced teaching or "solid food" of Scripture (Heb. 5:12–14) becomes more difficult.

New Christians are like miners eagerly and easily working a vein of gold near the surface. However, as the gold vein goes deeper into the earth, the miners must work harder to extract the gold. It takes more time and effort to tunnel deeper, to shore up the tunnel, to mine the gold, and to bring the gold to the surface. Similarly Christian "miners" must expend time and energy to dig deeper into Scripture to discover its valuable and nourishing spiritual truths. Greater spiritual growth also requires discipline and accuracy in Bible study, as taught in 2 Timothy 2:15, "Be diligent to present yourself approved to God as a workman who does not need to be ashamed, handling accurately the word of truth."

Our Bibles are spiritual gold mines, and they give us spiritual guidelines for spiritual growth. David described the Scriptures as "more desirable than gold, yes, than much fine gold; sweeter also than honey and the drippings of the honeycomb" (Ps. 19:10). No material wealth can compare with the spiritual value of knowing God and His wisdom through His Word (119:24, 97–100). In Christ "are hidden all the treasures of wisdom and knowledge," and we learn of Christ and His wisdom in His Word (Col. 2:3), and we learn of Christ and His wisdom in His Word.

If believers neglect to learn, apply, and obey Scripture, they will not be effective in their Christian life and service. Think of Christian leaders who have fallen into sin and thereby caused incalculable harm to their lives, families, and ministries. They all had two things in common—knowledge of biblical truth and blatant disobedience of biblical truth. Determine to obey God's Word by His Spirit (Rom. 8:4), not just because someone else failed, but because you love the Lord too much to disobey Him.

CHAPTER ELEVEN

Training for Godliness:
Discipleship and Disciplines for Sanctification

CAN YOU IMAGINE ANYONE comparing the Christian pursuit of godliness with training for athletic games? Yet Paul did that when He commanded Timothy, "train yourself to be godly" (1 Tim. 4:7, NIV). The word Paul used for "train" (Greek, *gymnazō*) referred to training in the Greek gymnasium for athletic events, and the noun *gymnasia* (training or discipline) in 4:8 is the source of the English word "gymnasium."

Athletic training and competition is one of the most frequent biblical analogies for Christian living (1 Cor. 9:24–27; Phil. 3:13–14; 1 Tim. 4:7–8; 2 Tim. 2:5; Heb. 12:1–2). Paul compared himself to a runner in a race to express his utmost effort in sanctification to become more Christlike (Phil. 3:13–14).[1]

But how do Christians train for godliness or sanctification? Christ trained His followers for sanctification mainly by calling them to discipleship. And Christ required some specific disciplines for His followers: obeying His Word (John 8:31–32), learning to pray (Matt. 6:9–13), self-denial (Luke 9:23), bearing one's cross (9:23), following Him (9:23), serving Him (John 12:26), and others that will be mentioned later. Thus practicing discipleship[2] and practicing spiritual disciplines are two ways Christians train for sanctification.

SANCTIFICATION THROUGH BIBLICAL DISCIPLESHIP

Every believer is "a disciple of Jesus in a general sense"[3](Matt. 28:19 John 8:31–32; Acts 4:32; 11:26). And a disciple in a general sense is "one who has come to Jesus for eternal life, has claimed Jesus as Savior and God, and has embarked upon the life of following Jesus."[4] Therefore all believers are involved both in the process of discipleship and in progressive sanctification (Heb. 2:11; 10:14; 12:14).

Jesus also spoke of a disciple in a specific sense in verses such as Luke 14:26 ("If anyone comes to Me, and does not hate his own father and mother and wife and children and brothers and sisters, yes, and even his own life, he cannot be My disciple"); 14:27 ("Whoever does not carry his own cross and come after Me cannot be my disciple"); and 14:33 ("So therefore, no one of you can be My disciple who does not give up all his own posessions"). Discipleship in a specific sense includes only mature disciples who are meeting the discipleship requirements stated in verses such as these. Discipleship in a general sense also includes new believers or disciples who have begun the process of learning and obeying the requirements to become mature disciples. Both development in discipleship and progressive sanctification have the same goal, namely, Christlike maturity, and both are practically the same in their requirements and in their process.

Requirements for Discipleship

The basic requirements for mature discipleship (being a disciple in the specific sense) are difficult to follow, and Christ did not soften them at all. Christ declared and the Gospels record the demands of discipleship in clear, challenging, and uncompromising language. So do not expect to find the conditions for discipleship in fine print or in ambiguous language.

The requirements for mature discipleship are particularly austere for people in cultures that value comfort, convenience, self-gratification, and non-commitment. Most of us can easily identify cultures that fit this description.

Discipleship is costly, but not so much so as the price of our salvation through Christ's blood (1 Pet. 1:18–19) or as life without Christ (Rom. 5:6–10). Furthermore, the rewards Christ's faithful disciples will receive far outweigh the costs of wholeheartedly following Him (Matt. 19:27–29).

The following are eleven elements involved in effective discipleship.

Deny yourself. Christ said, "If anyone wishes to come after Me, *he must deny himself*" (Luke 9:23, italics added). Jesus did not mean disciples must hate or loathe themselves or lose their personal identities. Rather, self-denial is a conscious choice to discover one's true identity and value "in Christ" (see chapter 3, "Discovering the New You in Christ") and to abandon the self-centered life and to live for God and others. In the path of discipleship we begin to discover the person God wants us to be, and that should be the person *we* want to be.

Love for Christ is the right motive for our self-denial (1 John 4:19). Christ's love for us motivated Him to deny Himself and to die for us (3:16). "For the love of Christ controls us, having concluded this, that one died for all, therefore all died; and He died for all, that they who live should no longer live for themselves, but for Him who died and rose again on their behalf" (2 Cor. 5:14–15).

Take up your cross daily. "If anyone wishes to come after Me [Jesus], let him deny himself, and take up his cross daily, and follow Me" (Luke 9:23). Christ had His cross on which He died to redeem others (John 19:17). Each Christian has his or her cross (Luke 14:27) which indicates death to self (see Gal. 2:20) and willingness to die for Christ, for His gospel, and for others (Mark 8:34–35). Anyone ready to die for Christ's sake is ready for any experience less than death.

The disciple's cross is more restrictive than general trials, burdens, suffering, problems, and painful relationships, since both believers and unbelievers can experience these adversities. Bearing one's cross daily involves a "voluntary acceptance of the responsibilities and sufferings incidental to being a disciple of Christ."[5]

Keep on following Christ. "If anyone wishes to come after Me, let him deny himself, and take up his cross daily, and follow Me" (Luke 9:23). To follow Him means that we are willing to be what He wants us to be, to go where He wants us to go, and to do what He commands us to do at any cost.

Believers must not let anyone or anything keep them from following Christ (9:59–61). Discipleship requires that we first count the cost and be willing to pay it (14:28–33). Jesus' disciples literally left everything behind to follow Him and to proclaim God's kingdom (5:10–11). Following Jesus might cost you your vocation (Matt. 4:18–22; 9:9), a certain dwelling place (Luke 9:57–58), or fulfillment of customary family responsibilities (9:59–62). Peter expressed this requirement when he said to Jesus, "Behold, we have left everything and followed You" (Matt. 19:27). In Christ's call to follow Him, He allows for no excuses and no delays (Luke 9:57–62).

Relinquish all your possessions to Christ. Christ said, "No one of you can be My disciple who does not give up all his own possessions" (14:33). Christians should place all they have at Christ's disposal.

Since Jesus is not physically walking and ministering on earth now, how do Christians give up everything to follow Him? We must be willing to submit to the Lord everything we are and have so that He can use us and our possessions for His purpose. In biblical terminology, we sanctify or set apart ourselves and our substance to the Lord. God owns each Christian by creation and redemption (Isa. 43:7; 1 Cor. 6:19–20). And all our possessions are on loan from God (John 3:27) so that we serve as His stewards. Each believer should ask, "Have I turned over to the Lord the title deed to myself and my possessions?"

Much as the Lord multiplied five small barley loaves and two small fish, so He will take our offerings, bless them, use them, and multiply them in ministry to others (6:10–13).

When we put our possessions at God's disposal, He may return them to our care and direct us to administer them faithfully for Him. Then God will multiply our resources so that we have more with which to minister to others (Matt. 25:29; 2 Cor. 9:10–11).

Continue in Christ's Word. Jesus said, "If you abide in My word, then you are truly disciples of Mine; and you shall know the truth, and the truth shall make you free" (John 8:31–32). Those loyal to Christ's Word demonstrate that they are true disciples, and they experience liberation from sin by learning and obeying His truth (8:32, 34, 36).

Practice prayer according to Christ's teaching. Jesus taught His disciples how to pray (Matt. 6:6, 9–13; 7:7–8) and how not to pray (6:5, 7–8; Luke

18:9–14). He encouraged and commanded them to pray (Matt. 26:41; Luke 18:1; John 16:24).

Abide in Christ. Abiding in Christ, the theme of John 15:1–11, is based on the believer's spiritual union with Christ, which He mentioned in 14:20, "In that day you shall know that I am in My Father, and you in Me, and I in you." This spiritual union first occurred at Pentecost when the Spirit came on the assembled believers (Acts 2:1–4). Now believers are spiritually united with Christ "by [or 'in'] one Spirit" (1 Cor. 12:13) at the moment of their salvation. All Christians are responsible to experience this spiritual union with Christ by abiding in Him (John 15:4–5).

Abiding in Christ means the believer shares an intimate relationship with Christ as they spiritually reside together. Christ commanded His disciples to "abide [Greek, *meinate* from *menō*] in Me" (15:4), that is, to share their lives with Him in an intimate, spiritual sense. This same terminology is used of two disciples who resided or "abode [Greek, *emeinan* from *menō*] with Him [Jesus]" in a physical and social sense (1:39, KJV).

Abiding in Christ requires a life cleansed from sin and from anything else that would hinder the true branches (believers) from abiding in the true Vine, Christ (15:1–3). If we have something in our lives we do not share with Christ, then either it is sin and needs to be confessed, or it is an area of our lives such as a need, a problem, or a purpose we need to share with Him, though He already knows about it.

The comprehensive requirement for abiding in Christ is obedience to His commandments (15:10; 1 John 2:6). John taught the same requirement for the believer's relationship to God: "The one who keeps His [God's] commandments abides in Him, and He in him" (3:24).

By abiding in Christ, we experience a fruitful life (John 15:4–5, 8), a prayerful life (15:7), and a joyful life (15:11). Prayer and joy are fairly familiar concepts to most Christians, but what is the spiritual *fruit* that abiding in Christ produces (15:4–5, 8)? John 15:1–11 does not give specific examples of spiritual fruit, but other New Testament references suggest what spiritual "fruit" includes, such as (a) manifestation of Christlike character (Gal. 5:22–23), (b) presentation of praise and thanks to God through Christ (Heb. 13:15), (c) contribution to Christian works and workers (Phil. 4:17), (d) salvation of souls through evangelism (John 4:35–37; 15:16; 2 Tim. 4:5),

(e) edification of other believers (Rom. 1:13), and (f) production of good works (Col. 1:10; see also 1 Tim. 5:9–10).[6]

Love Christ supremely. Christ taught, "He who loves father or mother more than Me is not worthy of Me; and he who loves son or daughter more than Me is not worthy of Me" (Matt. 10:37). Disciples should love God's Son so much that their love for any humans, even dearest relatives, would seem like hate compared to their love for Him. "If anyone comes to Me and does not hate his own father and mother and wife and children and brothers and sisters, yes, and even his own life, he cannot be My disciple" (Luke 14:26). A comparison of this verse with other relevant passages and a consideration of Hebrew usage show that Jesus was not asking His followers literally to hate their close relatives.[7] Jesus expects us to love our relatives and even our enemies. Still, disciples should always love Christ supremely (Matt. 22:37–38; John 21:15–17).

Love for Christ is the foundational and foremost requirement of discipleship because Spirit-produced love for Christ is the necessary motive and dynamic to meet the other requirements for discipleship (14:15, 21). Every church-age believer has God's Spirit (Rom. 8:9; 2 Cor. 1:22) and therefore has the spiritual resource for becoming a mature disciple (Phil. 2:12–13).

Love one another. If we love Christ, we will show practical love for His followers (John 13:34–35; 1 John 3:16–18; 4:19–21). This Christlike love that disciples have for each other is the main proof to the world that they are indeed His disciples. "By this all men will know that you are My disciples, if you have love for one another" (John 13:35).

Serve others. Christ gave His disciples an unforgettable example of humble service when he washed their feet (13:4–11), and then He commanded them to follow His example (13:14–15). Christ also taught His disciples that greatness comes through servanthood (Luke 22:24–27), and He lived and died as a servant among them (Phil. 2:5–8).

Make disciples of others. This requirement is stated most clearly in Matthew's account of the Great Commission (Matt. 28:19–20). All who become Christ's disciples have the great responsibility and privilege of leading others to trust Christ.

Rewards for Discipleship

Christ promised His twelve apostles they would rule over Israel (Matt. 19:28–30), and He promised a great return to all His disciples who faithfully follow Him.

Perhaps the greatest reward of serving Christ through discipleship is His promise in John 12:26, "If anyone serves Me, let him follow Me; and where I am, there shall My servant also be; if anyone serves Me, the Father will honor him." We can have no greater privilege than following Christ and no higher tribute than receiving honor from the Father.

SANCTIFICATION THROUGH SPIRITUAL DISCIPLINES

Training for sanctification includes practicing certain spiritual disciplines.

Wrong Approaches to the Spiritual Disciplines

In the history of Christianity the spiritual disciplines have often suffered neglect, misuse, or abuse. It is crucial then to take a proper approach to the spiritual disciplines so that we help rather than hinder our sanctification.

First, avoid a perfectionistic approach to the spiritual disciplines. Perfectionistic Christians tend to be so uptight and introspective in practicing the disciplines that they are like a tightrope walker who is so concerned about her next step that she loses her balance and falls. And ironically, perfectionism tends to increase a Christian's liability to fall into sin and fail in sanctification. Instead of producing more mature Christians, a perfectionistic approach to the disciplines often produces self-conscious and guilt-ridden Christians with shriveled spiritual lives.

Second, avoid a casual approach to the spiritual disciplines. Church going, occasional Bible reading, socializing with other Christians, and a few other related activities are important Christian practices, but they will not automatically produce Christlike maturity, especially if they are practiced in a perfunctory way. God's command to pursue sanctification (Heb. 12:14) requires intentional, dynamic, and enthusiastic practice of serious Bible study, prayer, Christian service, and other spiritual disciplines. Merely conforming to one's cultural version of Christianity yields lukewarm spirituality that nauseates Christ (Rev. 3:15–16). Following Christ's teaching on the demands of discipleship and the biblical exhortations to spiritual growth help prevent a lackadaisical approach to Christian living.

Biblical Concept of a Spiritual Discipline

A spiritual discipline is a God-appointed Christian practice to help believers become more Christlike. The term *spiritual* emphasizes the purpose of the biblical disciplines to nurture Christian spirituality. However, the spiritual disciplines involve the body, and thus in a functional sense they are also disciplines of the body.[8] Try to imagine personal Bible study without the use of your body. So the crucial role of the body in practicing the spiritual disciplines shows that sanctification is not opposed to the body but is vitally related to it.

Physical exercise can indirectly aid sanctification by promoting the health, strength, and functioning of the Christian's body as the temple of the Holy Spirit (1 Cor. 6:19–20). That's why 1 Timothy 4:8 says that "physical training is of some value" (NIV).

Christians may discover activities that are not explicitly commanded in Scripture but are helpful in practicing the biblical disciplines. For example, some Christians find that walking helps them stay alert and invigorates their praying and meditation. So we should freely use activities such as vigorous exercise to enhance our practice of biblical disciplines.

Purpose of the Spiritual Disciplines

The purpose for general spiritual discipline or training and the specific disciplines is that Christians might be godly. Paul told Timothy, "Discipline [a form of the Greek verb, *gymnazō*] yourself for the purpose of godliness" (1 Tim. 4:7). This same verb "to discipline or train" appears in three other verses where it is used of (a) believers "who because of practice have their senses trained [from *gymnazō*] to discern good and evil" (Heb. 5:14); (b) believers who are "trained" [from *gymnazō*] by divine "discipline" which "yields the peaceful fruit of righteousness" (12:11);

and (c) false teachers who have "a heart trained [from *gymnazō*] in greed" (2 Pet. 2:14; see v. 1). Thus a person's discipline or training can be for godly purposes such as spiritual discernment and righteous character, or for an ungodly purpose such as greed.

Proper Practice of the Spiritual Disciplines

What guidelines should we follow in exercising spiritual disciplines?

First, use the disciplines as means to godliness. Christians can become so enamored with the disciplines that they become ends in themselves, and then the spiritual purpose of the disciplines to make us godly is diminished or even obscured. For example, a Christian can become so absorbed in the experience of solitude and silence at a retreat center that the purpose of godliness in his or her everyday life is overshadowed by the experience and the location of the solitude and silence. If we are not becoming more Christlike through the spiritual disciplines, then either we are not properly practicing them or else we are missing their purpose, or both.

Second, give the same emphasis to the spiritual disciplines that Scripture does. In reaction against an unbiblical form of asceticism (see Col. 2:16–23), some evangelical Christians have dismissed the spiritual disciplines as having little or no value, even though the biblical disciplines can promote godliness when properly practiced. Thus we should not neglect the spiritual disciplines as most of the twentieth-century church has done. Neither should we overemphasize the disciplines and thereby depreciate or even neglect other biblical means of sanctification. It is misleading when Christians are told, "The only way you can overcome the lusts of the flesh is by fasting." Fasting can be a proper discipline in Christian living (Acts 13:2–3), but the teaching of Galatians 5:16 is certainly a more significant principle for victory over personal lusts: "Walk by the Spirit, and you will not carry out the desire of the flesh."

Prayer is a primary biblical discipline but even a radical practice of prayer or some other spiritual discipline by itself is not a cure-all for what ails your spiritual life. We also need to study and obey the Word and practice other biblical disciplines.

Third, depend on the Spirit for self-discipline and power to practice the spiritual disciplines.

A Sampling of the Spiritual Disciplines

The recent revival of interest in Christian spirituality has been accompanied by some books devoted primarily to the spiritual disciplines such as Richard J. Foster, *Celebration of Discipline;* Donald S. Whitney, *Spiritual Disciplines for the Christian Life;* and Dallas Willard, *The Spirit of the Disciplines.*[9] These books discuss the spiritual disciplines extensively,[10] but our purpose here is to discuss briefly a select list of primary biblical disciplines.

Studying the Scriptures is the foundational discipline. Through Scripture we learn about the triune God and His will and how to relate properly to the Father, the Son, and the Spirit (John 5:39; 16:13–15; 17:17; Eph. 5:17). The Spirit uses Scripture as His instrument in sanctification (John 17:17; 2 Cor. 3:18). By studying Scripture and relying on the Spirit we can learn and live God's truth so that we become mature in Christ.

Biblical meditation helps us understand Scripture and integrate it into our lives. The purpose of meditation is to reflect on God, His Word, His character, His works, and our relationship to Him (Josh. 1:8; Pss. 1:2; 48:9; 77:12). True biblical meditation is with the heart (19:14) and is pleasing to the Lord (104:34).

Prayer is a primary discipline because it is our means of communicating with God, just as Scripture is God's main means of communicating with us. Open and continual communication with God is essential for a right relationship to God. We are commanded to practice the discipline of prayer "without ceasing" (1 Thess. 5:17).

The discipline of *resting before the Lord* gives needed balance to the discipline of serving Him (Mark 6:31). God commands His people to "Be still and know that I am God" (Ps. 46:10, KJV). This may be the most disobeyed command in Scripture, especially by Christians who live in a performance-oriented society. Some conceive of God as a relentless slave driver who demands constant work or other activity. Believers with this wrong concept of God may wrongly believe they are more spiritual if they frantically participate in every Christian activity their schedule will allow.

Of course, disciplined Christian living does include some diligent, dynamic activity. However, Jesus showed us by His teaching and example that times of rest, relaxation, quietness, and waiting before God should undergird and alternate with our activity for God (Mark 1:35–39; 6:31; see Pss. 37:7; 62:5). Wise Christians will nurture their spiritual growth by appropriately balancing rest with work and periods of reflection with periods of rigorous activity.

The discipline of *solitude* is needed for focus on God (Mark 1:35; 6:45–47), for rest from interaction with people (6:31–32), for study, for prayer (1:35), and for concentrated practice of other disciplines.

Solitude is important for all Christians, and solitude is a special challenge for Christians who cannot stand to be alone, even with God. Some Christians crave constant involvement with other humans or input from TV programs or sound systems. We are deficient in our relationship with God if we lack the desire to be alone in His presence and without distracting sights and sounds (see Matt. 6:6). Learning to have intimate fellowship with God through solitude can whet our appetite for more time alone with God and nurture our Christian growth. Special times of intimacy with the Lord should be the highlights of our spiritual journey.

The main purpose of solitude is to reflect on our relationship to God and to grow in Christ. Disengaged from the frantic pace of life, we can consider where we have been in our spiritual journey, where we are, and where we need to be. Only as we get to know God and His will do we gain the proper spiritual perspective to evaluate ourselves and renew our spiritual passion.

Solitude with the Lord does not require that a Christian become reclusive, since this would oppose our relationship and responsibility to other members of Christ's body. Believers need interaction with groups of Christians for mutual fellowship and edification and for corporate worship. Yet Christians can develop intimate fellowship with the Lord only through special periods of solitude just as we develop an intimate relationship with a spouse or a friend only through time spent in one-on-one fellowship.

The biblical discipline of *fasting* involves refraining from food in order to concentrate on Bible study, biblical meditation, prayer, solitude, or
other spiritual exercises. Christians should not practice fasting as a fad or
with the questionable notion that fasting has spiritual value in itself (Rom.
14:6b; 1 Cor. 8:8).[11] However, if you voluntarily refrain from food to focus on some other biblical discipline such as prayer (Neh. 1:4; Dan. 9:3;
Luke 5:33; Acts 13:2–3), then fasting can have indirect spiritual value by
promoting your praying.

Believers should fast with the proper motive—that God, not men, will
see them fasting (Matt. 6:16–18)—and with the proper purpose—that
they may enhance their practice of other spiritual disciplines and become
more Christlike.

Simplicity in living is a spiritual discipline that can help us concentrate on our spiritual life and service. Paul told Timothy, "No soldier in
active service entangles himself in the affairs of everyday life, so that he
may please the one who enlisted him as a soldier" (2 Tim. 2:4).

Simplicity in living includes the practice of frugality. The value of fru-
gal living is presented in *Living on Less and Enjoying It More*, by Maxine
Hancock. Richard J. Foster's book, *Freedom of Simplicity*, is also helpful.

Christ taught and modeled simplicity (Matt. 8:20; 10:9–10; Mark
12:43–44; Luke 12:15). Such simplicity helps our spiritual growth in three
ways. (a) We can follow Christ with less distraction from earthly things.
(b) We can more easily give spiritual values priority over material things
(Matt. 6:33–34). (c) We are better prepared to love people and properly
use things instead of loving things and using people (Matt. 22:39).

Service is a very broad spiritual discipline because it relates to the whole
Christian life. Christians are God's servants in this life (1 Pet. 2:16, NIV)
and forever (Rev. 22:3). Christ's disciples are to serve Christ and others
(Matt. 20:26–28), and serving Christ requires following Him.

Christian service goes beyond our personal, family, church, civil, and
vocational responsibilities and includes areas such as ministry in our
neighborhood. For instance, a neighborhood usually has some needy widows who can use our help without our usurping the responsibility of their
family members. Scripture teaches us to "visit orphans and widows in
their distress" (James 1:27). I know a Christian woman who spends sev-

eral hours each week helping a neighboring widow who lives alone, is virtually blind, and needs to understand the gospel better and to trust Christ as her Savior. This helpful Christian woman is my wife.

Serving Christ may cost us some extra sleep, leisure time, TV watching, and personal pleasure. However, Jesus exemplified the kind of service He calls us to do (Matt. 20:28; Luke 22:27), and that service allows time for prayer, rest, recreation, solitude, and interaction with family and friends.

We obey God by practicing the discipline of Christian service ("Serve one another," Gal. 5:13), and obeying God promotes our sanctification ("Having been freed from sin . . . you derive your benefit, resulting in sanctification," Rom. 6: 22).

The discipline of *worship* should pervade our Christian life so that all we think, say, or do is offered as worship to God. For example, presenting our bodies to God as "a living and holy sacrifice" is considered our "spiritual service of worship" (12:1).

We can worship anywhere and anytime, but we cannot worship just any way. Biblical worship must be done "in spirit and truth" (John 4:23–24), that is sincerely, from the inner person, in the Holy Spirit, and according to God's truthful Word.

Christians should practice worship both privately (Matt. 6:6;) and corporately (Ps. 116:18; Eph. 5:19). Worship includes appropriate expression to God of our prayer, praise, thanksgiving, and singing.

As we properly practice worship and the other biblical disciplines, we will be training and gaining in godliness (1 Tim. 4:7).

CHAPTER TWELVE

Communicating with God:
How Prayer Promotes Sanctification

"TELL ME HONESTLY ABOUT your prayer life," your Christian friend insists. Do you feel embarrassed by this question because you have little to tell and much to hide about your personal prayer life? Any hesitation we have to share honestly with others about our intimate communication with God (or lack of it) is increased when we consider the great prayer warriors of Scripture. In the Old Testament we encounter effective intercessors such as Abraham, Job, Moses, Samuel, and Daniel. Consider also the miraculous answers to Elijah's prayers: the child restored to life (1 Kings 17:21–22), the fire from heaven (18:36–38), and the drought and then the rain (18:42–45; James 5:17–18). In the New Testament we learn of Christ's perfect prayer life (John 11:42; 17:1–26) and Paul's incessant prayers for the churches and for particular Christians (for example, Phil. 1:1–4; 2 Tim. 1:3). In comparison to the astounding prayer records of these biblical characters, many of us would have to grade our prayer life with an "F" for "failure" and not for "fantastic."

Each Christian should evaluate his or her prayer life, correct it in needy areas, and continue developing a more effective prayer life. The Bible gives us principles, exhortations, and examples concerning prayer and an opportunity to improve our praying (Luke 11:1–4, esp. v. 1). However, if Christians only focus on comparing themselves with the giants of prayer in the biblical record and in church history, they are setting themselves up for frustration. Do set high ideals for your prayer life, learn more about prayer from Scripture and from appropriate literature on prayer, and then focus on practicing the truth learned about prayer.

GENERAL PRINCIPLES ABOUT CHRISTIAN PRAYER

True praying is a believer's effective communication with God. The general New Testament formula for prayer is to pray in the Spirit (Eph. 6:18), through (or in the name of) Jesus Christ (John 14:6, 13), and to the Father (Eph. 2:18; 3:14). Prayer is generally addressed to the Father, but sometimes prayer is addressed to the Son (Mark 9:22–24; John 16:24; Acts 7:59–60).

Our Prayer Life Reflects Our Spiritual Life

Our prayer life is a good mirror of our spirituality. If our prayers are fresh, dynamic, and growing closer to the biblical pattern of prayer, then probably our spiritual life is dynamic. But if our prayers are stale, dull, and forced, then probably our spiritual life has similar negative qualities.

Prayer Is Every Christian's Responsibility

We sometimes hear that prayer should be as natural to the saint's soul as breathing is to the body. This is an idealistic view of prayer because prayer is quite different from breathing in some significant ways. Christians must decide to initiate prayer, because prayer is not involuntary like breathing. Scripture commands us to pray (Luke 18:1; John 16:24; 1 Thess. 5:17), and thus failure to pray is sin (1 Sam. 12:24; James 4:17).

Furthermore, breathing takes little physical effort in healthy individuals. But prayer can involve very intense effort from our whole being.

Other people can pray for us, but they cannot pray in our place. There are no subs or pinch hitters in praying. The newest and most immature Christian can and should pray. Imagine parents who have a teenage son who wins first place in a speech contest and who are thrilled with his accomplishment. But imagine that these same parents also have a baby who smiles, coos, and makes a sound like "gargle-de-goo-goo." They are just as thrilled with their baby son's earliest efforts at communication and expression as with their older son's outstanding speech ability. And God our Father is just as pleased when a new believer attempts to express prayer to Him as when the most mature saint communicates with Him. God wants each Christian to pray to Him and no one else's prayers can substitute.

Prayer Involves Work and Warfare

Prayer requires human decision and initiative. Prayer then is like an effective method of communication such as a telephone, but we must take certain steps to communicate over the telephone. Prayer also requires human effort along with reliance on the Spirit to help us know how to pray and for what to pray (Rom. 8:26–27; Eph. 6:18; Jude 20). Jesus showed that prayer can involve agony and hard work: "And being in anguish, he prayed more earnestly, and his sweat was like drops of blood falling to the ground" (Luke 22:44, NIV). Now that is earnest effort in prayer!

Prayer involves spiritual warfare as well as work, and both activities were involved in Epaphras's prayer for the Colossian Christians. Paul presented Epaphras as a front-line prayer warrior for them: "He [Epaphras] is always wrestling in prayer for you" (Col. 4:12, NIV). Praying can require stupendous effort which Satan opposes just as gravity opposes us when we try to carry a heavy pack up a steep hill.

The weapons for spiritual warfare also include prayer: "With all prayer and petition pray at all times in the Spirit, and with this in view, be on the alert with all perseverance and petition for all the saints" (6:18).[1] Christians can fight and win some of their greatest spiritual battles on their knees. Communicating with our heavenly Father is a delightful privilege, but it also requires strenuous work and engages us in spiritual warfare.

149

NEW PRINCIPLES OF PRAYER TAUGHT BY CHRIST

The Lord Jesus prayed, and He encouraged others to pray. "Now He was telling them a parable to show that at all times they ought to pray and not to lose heart" (Luke 18:1). Jesus taught His disciples how to pray (Matt. 6:5–13),[2] and He emphasized the importance of prayer (26:41; Mark 9:29; John 16:24).

The Gospels indicate Jesus prayed often and on various occasions. He rose early in the morning to spend time alone in prayer before preaching (Mark. 1:35, 38). He spent all night in prayer before He chose the twelve disciples (Luke 6:12–13). He prayed in public as well as in private (Matt. 15:36; Luke 23:34).

The Old Testament has much to say about prayer. Yet Christ taught His disciples two new principles that must have astounded His Jewish followers with their Old Testament background.

First, He taught the disciples to address God as "our Father" (Matt. 6:9). For the disciples to approach God on such intimate terms as their personal Father was foreign to their understanding of the Old Testament, though God was Father to His Old Covenant people (Isa. 63:16). Praying this way was blatant irreverence to pious Jews. Yet Jesus went a step further and addressed God as "Abba," an Aramaic term equivalent to "Papa" or "Daddy" (Mark 14:36). And Christians are prompted by the Spirit to address God their spiritual Father as "Abba" or "Daddy" (Rom. 8:15; Gal. 4:6).

Second, Christ promised His disciples, "If you ask Me anything in My name, I will do it" (John 14:14; see also v. 13; 16:24). This was a stupendous promise that would test both His credibility and their faith.

Prayer was one of the key characteristics of Christ's life and ministry. To pray like Christ we should do three things: (a) study Christ's teaching on prayer while He was on earth and through His apostles after His ascension, (b) study Christ's practice of prayer, and (c) practice the principles of prayer He taught and practiced. Believers who pray more as Christ prayed develop spiritually and become more like Christ.

REQUIREMENTS FOR PRAYING
ACCORDING TO GOD'S WILL

Saving faith in Christ gives us access to our Father (John 14:6; Heb. 10:19–22). And praying according to God's will assures us that He will answer our prayers. "This is the confidence which we have before Him, that, if we ask anything according to His will, He hears us. And if we know that He hears us in whatever we ask, we know that we have the requests which we have asked from Him" (1 John 5:14–15).

Praying according to God's will includes seven requirements which are some of the same requirements for sanctification. Meet the requirements for praying in God's will, and you will also progress in your sanctification.

Pray from a Pure Heart

To pray effectively we need to "call on the Lord from a pure heart" (2 Tim. 2:22; see also Ps. 24:3–4). The psalmist warned, "If I regard wickedness in my heart, the Lord will not hear" (Ps. 66:18). Praying from a pure heart does not mean God requires perfection before He will answer our prayers. Otherwise, no prayers could be answered during our earthly life.

Psalm 66:18 does mean we cannot expect God to answer us if we are tolerating sin in our lives. Christians who coddle a pet sin and cling to it like a child hugging a favorite teddy bear make their prayer life ineffective. Sins such as fantasizing about illicit romance or personal fame are so deceptive that they may seem to be a comforting pleasure or a harmless pastime. But any sin severely hinders our spiritual life and shuts down our prayer life.

Sin acts like a pair of snips that severs our prayer line. Personal sin cuts off personal communication with God. God has graciously provided a flawless repair kit so we can restore our communication with Him. God's repair kit is given in 1 John 1:9, "If we confess our sins, He is faithful and righteous to forgive us our sins and to cleanse us from all unrighteousness." Believers must confess and reject all their known sin, and then they can claim God's promise to forgive and cleanse them from all sin.

Christians who want a productive prayer life must keep a pure heart.

Pray with a Stable Faith

Christ promised that "all things you ask in prayer, believing, you shall receive" (Matt. 21:22). Christ was not teaching a blank-check approach to prayer. Praying with faith is not a magical formula to satisfy our selfish desires (James 4:2–3). True faith desires and discerns God's will in prayer (1 John 5:14–15). Faith assures us that when our prayers align with God's purposes and promises, He answers our prayers.

God answers prayer in response to stable faith, as James emphasized. "But if any of you lacks wisdom, let him ask of God, who gives to all men generously and without reproach, and it will be given to him. But let him ask in faith without any doubting, for the one who doubts is like the surf of the sea driven and tossed by the wind. For let not that man expect that he will receive anything from the Lord, being a double-minded man, unstable in all his ways" (James 1:5–8).

Stable faith does not waver between doubt and confidence like a float on the surf of the sea (1:6). Stable faith is like an anchor firmly embedded in God's sure promises (Rom. 4:20–21).

Many believers become frustrated when they sincerely want to trust God but come down with a bad case of doubt. This happened to a father who desperately wanted Jesus to help his demon-afflicted son (Mark 9:20–22). Jesus affirmed God's ability to do anything and then challenged the father to believe (9:23). The father "cried out and began saying, 'I do believe; help my unbelief'" (9:24). Was this man contradicting himself by affirming both his belief and his unbelief? No. Instead of contradicting himself, I believe that this father profoundly evaluated his condition as if to say, "Lord, I have some faith, but it is weak faith; I have a little faith but I am struggling with a lot of doubt. Please remove the doubt and give me sufficient faith to see my son healed." Jesus must have answered this father's request because He delivered his son.

Likewise, a Christian may confess, "I am a true believer in Christ, but my faith is very weak. I don't have a mustard seed of faith to move a mountain (Matt. 17:20); I don't even have enough faith to move a mustard seed!" Your faith may be very small, but the Lord can increase any believer's faith (2 Thess. 1:3). And if we ask for more faith (Luke 17:5), we should get ready for more trials, because God uses our trials to help our faith grow (James 1:2–4; 1 Pet. 1:6–9). And as our faith grows stronger and steadier, our spiritual life and our prayer life grow also.

Pray from an Obedient Life

Trouble in our prayer life is usually a symptom of a deeper problem in our spiritual life—disobedience. A light on the dashboard of our car may indicate we have engine trouble, but we cannot cure our engine problem by cutting the wire to the dashboard light. That only cures the symptom. We need to find and treat the real cause of the engine problem. The root cause of ineffective prayer is some form of disobedience.

The cure for disobedience is to confess and forsake our disobedience so that God will forgive it. And the prayer of confession is the only prayer God will hear when believers have knowingly disobeyed.

If we deal with disobedience and obey God, then He promises to hear our prayers, "And whatever we ask we receive from Him, because we keep His commandments and do the things that are pleasing in His sight" (1 John 3:22). We could paraphrase God's promise this way: "Listen to me when I command you, and I will listen to you when you call on me in prayer." Consistent obedience gives us confidence in our prayer life and growth in our Christian life.

Pray according to Christ's Words

In John 15:7 Christ stated the crucial connection between prayer and His words. "If you abide in Me, and My words abide in you, ask whatever you wish, and it shall be done for you." Christ's words reveal God's will. Thus when Christ's words abide in our lives, our prayers will align with God's will (1 John 5:14–15). As John Stott notes, "It is only when Christ's words abide in us that our prayers will be answered. Then we can ask what we will and it shall be done, because we shall will only what he wills."[3]

Christ's words and God's Word are interchangeable (John 14:24; 1 Pet. 1:10–11). So having God's Word abide in us is the same as having Christ's words abide in us (John 15:7). Having God's Word abide in us helps us pray according to His will in two main ways.

First, God's Word can function as a spiritual strainer to remove improper requests, wrong methods, and wrong motives from our prayers.

It would be an improper request for a single Christian man to pray that an unsaved woman would become his wife. God has already said no to that request based on the command, "Do not be bound together with unbelievers" (2 Cor. 6:14).

An example of a wrong method of prayer is "meaningless repetition" (Matt. 6:7). God is not impressed by the sheer number of times we repeat the same words in prayer whether the words are, "Yes, Jesus; Yes, Jesus . . ." or some other pious-sounding expression. Such vain repetition of words is no more effective in prayer than increased talking on a broken telephone.

James explained that wrong motivation thwarts answered prayer. "You ask and do not receive, because you ask with wrong motives, so that you may spend it on your pleasures" (James 4:3). Praying in God's will means that we pray for things that will please God rather than for things that will simply satisfy us.

Second, God's Word can function as a guide to show us how to pray and for what to pray. When God's Word fills His people, their prayers are brought in line with His will so that they can pray confidently (Ps. 37:4; John 15:7).

Pray for Things That Will Glorify God

Believers are commanded to "do all to the glory of God" and that includes asking requests of Him (1 Cor. 10:31). We waste our breath and time requesting things that will not glorify God. So before you pray, ask, "Can my request glorify God?" This criterion excludes requests that fulfill our selfish lusts (James 4:2–3). Genuine personal needs do qualify for requests that glorify God because God, who only wills what is for His glory, wills to provide His people's needs when they seek Him first (Matt. 6:8, 33; Phil. 4:19).

God can be glorified in three main ways through our prayer requests, though He is the Giver and we are the recipients and beneficiaries of His provision: (a) God's provision to meet our needs manifests His grace, goodness, and other perfect attributes, and God glorifies Himself when He manifests His attributes; (b) God accomplishes His will through answered prayer, and He is glorified whenever His will is done; (c) God gets glory when we thank and praise Him for providing our needs through prayer (see Ps. 50:23). For example, one of the ten lepers whom Jesus healed thanked Jesus for his healing (Luke 17:11–16). Jesus acknowledged that this healed leper glorified God through his thanksgiving and was healed through his faith (17:16–19).

Prayer requests that align with the will of God must be requests that we can ask and use for the glorify of God.

Pray for Things That Are Spiritually Helpful

God wills that Christians grow in Christ (1 Thess. 4:3; 2 Pet. 3:18). Therefore praying in God's will includes only requests that will advance our spiritual growth.

Believers can request things that will harm instead of help their spiritual life. When they insist on spiritually harmful requests against God's will, He may grant those requests if they will learn in no other way to accept His will in their prayers. Israel requested meat in the wilderness because they were dissatisfied with the manna or "bread from heaven" God gave them (Exod. 16:4; Num 11:1–35). God granted their desire but judged them for their sinful request (Ps. 78:21–33; 106:13–15). Israel also demanded to have a human king like the other nations rather than trusting their invisible God as their king (1 Sam. 8:19–20). The Israelites rejected God by rejecting God's voice through Samuel, and they suffered terrible consequences (8:7–18). The lesson Israel learned in making requests to God is clear: Once you know God's will, do not try to it. Otherwise, you may receive your wrong requests and harm your spiritual life.

Not even the apostle Paul could always determine whether a request was spiritually helpful or harmful. Paul prayed three times for God to remove what he described as "a thorn in the flesh, a messenger of Satan to buffet me" (2 Cor. 12:7–8). God denied this request because He had a better answer to the apostle's prayer. God left this thorn in Paul's flesh so that he would be humble and experience God's sufficient grace and more of Christ's power (12:9). Though God's answer to Paul's specific request was no, God gave him a yes answer to something better. We can thank God for His no answers to our requests, even when our requests seem to fit His will. We should learn to accept God's better answers to our requests because they will bring more spiritual good to us and more glory to Him.

In His perfect wisdom God knows and does what will spiritually benefit us. Consider Brad, who sees his little daughter, Heather, reaching for some shiny razor blades. Brad says firmly, "No, no, Heather; those will hurt you." Heather still tries to grasp the razor blades because they are so shiny and appealing. As a loving Father, Brad prevents Heather from having the razor blades because he knows they will hurt her. Similarly our wise heavenly Father may withhold things that appeal to us because He knows they will not work for our spiritual good (Rom. 8:28). The earthly father may permit rather than prevent some of the child's choices and actions. And like the Israelites, the child may receive some bad consequences from some bad choices and learn some hard lessons. Do we trust our heavenly Father enough to accept His negative answers to our requests, even when our requests seem helpful to us and according to His will? Like Paul, we are challenged to trust that our all-knowing Father has something better for us or is waiting for a better time to grant our request.

Pray in the Holy Spirit

Twice Scripture commands believers to pray "in the Spirit" (Eph. 6:18; Jude 20). To pray in the Spirit requires that we rely on the Spirit to control and direct our prayers.

When we pray "in the Spirit," He enables us to pray according to the will of God. Romans 8:26–27 says, "In the same way the Spirit also helps our weakness; for we do not know how to pray as we should, but the Spirit Himself intercedes for us with groanings too deep for words; and He who searches the hearts knows what the mind of the Spirit is, because He intercedes for the saints according to the will of God." The Spirit helps us know how to pray and for what to pray. And God who searches our hearts (1 Sam. 16:7; Heb. 4:12) understands perfectly the Spirit's expression of our prayer requests.

We all know the frustration of trying to connect on an important long-distance telephone call and then hearing the words: "Your call cannot be completed as dialed." And we can be even more frustrated when the gist of God's response to our important prayer is, "Your request cannot be answered as prayed." How different when the Father can respond to our prayer this way: "Your request can be answered because you prayed in the Spirit, through my Son, and according to My will."

Praying in the Spirit is not just one way to pray; it is the only way for Christians to pray in God's will.

PRACTICING PRAYER TO ADVANCE SANCTIFICATION

The Boy Scout motto, "Be prepared," also applies to prayer. However, preparation for prayer is not enough. Christians need this expanded motto, "Prepare for prayer and practice prayer." People spend billions of dollars on programs and equipment for physical exercise. Their preparation is maximum, but often their time and effort in exercising is minimal. The results for their physique and health are also minimal. If we want abundant prayer answers and spiritual growth, we must pray persistently and consistently (Matt. 7:7–8; Luke 18:1; 1 Thess. 5:17).

Believers should pray for their personal sanctification and for the sanctification of other Christians. Christ asked His Father to "sanctify them [His believers] in the truth" (John 17:17), and His prayer request included the sanctification of future believers (17:20).

Pray for Personal Sanctification

Praying for oneself to grow in Christ for God's glory is not egotistical; it is biblical. Believers can pray to receive daily meals (Matt. 6:11), to love God and their neighbors more (22:37–40), to know and do God's will (Eph. 5:17; 1 John 2:17), to have more faith (Luke 17:5), to know Christ more (Phil. 3:10; 2 Pet. 3:18), and to progress in sanctification (1 Thess. 4:3). All these requests are God's will for believers. Likewise, under the Old Covenant God willed to answer appropriate prayers for personal blessing, as Jabez illustrates. "Now Jabez called on the God of Israel, saying, 'Oh that Thou wouldst bless me indeed and enlarge my border, and that Thy hand might be with me, and that Thou wouldst keep me from harm, that it may not pain me!' *And God granted him what he requested*" (1 Chron. 4:10, italics added). God's response to this simple, sincere prayer shows that such prayers for personal requests need not be selfish. Jabez prayed with a pure motive and a godly goal, and God honored his servant's request with bountiful blessing. We misrepresent God's character when we consider Him stingy, begrudging, and meager in responding to our prayers for personal needs. I am not suggesting a name-it-and-claim-it approach to asking and receiving from the Lord. Instead, I am urging a confident approach to our gracious God who delights to mature, bless, and use His children.

Requests for spiritual needs for oneself and for others is a major neglect in most Christian prayers. Anyone who doubts this contention should note the far greater emphasis on physical needs in both spoken and printed prayer requests shared in most evangelical churches. Why are our requests and prayers for physical things so much more prominent than our prayers for spiritual things such as our sanctification? It is because we are more sensitive to our physical condition than to our spiritual condition, and we cherish our comfort and convenience more than we desire spiritual growth. We would rather that God change our physical and material circumstances than our character.

I believe a study of the principles and practice of New Testament prayer supports the priority of spiritual requests. For example, Paul's prayer in Ephesians 3:14–21 clearly emphasizes spiritual requests for believers and particularly for their personal spiritual growth.

For this reason I bow my knees before the Father, from whom every family in heaven and on earth derives its name, that He would grant you, according to the riches of His glory, to be strengthened with power through His Spirit in the inner man; so that Christ may dwell in your hearts through faith; and that you, being rooted and grounded in love, may be able to comprehend with all the saints what is the breadth and length and height and depth, and to know the love of Christ which surpasses knowledge, that you may be filled up to all the fulness of God. Now to Him who is able to do exceeding abundantly beyond all that we ask or think, according to the power that works within us, to Him be the glory in the church and in Christ Jesus to all generations forever and ever. Amen.

The prayers of Epaphras for the Colossian Christians also emphasize spiritual requests, since Paul described him as "always laboring earnestly for you in his prayers, that you may stand perfect and fully assured in all the will of God" (Col. 4:12). This would be an appropriate spiritual request to ask for any Christian.

We can reorder our priorities about prayer requests by studying the biblical prayers, and by noting the strong emphasis on spiritual requests. Studying Paul's prayers is a good way to begin learning the appropriate place of spiritual requests in prayer (Eph. 1:15–23; 3:16–21; Col. 1:9–14).[4] Also, we will benefit spiritually by repeating and personalizing Paul's prayers.

Pray for the Sanctification of Other Christians

Many Christians not only fail to give spiritual requests proper place in their prayers, but they also fail to emphasize intercessory prayer, praying for the spiritual and physical needs of others. Paul valued the prayers of other believers for His missionary team, as seen in his request, "Brethren, pray for us" (1 Thess. 5:25; see also 2 Cor. 1:11). Scripture commands us to engage in intercessory prayer. "Pray for one another, so that you may be healed" (James 5:16). Failure to pray for others is sinful (1 Sam. 12:23). Christ perfectly exemplified intercessory prayer after His time with the disciples in the Upper Room and in the Garden of Gethsemane. Intercessory prayer for others is a major means by which we can show Christian love for others.[5]

When we intercede in prayer for the sanctification of other believers, we follow Jesus' example in praying for the sanctification of His own (John 17:17), and we align with God's main purpose for Christians—to make them more Christlike (Rom. 8:29).

Paul gave himself wholly in sacrificial service to other Christians. He also gave his time and energy in frequent, fervent prayer for the spiritual welfare and progress of other Christians. Passages such as Philippians 1:9–11 and 2 Thessalonians 1:11–12 clearly show that Paul prayed primarily for the spiritual growth of other Christians. Each Christian should ask, "Am I faithful in praying for the sanctification of fellow Christians and for their specific spiritual needs as well as their physical needs"?

CHAPTER THIRTEEN

Handling Our Circumstances:
How God's Providence Works in Sanctification

"HOW IS LIFE TREATING YOU TODAY?" you ask your neighbor. He answers, "Well, the stock market fell drastically; my favorite sports team lost its game; our sewer is plugged; and I have a terrible cold." Would only an unbeliever give this answer because it reflects viewing life from secular circumstances and not from inner spiritual values? Not necessarily, because a believer, too, can sometimes view life only from outer, temporal circumstances.

We should acknowledge our temporal, earthly circumstances just as the apostle Paul recognized that he was "aged" and imprisoned (Philem. 9). But we should also see and handle our circumstances from God's viewpoint because He controls all our circumstances for our good and His glory. This is supported by Romans 8:28, "And we know that God causes all things to work together for good to those who love God, to those who are called according to His purpose." The promise in this verse is directed only to believers, who are identified as "those who love God . . . those who are called according to His purpose." The phrase "all things" includes good things and bad things, favorable and unfavorable events, joys and sorrows, and every other circumstance. Thus God can bring good even out of adversity and human failure, though human failure is never excusable. Also, it is important to note that the "good" is clarified by the next verse, "for whom He foreknew, He also predestined to become conformed to the image of His Son" (8:29).

THE CHALLENGE OF HANDLING
ALL OUR CIRCUMSTANCES

We should readily respond to our circumstances in God's way since God controls them. This is a formidable task because of the number and variety of events to which the average Christian must respond. But with God in control and through Christ's strength (Phil. 4:13), Christians can handle all situations in God's way. Two areas that are unusually daunting are the challenge of routine circumstances and the challenge of poverty and prosperity.

The Challenge of Routine Circumstances

Most of life is routine, and routine procedure may cover over 90 percent of the average person's activity. When a person claims to have an exciting life, he or she means it is exciting some of the time and routine the rest of the time. I heard a prominent Bible teacher remark that one of his greatest struggles was to overcome the monotony of the ministry. Even a committed, dynamic, and popular Bible teacher may struggle with the routine of preparing and delivering hundreds of messages. Other major Christian leaders admit that at times they would like to walk away from their desk and say, "I'm out of here for good." Even significant service to the Lord can become routine and wearisome for both Christian leaders and beginners. So believers talk about rejuvenating their personal passion for Christ and for Christian service. And we may sense a need for renewal in our family life and for new zest in our vocation because of the rut of the routine.

True, much of personal, family, church, and vocational life is unavoidably routine. Yet Christians can rise above the dampening effect of life's routine and live in a spiritually significant way by following eight principles. *First,* practice discipleship by denying yourself, taking up your cross daily, and following Christ (Luke 9:23). *Second,* trust the Lord to provide your daily needs and to help you handle all your circumstances (Matt. 6:11, 33–34; Rom. 8:28, 37). *Third,* spend time daily in Bible study, meditation, prayer, and fellowship with the Lord (Josh. 1:8; Ps. 1:2; Mark 1:35; 2 Tim. 2:15). *Fourth,* keep pursuing sanctification toward Christlike maturity (Heb. 12:14). *Fifth,* keep your priorities in biblical order and by the Spirit's power fulfill your responsibilities in your personal, family, church, and vocational life (Eph. 5:18–6:9). *Sixth,* practice mutual fellowship, encouragement, and ministry with other believers in the church body for individual and corporate spiritual growth (Eph. 4:12–16; Heb. 10:25; 1 Pet. 4:10-11). *Seventh,* look for opportunities to serve others (John 4:34; Gal. 5:13). *Eighth,* keep your life Christ-centered and find your peace, joy, contentment, and strength in Him (Neh. 8:10; Ps. 16:11; John 14:27; 15:11; Phil. 4:4, 11–13). These are familiar truths already covered in this book, but if you diligently practice them they can remove you from some of the ruts of the routine.

The Challenge of Poverty and Prosperity

Poverty is a continuous problem for many humans. And abundant prosperity is not the total solution to the problem of poverty because too much prosperity in an individual's life can be problematic as Proverbs 30:8–9 teaches, "Give me neither poverty nor riches; feed me with the food that is my portion, lest I be full and deny Thee and say, 'Who is the LORD?' Or lest I be in want and steal, and profane the name of my God."

Prosperity can be a problem because Christians who have such things as wealth and good health tend to rely on their good circumstances as if they were permanent (1 Tim. 6:17). These Christians may fail to depend on God because their good circumstances give them a false sense of security, comfort, and well-being. Evidently God does not make Christians too prosperous or prosperous in every area of life because most Christians would not experience optimum growth through prosperity alone. God knows just the right set of circumstances to help each believer grow most, and that includes the right amount of prosperity for each believer

(1 Sam. 2:7–8). Therefore Christians are unwise to compare themselves and their circumstances with others (2 Cor. 10:12).

James 1:9–11 explains how Christians should handle both poverty and prosperity. "But let the brother of humble circumstances glory in his high position; and let the rich man glory in his humiliation, because like flowering grass he will pass away. For the sun rises with a scorching wind, and withers the grass; and its flower falls off, and the beauty of its appearance is destroyed; so too the rich man in the midst of his pursuits will fade away."

Some Christians are in "humble circumstances" (1:9). They are poor and needy in contrast to the rich who have abundant provisions (2:5–6; 5:1–5). At times Paul was impoverished and needy (Phil. 4:12). Christians in such "humble circumstances" must find their true riches in their spiritual inheritance through their Christian faith. "Did not God choose the poor of this world to be rich in faith and heirs of the kingdom which He promised those who love Him?" (James 2:5).

Still, the rich spiritual inheritance of Christians is no reason to neglect poor Christians. Jesus taught and practiced ministry to the poor (Mark 14:7; Luke 4:18; 11:41; 14:13). The apostles and the early churches shared with the poor (Acts 9:36; 24:17). We are to minister to needy fellow believers without neglecting the needs of others. "So then, while we have opportunity, let us do good to all men, and especially to those who are of the household of the faith" (Gal. 6:10). If we are in direct contact with other believers in genuine need and can help them, then we should do so. Otherwise, our love is merely talk because it lacks reality and practical expression (1 John 3:16–18).

Some Christians are prosperous, and most Christians in countries such as the United States enjoy financial and material abundance. But such abundant prosperity is not common among Christians in many other parts of the world such as Third World countries and former Soviet-bloc countries. The rich—and virtually all Christians in the United States are rich by worldwide standards—should be humble before God because rich persons and their possessions are temporary and will fade like a flower (James 1:10–11). Therefore rich Christians as well as poor Christians should find their true riches in Christ. "For not even when one has an abundance does his life consist of his possessions" (Luke 12:15).

We tend to think of the poor and the rich only in contrast to each other, but four biblical principles apply to both poor and rich Christians in relation to their circumstances.

(a) Both poor and rich Christians should have their treasure and hope in eternal, spiritual things and not in temporary, material things (Matt. 6:19–21; 2 Cor. 4:16–18). As long as physical and financial security is our main concern and goal in life, we will not fully trust and serve the Lord as we ought.

(b) Both poor and rich Christians need to trust the Lord in their circumstances. The poor need to trust the Lord to provide their needs (Matt. 6:30, 33). The rich need to trust the Lord humbly instead of trusting in their unsure riches. "Instruct those who are rich in this present world not to be conceited or to fix their hope on the uncertainty of riches, but on God, who richly supplies us with all things to enjoy" (1 Tim. 6:17). The rich are further instructed "to do good, to be rich in good works, to be generous and ready to share" (6:18).

God does not begrudge the riches He gives us, and Christians need not feel guilty about possessing riches legitimately received. For it is not having money but loving money that is "a root of all sorts of evil" (6:10). Christians can enjoy their possessions because they can thank God who gave them for their enjoyment (Eph. 5:20; James 1:17); they can use their God-given possessions as a stewardship to minister to the needs of others (2 Cor. 8:1–9:15; Eph. 4:28); and through Christ's strength they can be content without their possessions (Phil. 4:11–13). How we handle our money and material possessions (or lack of them) in relationship to God and other humans reveals our true spiritual condition.

(c) Both poor and rich Christians can have godliness with contentment and that is "great gain" (1 Tim. 6:6–8).

(d) Both poor and rich Christians need divine wisdom to handle their resources as faithful stewards (1 Cor. 4:2). The request for divine wisdom in James 1:5–8 is preceded by teaching about spiritual growth through trials (1:2–4) and followed by teaching about the proper response to poverty and to riches (1:9–11). So whether we are prosperous or poor, we can ask God for wisdom to handle either circumstance for Him. If we pray for wisdom with a stable faith, He will provide wisdom generously and without reproach (1:5–8). The Christian responsibility to handle poverty or riches is a test that God uses to help us grow spiritually (1:2–4).[1]

THE CHALLENGE OF HANDLING
OUR ADVERSE CIRCUMSTANCES

Adverse circumstances are a big problem for most people. Some Christians seem to struggle more than unbelievers with the problem of adverse circumstances, mainly because Christians emphasize God's goodness. I mentioned to a class of theological students that the existence of evil circumstances in the world (suffering, malnutrition, injustice, and other human adversities) is the most common problem raised by unbelievers about Christianity with its firm belief in a God of grace and goodness. These students tended to agree with me, but they reminded me that believers may struggle with the question of how a good God can allow adverse circumstances in the lives of His people. After all, Christians are supposed to be serving a God who is for them and not against them. Christians then need clear understanding and strong conviction that God indeed works all circumstances for their good and His glory (Rom. 8:28; 11:36).

Recognize That Biblical Christianity Includes Adversity

Samuel Johnson, eighteenth-century literary scholar, said, "He that never was acquainted with adversity has seen the world but on one side."[2] Christians may wrongly believe they can experience life on only one side—the painless side with only prosperity and pleasure. Larry Crabb notes that "modern Christianity, in dramatic reversal of its biblical form, promises to relieve the pain of living in a fallen world."[3] And our personal pain may come in our spiritual, mental, emotional, social, or physical life or a combination of these areas. Christians are not exempt from difficult relationships in marriage, family, church, school, workplace, community, or in national or global contexts. We must realize that the arena of our Christian sanctification is a world pervaded, broken, and twisted by sin (Rom. 3:9–23). Even babies come into this world experiencing pain and tears before pleasure and smiles.

We are all destined for difficulties and adversities as Job's friend Eliphaz noted: "For man is born for trouble, as sparks fly upward" (Job 5:7). Jesus clearly presented both the peaceful, joyful side of Christian experience and also its painful side: "These things I have spoken to you, that in Me you may have peace. In the world you have tribulation, but take courage; I have overcome the world" (John 16:33). Paul indicated that Christians and creation both suffer and groan in this present age (Rom. 8:14–23). Thus "an aching soul is evidence not of neurosis or spiritual immaturity, but of realism"[4] Still, the idea of suffering Christians "is a theme radically different from many contemporary notions of American Christianity that emphasize the good life of American middle-class living as synonymous with Christian life."[5] Scripture and experience both teach that adversity is always an ingredient in the mix of human life and that includes the Christian life.

Adverse circumstances are not limited to a few struggling believers; all believers suffer to some extent. New converts exuberant with their "first love" for Christ soon discover that biblical Christianity does not eliminate their adversity. Believers who think Christians are always peaceful, joyful, carefree, and exempt from troubles are shocked by reality when they encounter difficult circumstances. More mature Christians admit that the conflict with adversity rages on and sometimes intensifies. Often the godliest people experience the most and severest troubles. As Paul wrote, "All who desire to live godly in Christ Jesus will be persecuted" (2 Tim. 3:12).

People who are wholeheartedly following Christ need not feel guilty for not suffering more for Christ. Neither should Christians go looking for suffering in order to appear more spiritual or to make up for suffering they may have missed in the past. We should focus on becoming Christlike through sanctification and then expect suffering only as God permits because of our godly living. Total relief from adversity will come only when believers go to be with Christ or He comes for them. So we can rightly say, "I'm done with adversity," only when we can say, "I'm home with the Lord."

Furthermore, believers avoid certain difficulties that unbelievers experience. Many of the unbelievers' difficulties we avoid are far more consequential than believers' troubles. The contrast between a godly and an ungodly lifestyle emphasized in Psalms and Proverbs reveals some of the difficult circumstances believers escape (Ps. 1:1–6; Prov. 4:10–19). As Willard notes, "To depart from righteousness is to choose a life of crushing burdens, failures and disappointments, a life caught in the toils of endless problems that are never resolved. Here is the source of that unending soap opera, that sometime horror show known as normal human life. The "cost of discipleship," though it may take all we have, is small when compared to the lot of those who don't accept Christ's invitation to be a part of his company in The Way of life."[6]

The path to enter the kingdom of God is "through many tribulations" (Acts 14:22), but the alternative path leads to eternal destruction (Matt. 7:13). When we become discouraged because of the difficulties of following Christ, we should reconsider the benefits of following Him and the stupendous difficulties of living without Him.

Expect a Variety of Adversities

Jesus experienced a great variety of adversities in His living and His dying. Through saving faith in Christ we become spiritually identified with Christ (John 1:12; 14:20; Rom. 6:3–4; 1 Cor. 12:12–13). And our identity with Christ includes some adversities such as trials, suffering, opposition, and persecution (John 15:18–21; 16:33; Phil. 1:29) beyond the adversities of normal human life. So like our Lord, Christians are to expect a variety of adversities in their lives.

Adversities are like boxes. They come in different forms and sizes. Even people with basically good health may still have some colds, other physical illnesses, and sometimes rather serious operations. Even Arnold Schwarzenegger, the bodybuilding champion, had to have a heart valve operation while he was still middle-aged. Add to this list achy muscles and joints, root canals, broken bones, bouts with cancer, heart disease, and many other medical problems, some or all of which an individual may experience in a lifetime. Our health is a major area where we can undergo adversity, but it is still just one area among many where a variety of difficulties can strike.

Adversity may come through a loss of job and the attendant loss of some financial income and possible loss of a sense of self-worth.

Present and prospective retirees wonder if their income will be sufficient to support them, especially with inflation continually decreasing the dollar's value. Better health measures have increased the average life span, but medical costs have increased even more rapidly.

City-dwellers experience stress from living in crowded conditions, breathing unhealthy air, and driving on gridlocked freeways. People living in smaller population centers or out in the country often face economic decline as population and jobs continue to shift from the rural areas to urban centers.

For many the greatest difficulties are strained or broken relationships with others. Some ignore their dysfunctional relationships while others try to get healing for past hurts, to rebuild shattered relationships, or just to cope with defective relationships.

This is a very limited survey of various adversities that we face. We have not included many other afflictions such as certain diseases more prevalent in less developed areas of the world. Our purpose is not to paint a gloom-and-doom picture of the Christian life or to keep wallowing in thoughts of hardship. We can indeed overcome adversity through Christ (Rom. 8:37), but first we must recognize the reality and variety of adversities that God permits. Then each Christian must accept adversity from God as a major means He uses to sanctify him or her toward Christ's image.

Accept Adversity as Part of God's Plan for Each Christian

The fact that Christians, too, face adversities impressed me personally and poignantly when I read about a celebrity's wish that her antagonist would have a root canal and a tax audit. Then I experienced these same two trials within several months of each other (and incidentally, I was not the celebrity's antagonist!). We may readily acknowledge that everyone, whether godly or ungodly, must face adversity in life. But we still ask, "Why me? Doesn't God realize that these adversities can cost me time, energy, health, and finances that I could better use for His service?"

Some Christians protest to God under their breath, if not out loud, "God let me down; He did me wrong!" Yet, at other times these same

Christians who ask these questions and make these protests confidently affirm, "Christ makes a big difference in my life; He gives me salvation, love, joy, peace, and purpose for living." Salvation and tribulation, blessing and adversity, joy and sadness, peace and turmoil, serenity and struggle, purpose and confusion—what a strange mix of experiences! Yet both blessings and adversities will occur in a believer's life. Job, Joseph, and Paul are only three of many biblical examples of this fact.

From Job's example we can learn how to accept both blessings and problems in our lives (Job 1:1–2:13; 42:11). After his first cycle of adversity Job said, "Naked I came from my mother's womb, and naked I shall return there. The LORD gave and the LORD has taken away. Blessed be the name of the LORD" (1:21). Job accepted serious setbacks with worship and praise to the Lord. He did not sin in his speech or charge God with wrongdoing (1:20–22).

In his next cycle of adversity, Job asked rhetorically, "Shall we indeed accept good from God and not accept adversity?" (2:10). Job was human and he did struggle in his suffering, but he came to realize his difficulties came from God. Through his problems Job showed that he was indeed godly (1:8), and he grew spiritually (42:5–6, 8) and prospered physically (42:10). Have we like Job learned to accept adversity as well as prosperity from the Lord? We must watch how we answer that question if things are going well for us right now.

When Christians reflect on their past, they may thank God for the trials He has brought into their lives, realizing they grew because of them. But these same Christians may ask the Lord not to put them through any more adversity. After all, it would seem that Christians could grow enough through adversity to reach spiritual maturity and then leave adversity behind, just as an adult grows through adolescence and then leaves it behind. But adversity, unlike adolescence, is not a stage we overcome. Difficulties are a main means of spiritual growth which God continually uses to help His people grow, whether they are brand-new believers or the most mature Christians.

Some form of adversity is almost constantly occurring in the Christian life. This means that we just exited adversity, or we are in it, or we are about to enter it again. As we progress in sanctification, our problems may tend to increase in number and severity, just as they did for Job and

Abraham (Gen. 12:1; 13:1–13; 21:9–19; 22:1–14). But our progress in sanctification also prepares us to have greater victory over our adversities through Christ and by God's grace (2 Cor. 12:7–9; 2 Tim. 2:1). We grow most through problems when we willingly and joyfully accept them as friends from God to help us rather than as enemies to hurt us.

Receive Promised Benefits from Adversity

I have used the word *adversity* and *adversities* frequently in this chapter because they best encompass those unfavorable events and circumstances humans experience. *The Book of Common Prayer* refers to Christians "in trouble, sorrow, need, sickness, or any other adversity."[7] The word *adversity* comes from the Latin word *adversus*, which means "turned against." It does appear that some circumstances are turned against us, but we know that God is for His people. The psalmist said, "This I know, that God is for me" (Ps. 56:9). Believers who trust God's providence and respond biblically to adversity find that God transforms their adversity into their advantage. Jacob's son Joseph experienced this principle: "As for you, you meant evil against me, but God meant it for good in order to bring about this present result, to preserve many people alive" (Gen. 50:20).

God's Word promises the following beneficial results from our adversity.

- *God uses adversity to make us more Christlike.* The Christian's adversities become sculpting tools in God's hands to shape each believer into His Son's image. Troubles can make us more Christlike by building our character (Rom. 5:3–5), developing our maturity (James 1:2–4), and strengthening our faith (1 Pet. 1:6–9).

- *We can learn obedience through adversity.* Christ "learned obedience from the things which He suffered" (Heb. 5:8). His suffering was never corrective because He never did wrong (John 8:29; 1 Pet. 2:22). Christ's obedience was already perfect at every stage of His life, so His suffering further matured and reinforced His obedience. God uses suffering in our lives to correct our disobedience and to develop our obedience so that we mature in holiness and righteousness As the psalmist wrote, "Before I was afflicted I went astray, but now

171

I keep Thy word" (Ps. 119:67). And the writer to the Hebrews taught that God's discipline enables us to "share [God's] holiness" and results in "the peaceful fruity of righteousness" (Heb. 12:10–11).

- *God uses our adversity as an opportunity to minister to others.* He used Joseph's adversity to help his extended family. Paul taught that God "comforts us in all our affliction so that we may be able to comfort those who are in any affliction" (2 Cor. 1:3–4). Then we can say with true sympathy to other Christians encountering the same adversity that we have experienced, "I know what you are going through because I have been there, too, and God will help you as He helped me."

- *God rewards us for the costs and adverse circumstances involved in following Christ.* The difficulties of true Christian discipleship are small compared to the great privilege and reward of being Christ's servants.

Respond to Adversity in God's Way

God promises to handle our adversity so that it works for our benefit, and we can handle our adversity in God's way by practicing the following principles.

Accept adversity as a major means God uses to sanctify Christians and to provide the benefits in the previous list. Willingness to accept adversity from God is essential to practicing the next three responses to adversity.

Submit to God's sovereign plan and trust Him through all your adversity (1 Pet. 4:19; 5:6). God expected Job to trust His sovereign purpose and to hope in Him through all his suffering (Job 13:15; 42:1–6). Likewise, God's challenge to all His people may be summarized this way: "Trust Me that I know what I am doing as the sovereign Lord of your life. Humbly submit to Me through all the adversity I am permitting in your life for your good and My glory." Through his suffering, Job became better acquainted with himself and with God, grew in his relationship to God, and received multiplied blessings from the Lord.

Suffering played a major role in Jesus' earthly experience. Jesus expressed total submission to His Father's will in facing the most severe adversity any person has ever undergone: "My Father, if it is possible, may this cup be taken from Me. Yet not as I will, but as You will" (Matt. 26:39, NIV). Are we, like Christ, willing to face suffering, trials, and other adversities with total trust and submission to the Father's will?

Conquer your adverse circumstances through Christ so that you can maximize your spiritual growth. Scripture assures believers they can "overwhelmingly conquer" all their adversities "through Him who loved us" (Rom. 8:37). In any adverse circumstances we must choose either to be victors over our circumstances or to be victims of our circumstances.

Often God's way for His people to conquer adversity is not immediate but through long endurance. If we endure rather than crumble under various trials, God strengthens and matures our Christian character (Rom. 5:3–4). James reminded Christians that "when [not 'if'] you encounter various trials . . . the testing of your faith produces endurance" (James 1:2–3). Then we should "let endurance have its perfect result, that you may be perfect and complete [spiritually mature], lacking in nothing" (1:4). Be warned: Adversity can make you bitter instead of better if they respond to it in the wrong way by failing to accept it from God and submit to His will. Adversities work for us only if we respond to them in God's way.

Claim God's promises of inward peace, joy, and contentment in the midst of all your circumstances. The apostle Paul experienced a variety of severe external pressures (2 Cor. 11:23–28a) along with what he described as "the daily pressure upon me of concern for all the churches" (11:28b). He was squeezed in a viselike grip between pressure on the inside and pressure on the outside—a very stressful situation (7:5). Yet, as he rejoiced while in jail for Jesus, he commanded us to "rejoice in the Lord always" (Phil. 4:4). Paul could even say that in all his "affliction" he was "overflowing with joy" (2 Cor. 7:4). Thus our inner condition of heart need not be controlled by our outer circumstances.

Growth in Christ often sharpens the contrast between our inward spiritual experience and our outward circumstances. Through our severest trials we may realize the deepest peace and joy in Christ and the greatest growth in Christ.

Some Christians want to claim the promises of spiritual benefits but do not want to accept the promises of adversity. Believers must learn to endure adversities in the Christian life as well as enjoy the blessings of Christian living. God provides both.

We need to handle adversity in God's way and not in the usual human way. People usually respond to adversity as an enemy to escape from as soon as possible and without any consideration of how they might benefit from it. Sometimes believers can legitimately avoid adverse circumstances, such as unjust imprisonment, or gain freedom from adversity such as slavery (Acts 16:35–40; 1 Cor. 7:21). But when God permits us to remain in adversity, then our proper response should not be "Why me?" but "Why not me?" and "Lord, help me to respond biblically to You and to this problem so that I can grow in Christ and minister to others."

Our response to adversity makes all the difference. Job had two choices when he faced adversity: to bless God, grow in his faith, and become a better person, or to become a bitter person, curse God, and die, as his wife advised (Job 2:9). Job chose the former, and so should we, because adversities serve as God's construction crew to make us more like His Son.

CHAPTER FOURTEEN

Winning in Spiritual Warfare:
Satan's Opposition to Sanctification

"WINNING IS EVERYTHING," said Vince Lombardi, the
famous coach of the Green Bay Packers. Others would contest that statement and affirm that it is more important how
you play the game than whether you win. People interested
in athletics will continue to debate this issue. But in spiritual warfare winning *is* everything because losing to Satan
is always less than God's plan and His provision for Christian living. God makes it possible for His people to win
overwhelmingly over all circumstances in this earthly life,
including Satan's opposition to our sanctification. "But in
all these things we overwhelmingly conquer through Him
who loved us" (Rom. 8:37).

Spiritual struggle and warfare are not limited to a few
halfhearted Christians who are prone to fail. New converts
with their burst of "first love" for Christ soon discover spiritual conflict in their Christian life. More mature Christians
admit that the spiritual battle rages on and intensifies. Christians face strong spiritual opposition, and probably it will
get stronger until it ceases when we are forever with Christ.
Does this mean that Christians should become spiritual pas-
sivists and that they should accept defeat in spiritual warfare

and wait for heaven to become mature in Christ? Absolutely not! Relentless spiritual warfare is not our signal to put up a white flag and surrender to our spiritual enemies. Spiritual warfare is a challenge to conquer through Christ and to grow in Christ.

The world, the flesh, and the devil are our primary opposition to Christian living. They promote sin, and God promotes our spirituality. Satan and demons are evil personalities, while the world and the flesh are impersonal forces which the devil may use in warfare against us (Gen. 3:1–6; Matt. 4:1–11; 1 John 2:15–16). In chapters 4 and 5 we discussed how Christians can conquer sin, the flesh, and the world by applying our position in Christ, relying on the power of the Spirit, and by obeying the Word. And these same responses are also essential for victory over the devil and demons. However, in this chapter we want to focus more specifically on the devil and His demons as our main personal enemies and to present more specific methods for dealing with them. The basic principles for winning in spiritual warfare with Satan also apply to our spiritual warfare with demons, particularly since Satan is "the ruler of the demons" (Matt. 12:24).

God planned that our spiritual growth occur in the same arena where Satan and his demons operate. A new believer may express this realization in this way: "Soon after becoming a Christian I find myself in the middle of a spiritual battle." We change sides when we trust Christ, and we feel Satan's full enmity vented against us. Christ has delivered us from Satan's kingdom of darkness, and now we have entered Christ's kingdom of light (Col. 1:12–14). Our allegiance is to God, and Satan attacks God's person, His people, and His plan. Spiritual warfare goes with the territory of sanctification, and spiritual warfare requires spiritual weapons. So we need to discover what our spiritual weapons are and how to use them so that we can win over Satan and his evil spiritual powers.[1] But before we talk about battling with Satan, we need to note the reality of Satan and his demons.

REALITY OF SATAN

Some people believe that Satan is merely a personification of evil. They deny the reality of Satan but not necessarily the reality of evil in the world.

Satan then personifies evil just as the "green-eyed monster" personifies jealousy or as Uncle Sam personifies the United States government.

Scripture gives clear and abundant evidence for a personal devil. Satan is mentioned in seven books of the Old Testament (Genesis, 1 Chronicles, Job, Psalms, Isaiah, Ezekiel, and Zechariah) and by every writer of the New Testament. Twenty-nine passages in the Gospels refer to Satan, and in twenty-five of those passages Christ is the speaker. Christ also mentioned and confronted demons rather frequently (Mark 1:32, 34, 39; 3:13–15, 22–27; 5:1–20; 16:9). If we believe the Scriptures, then we must believe in the reality of the devil and demons and our spiritual warfare with them (2 Cor. 2:11; 10:3–5; Eph. 6:10–18).

The biblical record of Christ's words and other verses teach these basic truths about Satan: (a) he personally exists (Job 1:7–8, 12; 2:2–3, 6; Matt. 4:1–11; 2 Cor. 2:11); (b) he is an intelligent, powerful, and evil spirit being (Job 1:6–12; John 17:15; 2 Cor. 2:11; Eph. 6:11; 1 John 3:8; Rev. 12:4, 9); and (c) he is engaged in spiritual warfare with God, the good angels, and believers (1 Chron. 21:1; Zech. 3:1–5; Eph. 6:10–12; 1 Pet. 5:8).

Redemptive history in Scripture and human history in general support the reality and activity of Satan, whose name means "the adversary." When one reads and sees the daily news, it is difficult to deny that Satan is unusually active. Christian experience confirms the biblical teaching that Satan is not a myth but that he is a powerful and evil supernatural being who relentlessly tries to counter all that God stands for and all who stand for God.

When Christians aggressively pursue sanctification, they soon discover that Satan's temptations and spiritual opposition are extraordinary and not imaginary. Satan resists our spiritual progress just as air or water resists physical progress. The more we pursue sanctification and oppose Satan's, the more spiritual resistance and attacks we can expect from him. So God's work of maturing Christians involves their battling with Satan.

True, evil can originate from sinful human nature apart from Satan's temptation and prompting (Mark 7:21–23; James 1:14–15). Yet we sense that much of our spiritual struggle involves something more than evil in general or the world and the flesh in particular. The uncanny methods and timing of some temptations and spiritual conflicts point to a mastermind behind them. When you entertain a covetous or lustful idea, Satan seems to put glue on your sinful idea and to lubricate your process of evil thinking. You need God's spiritual weapons to demolish the strongholds Satan has established in your thought life and to prevent your mind from further influence by Satan (2 Cor. 10:3–5; Eph. 6:10–18; Phil. 4:6–8). But whether Satan attacks our mind, will, emotions, or body, or a combination of these, our spiritual warfare is winnable through God's victorious Son, God's all-powerful Spirit, and God's truthful Word.

FACTS ABOUT SATAN

Satan is an evil spirit with stupendous might and cunning. He operates throughout the earth and in the heavens through his demons. Satan described himself as "roaming about on the earth" (Job 1:7), and Paul spoke of "the spiritual forces of wickedness in the heavenly places" (Eph. 6:12). Still, Satan focuses much of his attention on earth, where the drama of redemption unfolds in the human race (Gen. 3:15; Eph. 2:1–3; Heb. 2:14; Rev. 12:12). Despite his great wit and strength, Satan remains a finite creature and is no match for our infinitely wise and powerful God (Isa. 14:12–15; Ezek. 28:12–19; 1 John 4:4; Jude 9).

Satan Is Limited in Knowledge, Power, Presence, and Activity

Though Satan carries on universal spiritual warfare with skill and supernatural power, his evil activity is completely controlled by our God who is all-knowing (Ps. 147:5), all-powerful (Gen. 17:1; Job 42:2), and everywhere present (Ps. 139:7–12; Jer. 23:23–24). God's Word and His ability assure us that whatever comes into the Christian's life must have His stamp of approval upon it (1 Cor. 10:13; Rev. 2:10). Every temptation can be resisted; every trial can be overcome; every need can be met; and every problem can be solved or handled with God's sufficient grace.

Satan Has Been Judicially Conquered through Christ's Work on the Cross

A main purpose for Christ's coming was to "destroy the works of the devil" (1 John 3:8). This purpose required Christ's incarnation so "that through death He [Christ] might render powerless him who had the power of death, that is, the devil" (Heb. 2:14). Judgment against sin, the world, the flesh, and the devil was provided at the cross (John 12:31–33; Rom. 8:2–3; Gal. 2:20; Heb. 2:14).[2] The judicial sentence against Satan and his allies has been proclaimed (John 12:31; 16:11; Col. 2:14–15), though final judgment of Satan and his allies has not yet been executed (Matt. 25:41; Rev. 20:10). Since believers are identified with the person and work of Christ (Rom. 6:3–4; Gal. 2:20; 5:25), by faith we can claim Christ's victory over sin, the world, the flesh, and the devil as our victory (Rom. 6:8–11; 16:20; Gal. 5:24). Then by the Spirit's power and God's Word we experience Christ's victory over sin, the world, the flesh, and the devil in our lives.

Satan Uses Strategies and Tricks in His Spiritual Warfare against Believers

Satan's "schemes" (2 Cor. 2:11) and his "strategies and tricks" (Eph. 6:11, NLT) emphasize his focused and well-planned attacks against believers. Satan has battle plans tailored for each believer's particular weaknesses. David was susceptible to Satan's temptation because of his pride in the size of his army (1 Chron. 21:1–17), and Ananias and Sapphira were susceptible to Satan's temptation because of their covetousness and desire for recognition (Acts 5:1–11). Satan knows where we are weak and when we are weakest.

Christians may feel good about gaining victory 90 percent of the time. But Satan knows about the 10 percent where we are most susceptible, and that is where he aims his "flaming arrows" (Eph. 6:16, NIV). Partial victory is little better than no victory at all because we still leave areas for Satan to cause major defeat in our lives. Who would want to go out on the ocean in a boat with only 90 percent of the bottom in it? It would sink almost as quickly as a boat with no bottom. God has provided adequate power for us to experience victory in every area of life through His Son (1 John 2:1–2; 5:18), His Spirit (Gal. 5:16; 1 John 4:4), and His Word (Matt. 4:1–11; Eph. 6:17). So aim for nothing less than total victory in your spiritual warfare with Satan.

Satan Operates Primarily through Deceit and Imitation

People usually portray the devil as a physical creature who has horns, a spear-pointed tail, and cloven hooves, is clothed in red thermal underwear, and armed with a pitchfork. Does such gross misrepresentation upset Satan? Not at all. It just shows how easily he can deceive humans. He sometimes "disguises himself as an angel of light,:" that is, as a good angel (2 Cor. 11:14), and he even "deceives the whole world" (Rev. 12:9).

Paul warned believers about the devil's deceptive designs: "In order that no advantage would be taken of us by Satan; for we are not ignorant of his schemes" (2 Cor. 2:11). This warning grew out of a serious situation in the Corinthian church. At first the Corinthian believers were arrogant in tolerating the behavior of a professing believer who was guilty of incest (1 Cor. 5:1–2). Paul told them that their boasting was not good (5:6) and that they should remove this wicked man from their assembly (5:13). Satan had deceived the Corinthian believers into letting known gross sin go uncorrected because of their arrogance (5:2). Evidently this man (or possibly another) guilty of serious sin had repented after the church had exercised discipline (2 Cor. 2:5–8). Now Satan had influenced the church to go to the other extreme of not forgiving the repentant man (2:7–11). The Corinthian Christians were probably patting themselves on the back because they had become intolerant of the man though he had now repented of his sin. And the devil was probably patting some backs too!

This account shows two main ways by which Satan tries to hinder Christian progress in sanctification.

First, Satan tempts Christians to tolerate rather than confront and correct sin in their personal lives and among believers in their local church (Acts 5:1–11; 1 Cor. 5:1–5). Satan encourages toleration of sin because it directly opposes Christian sanctification and service.

Second, Satan tempts Christians to withhold forgiveness from a genuinely repentant person already forgiven by God. We are to forgive others as God in Christ has forgiven us (Eph. 4:32). To withhold forgiveness does severe spiritual, mental, and emotional damage to the unforgiving person as well as to the unforgiven person. People who do not forgive because of bitterness or some other wrong motive wound their own souls just as though they ingested hot cinders and wounded their stomachs. Repentant people who are not forgiven can be overwhelmed with guilt and grief, and suffer severe spiritual and psychological damage. How should we respond to a repentant person? "Forgive and comfort him, lest somehow such a one be overwhelmed by excessive sorrow" (2 Cor. 2:7).

When my wife and I travel east from the Los Angeles area by car we often go through Las Vegas at night to avoid the extreme daytime heat, and the lighting there is strikingly beautiful. However, behind the gorgeous buildings and brilliant colors are people with empty lives still asking themselves, "Are we having fun yet?" Las Vegas, with its many glittering attractions to sin, is certainly a stronghold of Satan. Yet I doubt that Satan works as hard to hold the Los Vegas pleasure-seekers (since he seems to keep them numb to spiritual truth and often addicted to enslaving habits) as he does to keep Christians tolerant of sin in their personal and church life and unforgiving toward others. These are two of Satan's main spiritual fortresses right within the Christian camp. So resist Satan's attempts to establish tolerance of sin and an unforgiving attitude in your life. I have seen the "Las Vegas types" come to faith in Christ, and when they respond positively to Him, it is generally through Christians who are pure, joyful, loving, and accepting, as our Lord. People in Satan's clutches will hardly find freedom in Christ through us if Satan has established bulwarks of sin in our minds and hearts and an unforgiving spirit toward others.

Paul also warned that Satan tries to deceive us by using his false apostles, servants, and teachers to infiltrate the ranks of believers and to imitate Christ's servants of righteousness (2 Cor. 11:13–15; 2 Pet. 2:1–19). And Satan spreads false religious teaching through demonic spirits (1 Tim. 4:1–5; 1 John 4:1–4). Therefore we need to study "the word of truth" (2 Tim. 2:15) and rely on "the Spirit of truth" (John 16:13) in order to detect false teachers and teaching and to defend ourselves against them. Furthermore, we need to depart from all personal wickedness and sinful associations (2 Tim. 2:19–21) so that we will each be "a vessel for honor, sanctified, useful to the Master, prepared for every good work" (2:21).

Satan Can Tempt True Believers to Doubt Their Salvation

Believers can have assurance of salvation through the Word of God (John 3:16–18, 36; Rom. 5:1; 1 John 5:11–13) and the Spirit of God (Rom. 8:16–17; 1 John 5:10). Certainty of salvation and security in salvation are foundational for a holy life. We cannot fully focus on living the spiritual life unless know that we have spiritual life as a sure and irrevocable possession.

Believers in Christ are regenerated by the Spirit once for all (John 3:5; Titus 3:5). Regeneration cannot be undone and therefore never needs to be redone. Everyone who has faith in Christ has eternal spiritual life in Christ and can never perish (John 10:27–29). Therefore believers can never come into condemnation (5:24; Rom. 8:1). Nothing can separate us from the love of Christ (8:38–39), and nothing can ever sever us from the body of Christ (1 Cor. 12:12–13).

Since Satan knows that He cannot reverse our spiritual birth, he tries to resist our spiritual growth and service. Thus when Satan tempts true believers to doubt their salvation and feel insecure in their relation to God, they should counter satanic doubts with scriptural assurances that they have security for eternity.

God Permits Satan to Tempt, Sift, and Discipline Believers within His Sovereign Plan

God cannot be tempted and He does not tempt anyone (James 1:13), but He does permit Satan to tempt people (Gen. 3:1–6; 1 Chron. 21:1). The same event in a believer's life may be both a temptation to sin from Satan and also a test from God to strengthen and bless the believer (Job 1–2; 42; James 1:12). Whenever believers resist Satan's temptation, they also pass God's test.

Satan especially tempts people to doubt the goodness of God, to depart from the will of God, and to disobey the Word of God (Gen. 3:1–6). He also tempts believers to rely on human strength and wisdom (1 Chron. 21:1–8; James 3:14–16), to oppose God's plans (Matt. 16:21–23), to lie (Acts 5:3), to commit sexual sins (1 Cor. 7:5), to be conceited (1 Tim. 3:6), and to be preoccupied with earthly cares (1 Pet. 5:6–10). However, we never have to yield to Satan's temptations since God will not permit us to be tempted beyond our ability to resist or to endure any temptation (1 Cor. 10:13).

God may allow Satan to sift believers as Satan did in Peter's case (Luke 22:31–32). God may also discipline His children by using Satan to afflict them physically, even to the point of physical death (1 Cor. 5:5). Even the godliest believers such as Job and Paul can suffer affliction from Satan according to God's plan to make them even more godly, useful, and blessed.

Satan follows the principle that if at first he doesn't succeed, he keeps trying. He persisted in his attacks against Nehemiah, relentlessly using various tactics and human agents to try to stop Him from rebuilding the wall around Jerusalem (Neh. 2:19–6:19). Satan tried each of the three main channels of human temptation when he tempted Jesus in the wilderness (Luke 4:1–12; compare Gen. 3:1–6; 1 John 2:16). And Luke 4:13 says, "When the devil had finished every temptation, he left Him until an opportune time." Though the devil totally lost this battle with Jesus, he continued his warfare against Him (Matt. 16:21–23; John 13:2, 27). Even when a battle with the devil is won, the spiritual war is not over. We can be sure that Satan will come back after he has switched tactics and reinforced his allies.

By faith Christians can rely on God's Spirit and have grace and power to resist Satan's temptations and endure tests (2 Cor. 12:7–9; 1 John 4:4; 5:4). And winning in spiritual warfare can have great reward. When we overcome Satan's attacks and temptations by God's power, He increases our faith, our spiritual strength, our usefulness in service, and our blessings.

Satan Can Hinder the Spiritual Growth and Service of Believers

Satan has numerous ways to impede believers' sanctification and spiritual ministry. We have seen that Satan tries to hinder the spiritual growth of believers by their toleration of sin and by their unforgiving response toward a genuinely repentant person (1 Cor. 5:1–13; 2 Cor. 2:5–11).

He also tries to retard believers' spiritual growth by resisting their intake of the Word (1 Cor. 3:1–3). He hinders believers from helping other believers grow. Paul was very concerned about the young Christians at Thessalonica, and he explained to them, "For we wanted to come to you—I, Paul, more than once—and yet Satan thwarted us" (1 Thess. 2:18).

Satan especially preys on new converts just as beasts of prey look for young, vulnerable victims (1 Pet. 5:8). The new believers at Thessalonica had progressed in their faith, love, and hope (1 Thess. 1:3), but they were very susceptible to. So Paul told them, "For this reason, when I could endure it no longer, I also sent to find out about your faith, for fear that that tempter might have tempted you, and our labor should be in vain" (3:5). Christians often discover that when they try to follow up new converts to help them grow in Christ they encounter unusual difficulties in contacting and ministering to them because Satan wants new Christians to remain spiritually immature, weak, and vulnerable to His temptations.

But Satan's opposition is not our signal to give up or even to slacken our spiritual progress. Instead, we should keep growing and helping others grow because we have this promise: "The Lord is faithful, and He will strengthen and protect you from the evil one" (2 Thess. 2:3).

Satan Tries to Divert Our Minds from Simple, Pure Devotion to Christ

The devil strongly opposes devotion to Christ, and Paul was keenly aware of this when he wrote to the Corinthian Christians. "But I am afraid, lest as the serpent deceived Eve by his craftiness, your minds should be led astray from the simplicity and purity of devotion to Christ" (2 Cor. 11:3). Believers are to be occupied with Christ (Phil. 1:21; Heb. 12:2), with His interests, and with Christlike virtues.

Like Martha, believers can be busy with many good parts of life and miss the best part of life to which Martha's sister Mary devoted herself— Christ and His Word (Luke 10:38–42). Paul, too, focused on knowing more of Christ and becoming more like Him (Phil. 3:10–14).

Why do Christians sometimes fail to keep their lives Christ-centered? It is generally because they are pursuing many other good things but are not focused on sanctification toward Christlikeness with a passion (Heb. 12:14). I have a great passion to study Bible doctrine. But my growing doctrinal knowledge should be accompanied by more devotion to Christ and more obedience to His Word. Greater spiritual knowledge makes us liable to more severe judgment, particularly when we expect to teach others the biblical doctrines that we learn (James 3:1).

Christ desires His followers to maintain single, simple, and intense devotion to Him. When the resurrected Lord plumbed the depths of Peter's soul, the main issue was, "Simon, . . . do you love Me?" (John 21:15–16). "Love" in these two verses is related to the Greek word *agapē*, a volitional, sacrificial, stable love which the Spirit produces in Christians. Satan knows that if he can cause our *agapē* kind of love for Christ to diminish, he can hinder our growth in Christ and our service for Christ. When we have *agapē* love for Christ, we will obey His commands (John 14:15; 23), and we will truly love and care for His sheep (21:15–17).

The threefold repetition of Christ's question to Peter was a tacit reminder of Peter's threefold denial of Christ (Matt. 26:69–75). Peter had claimed that he would not deny Christ but would even die for Him (26:34–35). Evidently Peter was sincere in his claim, but he was also naive, arrogant, and unprepared for Satan's plan to sift him as wheat (Luke 22:31). Peter would fail, but not because his faith was unsupported by Christ's intercessory prayer. Peter's salvation was secure, but he would need restoration from his sinful denial to prepare him for ministry. Christ said to Peter in preparation for his recovery from the denial, "When once you have turned again, strengthen your brothers" (22:32).

Peter's faith did not fail him but led him to genuine repentance after his denial of Christ (Matt. 26:75). The risen Christ appeared privately to Peter and restored him to fellowship with Himself and to leadership among the other apostles (Luke 24:34; John 21:15–17; Acts 1:13; 2:14).

Peter's example shows two key principles about spiritual warfare: (1) Satan attempts to sift God's people to hinder their fellowship with Christ and their service for Christ. (2) After defeat by Satan and restoration from sin through repentance, Christians need to respond to Christ by loving Him and following Him. Even our best intentions to live for Christ and not to fall into sin will fail unless we have Spirit-produced love for Christ. Peter gained this kind of love at Pentecost when the Spirit came (2:1–4), and he demonstrated this love by boldly preaching for Christ at the risk of his own life (2:14–40).

We Can Defeat Satan Only through God's Power

After significant progress in sanctification or a great spiritual victory, Satan may tempt a Christian to think this way: "I'm doing very well in my spiritual life, and I think of myself as a super Christian, though I would not make that claim to other Christians because it sounds boastful." Satan is already at work promoting pride in such a person, because Satan knows that pride caused his fall (Isa. 14:12–14; Ezek. 28:17; 1 Tim. 3:6). If this self-confident Christian tries in his own power to defeat Satan, he will suffer spiritual defeat almost instantly and learn the hard way that he is not a super Christian but a susceptible one. And we can chalk up another believer defeated by Satan's superior power over mere human power. Paul warned, "Therefore let him who thinks he stands take heed lest he fall" (1 Cor. 10:12). Standing before Satan in our own power is like standing in the face of a wildfire with only a straw hut to protect us. Straw huts cannot protect us against fires, and human power alone cannot win in a spiritual struggle with Satan. Through the power of the Lord, who "will strengthen and protect you from the evil one" (2 Thess. 3:3), you can overcome Satan like an army tank overcomes someone attacking with a toy gun.

Christ Prayed for Our Protection from Satan

Christ asked the Father to keep His followers from "the evil one" while they remain in the world (John 17:15). Though believers cannot be reclaimed by Satan (17:12; Col. 1:12–14; 1 John 5:18), this prayer does not teach that believers automatically have victory over Satan's temptations and attacks. We are assured through Christ's intercessory prayer that Christians have adequate spiritual resources for victory over Satan, but we must by faith use our spiritual resources or suffer defeat by Satan. A woman in a burning building must choose either to stay in the building or to escape by using the fireman's ladder at her window. And we must use "the way of escape" from our temptation that God always provides for Christians (1 Cor. 10:13).

Even when Satan defeats us as he did Peter, we can be sure that Christ has already prayed for us as He did for Peter and that we can persevere in faith and recover from defeat.

RESPONSE TO SATAN

A chain is no stronger than its weakest link, and our spiritual resistance is no greater than our weakest moment and most vulnerable area. Listed below are ways we can defend ourselves against Satan.

Take Satan Seriously

Scripture teaches us not to disregard Satan or to treat him flippantly (2 Cor. 2:11; Jude 8–9). Satan is already a big winner over people who joke about his reality and activity. Dealing with the devil is serious business, which requires submission to God, appeal to His authority, and application of His Word (James 4:6–7; 1 Pet. 5:6–9).

Submit to God and Resist Satan

Once we realize that we must take Satan seriously, then our most important response is to "submit . . . to God" (James 4:7), which means putting ourselves under God's authority. Submission to God brings two significant results in spiritual warfare.

First, submitting to God enables us to resist Satan as James taught: "Submit therefore to God. Resist the devil and he will flee from you" (4:7). The country preacher was right when he said, "As long as you stay under God, you can stay on top of the devil." Satan knows we are invincible in spiritual warfare as long as we submit to God and obey Him.

Similarly, Peter exhorted Christians to "resist him [Satan], standing firm in the faith" (1 Pet. 5:9, NIV). This requirement shows that only believers, that is, those who are "in the faith," can win over Satan in spiritual warfare, since unbelievers are Satan's spiritual children (John 8:44; 1 John 3:10) and are under his control (Eph. 2:2–3). The moment Christians fail to submit to God and resist Satan, they become vulnerable instead of invincible in spiritual warfare.

Second, when we submit to God we can expect Him to exercise His authority against Satan. For example, Michael the archangel appealed to the Lord to exercise His authority against Satan. "Michael the archangel, when he disputed with the devil and argued about the body of Moses, did

187

not dare pronounce against him a railing judgment, but said, 'The Lord rebuke you!'"(Jude 9). Believers can have confidence that the Lord will also exercise His authority against Satan in their spiritual battles if they submit to Him and invoke His authority because "the battle is the LORD's" (1 Sam. 17:47).

In our Christian life and work we will face satanic attacks, just as Nehemiah faced satanic attacks when he led the Israelites in rebuilding the wall around Jerusalem. Like Nehemiah, we must commit the work of Satan to the Lord and persevere in our work (Neh. 2:19–20; 4:1–20; 6:1–19).

Stay Aware of Satan and His Plans

We should be able to say, "We are not ignorant of his [Satan's] schemes" (2 Cor. 2:11). The purpose of knowing Satan's schemes is not so that we will become experts in Satanology but so that he will not take advantage of us. And Satan mainly takes advantage of us by causing us to disobey God's Word such as withholding forgiveness from a repentant believer (2:5–8). To overcome Satan then, we need to know more than his schemes. We need to know and use the Scriptures as Christ did in resisting Satan's temptations, and we need spiritual discernment through spiritual maturity and the Spirit's ministry. Knowledge of biblical truth and discernment through the Spirit of truth help us to detect the devil's tactics and temptations and employ God's principles to defeat him (Eph. 6:14, 17).

Put on the Full Armor of God to Stand against the Devil and His Schemes

The kind of warfare we wage determines the kind of weapons we must use. Since we are engaged in spiritual warfare against Satan, we must use spiritual weapons from God. "For our struggle is not against flesh and blood, but against the rulers, against the powers, against the world forces of this darkness, against the spiritual forces of wickedness in the heavenly places" (Eph. 6:12). If our warfare with Satan and demons were physical, we could use guns and bulletproof vests and establish a Christian armed services with jet aircraft, guided missiles, and even nuclear weapons. But using physical weapons against a spiritual enemy would be like trying using a hearing aid to see in the dark; it will not work. The "full armor of God" does work, however, because this spiritual armor can defend us against our personal spiritual enemies, namely, Satan and his demons (Eph. 6:11–12). Therefore "we do not war according to the flesh, for the weapons of our warfare are not of the flesh, but divinely powerful for the destruction of fortresses" (2 Cor. 10:3–4).

"The full armor of God" is patterned after the Roman soldier's armament with its physical pieces corresponding to spiritual realities for spiritual warfare (Eph. 6:13–18). A detailed exposition of this passage is beyond our purpose here, but two main observations are relevant.

First, God's full armor covers everything from "the preparation of the gospel of peace" for the "feet" (6:15) to "the helmet of salvation" for the head (6:17). Twice this passage mentions "the *full* armor of God" (6:11, 13, italics added) which we must "take up" (6:13) and "put on" (6:11). We need full spiritual coverage with God's protective armor to face Satan, who looks for any area vulnerable to attack. No piece of the armor should be neglected because we can "stand firm" only after "having done everything" (6:13). All Satan needs is one unprotected area and that is where he will shoot his "flaming arrows" (6:16, NIV). Satan is not omniscient as God is, but Satan is a mastermind of sinful human nature. Evidently Satan is aware of susceptible areas in individual Christians as seen in Peter's case (Matt. 16:22–23; Luke 22:31–32) and in the experience of Ananias and Sapphira (Acts 5:1–11).

Satan has temptations tailor-made for each Christian's weakest areas and most susceptible moments. Our best defense is to be sure we are dressed fully in God's armor so that we can "stand firm against the schemes of the devil" (Eph. 6:11) and "resist in the evil day" (6:13).

Second, Christians must take up and put on each individual piece of the spiritual armor. God has provided the armor, but He expects believers to dress themselves in it promptly. Waiting until you are in the thick of spiritual battle to find out whether you are spiritually protected can be disastrous. Police SWAT teams do not wait until the bullets are flying toward them to see if they have put on their bulletproof vests.

Every Christian should carefully consider the meaning and practical application of each piece of armor mentioned in this passage (6:13–18) and then check to see that each piece is in place.

Do Not Give the Devil an Opportunity

The command, "Do not give the devil an opportunity [literally, 'a place']"
(Eph. 4:27), is related to instruction in the previous verse that warns against
prolonged, unrighteous anger. "Be angry, and yet do not sin; do not let
the sun go down on your anger" (4:26). Prolonged, uncontrolled anger
gives Satan a chance to take control of one's emotions so that hurtful
things are said and done to others. We can all say with regret, "I am guilty
of that." Thankfully we can find forgiveness from God through confession (1 John 1:9), seek the forgiveness of others (Matt. 5:23–24), and forgive
others for hurtful things said and done to us (Eph. 4:32).

Christians filled with the Spirit and with Scripture have no room left
in their lives for Satan to get a foothold. But this does not mean that Satan
no longer tempts and attacks them. It does mean that they can effectively
repulse the devil's temptations and attacks by yielding all their being,
thoughts, words, and actions to the control of the Spirit and Scripture.

If believers are not prepared for spiritual warfare, then they may have
a panic attack while under Satan's attack, and Satan like a lion moves in to
devour them spiritually (1 Pet. 5:8). Lions and other animals of prey are
stimulated to attack when their quarry runs in fear. Satan looks for believers who are young, weak, fearful, or away from fellowship with God.
So "be strong in the Lord" (Eph. 6:20) so that you can stand unafraid and
firm against Satan (6:11).

Pray for Deliverance from Satan

"Do not lead us into temptation"[3] precedes the request to "deliver us from
the evil one" (Matt. 6:13, NKJV). The latter request is evidently a prayer
for deliverance from Satan's temptations and influence. It is not a prayer
to avoid being possessed by Satan, for true believers cannot be repos-
sessed by him. They have been "delivered ... from the domain of darkness"
to the kingdom of God's Son (Col. 1:13).

Also, the prayer "deliver us from the evil one" is not a magic wand that
immunizes Christians against the devil's temptations and influence. We
are engaged in the most serious conflict in the universe—the war between God and His followers and Satan and his followers. Christians

should pray for victory over Satan's temptations and influence and then put feet to their prayers by obeying this list of biblical responses to Satan presented in this section. In Ephesians 6:10–18 the preparation for spiritual warfare ends with prayer: "With all prayer and petition pray at all times in the Spirit, and with this in view, be on the alert with all perseverance and petition for all the saints" (6:18).

Be Self-Controlled and Alert in Response to Satan

Peter warned Christians, "Be self-controlled and alert. Your enemy the devil prowls around like a roaring lion looking for someone to devour" (1 Pet. 5:8, NIV). Christians can fulfill God's requirement for self-control only by keeping their lives under the Spirit's control (Gal. 5:23; Eph. 5:18). Self-control of the Christian's thoughts is particularly crucial because the mind is a main target of Satan in his war against the saints (2 Cor. 10:3–5).

Wrong thinking gives Satan a great opportunity to do his spiritual damage in our lives. Satan is looking for Christians susceptible to his mind-control. He knows that wrong thinking will lead to wrong living because how people think largely determines how they live (Prov. 23:7). When Christians do not think right, they do not decide right, act right, or feel right. The biblical command, "Be transformed by the renewing of your mind" (Rom. 12:2) shows that God changes our living by changing our thinking. And God desires to change our thinking by His Spirit and through His Word so that we live like Christ because we think like Christ.

When people rely on "earthly, natural, demonic" wisdom (James 3:15), they experience mental confusion and other areas of their lives spin out of control (3:16). But by filling their minds with God's "wisdom from above" (3:17) believers can experience self-control, mental orderliness, and peace from God (3:13, 17–18).

Christians need to be "alert" as well as "self-controlled" because of the devil's lionlike prowling. Alert Christians are awake and vigilant, the opposite of what Peter and his companions were when they slept while Jesus was praying (Matt. 26:41–46). So Scripture warns us to be wise to Satan's tricks and traps (2 Cor. 2:11; Eph. 6:11) and watchful at all times for his attacks.

Overcome Satan through Christ's Blood and Your Personal Testimony

This principle of overcoming Satan is expressed in Revelation 12:11, "And they overcame him [Satan] because of the blood of the Lamb and because of the word of their testimony." Here the saints' overcome Satan's accusation against them for their sin, because in the previous verse he is called "the accuser of our brethren . . . who accuses them before our God day and night" (12:10). Satan's accusing ministry closely aligns with his title "the devil," from the Greek *diabolos*, "the slanderer."

Does Revelation 12:10–11 teach that we should plead the blood of Christ to overcome Satan, as some Christians believe? Pleading the blood of Christ may be done with good intention, and God may honor the sincere desire of believers to counteract Satan through Christ's blood. However, Scripture teaches us to overcome Satan not by pleading the blood of Christ but by believing that God is satisfied that Christ's blood has paid for our sins (Eph 1:7) and that Christ's blood continues to cleanse us from all sin (1 John 1:7). Our forgiveness and cleansing from sin by Christ's blood occurs the moment we trust Christ as our personal Savior (Acts 13:38–39; Rom. 3:24–26; Col. 2:13). Through our position in Christ (Rom. 8:1), Satan has no basis to accuse us before God (Rev. 12:10–11).

Christ is our "Advocate" (1 John 2:1) who acts as our defense lawyer to counter Satan's accusation of us. Some famous defense lawyers have won 90 percent or more of their cases. Christ has never lost a case for a believer. This means that Christ always perfectly defends and secures each believer against Satan's accusations. The basis for Christ's defense is His sacrificial death on the cross which provided "the propitiation for our sins" (2:2; 4:10). The Father is perfectly satisfied that the complete price for our sins has been paid in Christ's blood (John 19:30; Rom. 3:24–25). And we should believe and testify that Christ fully paid for our sins with His blood so that we realize victory over Satan and his accusations.

Christ's blood continues to provide forgiveness and cleansing in a relational or experiential sense as we confess our sins (1 John 1:7–9). Then through our position in Christ and our practice of confessing all known sins, none of our sins remain as leverage for Satan to accuse us and spiritually hinder us.

Pursue Sanctification

Each of the preceding practices is essential for Christians to win in spiritual warfare and to progress in sanctification. We cannot successfully pursue sanctification if we are losing in spiritual warfare.

Likewise, progress in sanctification better prepares us for spiritual warfare. But how does this work? Progress in sanctification increases our spiritual strength and maturity and thereby our ability to advance against our adversary, the devil.

Strong, mature Christians are not exempt from spiritual warfare or immune to Satanic attack. They may even become special targets of Satan because of their rapid spiritual growth, their positive spiritual influence on others, and their ministry in helping people trust the Savior and find freedom from Satan.

Advancing in sanctification then requires overcoming the opposing spiritual forces of Satan just as advancing upstream requires overcoming the opposing forces of the current. So a Christian who is gaining rapidly in spiritual growth is winning in spiritual warfare. And God want you to be that kind of Christian.

CHAPTER FIFTEEN

Helping Other Christians Grow:
Interpersonal Ministry for Sanctification

IN AN IDEAL FAMILY A CARING MOTHER and father expend much love, time, effort, and money to raise a child to healthy adulthood. Other family members, friends, teachers, medical personnel, counselors, leaders, dieticians, and many others contribute to the maturation of a person. A team of persons is required for every human to reach adulthood.

Likewise, ideal spiritual growth of a new believer to Christlike maturity requires a team of Christians. True, a new believer must choose to receive the spiritual food of the Word and engage in spiritual practices to become spiritually mature (Heb. 5:12–14) just as a physical infant must receive physical food and exercise to become physically mature. But both physical infants and spiritual infants need other persons to help nurture them to adulthood. And both physically mature persons and spiritually mature persons still depend on a team of persons to help meet their respective needs. Christ taught that both His lambs and His mature sheep require spiritual care (John 21:15–17).

Each Christian is responsible to pursue sanctification; no one else can pursue it for him or her. However, believers can and should help each other grow, and spiritual infants especially need more mature Christians to help them through the early stages of growth.

God intends for the Christian community to be a context in which Christians can help each other grow through mutual ministry. "We are to grow up in all aspects into Him, who is the head, even Christ, from whom the whole body, being fitted and held together by that which every joint supplies, according to the proper working of each individual part, causes the growth of the body for the building up of itself in love" (Eph. 4:15–16). As Les Steele says, "This is to be a community of mutuality and reciprocity; as the community contributes to our growth, we contribute to its growth and the growth of its members."[1] Christians should take "a mutual interest in each other's growth toward maturity."[2]

BIBLICAL RESPONSIBILITY
TO HELP EACH OTHER GROW

Though God uses human effort and relationships in spiritual development, He is the ultimate source of our spiritual growth as Paul indicated: "The entire body . . . grows with a growth which is from God" (Col. 2:19). We should practice interpersonal ministry to help each other grow, but Lawrence Richards reminds us that "only in God, by virtue of an intimate relationship with Jesus and the work of the Holy Spirit can any of us hope to live a vital spiritual life."[3]

Spiritual growth is rooted in the individual's relationship to God through Christ. The numerical and spiritual growth of the church depends directly on the addition of individual believers and the individual spiritual growth of its believers (Acts 9:31). Thus believers are first responsible to nurture their own personal growth. Others can teach us biblical truth, but we must personally receive, retain, and obey that truth to grow in Christ. Others can encourage us in biblical memorization and meditation and exemplify these practices to us, but only we can receive, chew, and digest our individual spiritual food. Surrogate spiritual development is not part of God's plan.

However, the responsibility of believers goes beyond nurturing their own spiritual lives and receiving help from others for their spiritual growth.

Believers are responsible to help others grow spiritually so that the whole body of Christ grows through reciprocal ministry (Eph. 4:11–16).

Christians may struggle with apathy and irresponsibility, which hinder their personal spiritual growth and their interpersonal ministry to help others grow. But we can overcome these negatives through discipline and responsible action empowered by the Spirit. Believers who are experiencing dynamic spiritual growth are best prepared to encourage and edify others in their Christian faith. "Therefore encourage one another, and build up one another, just as you also are doing" (1 Thess. 5:11).

Responsibility Based on Our Membership in Christ's Body

The Spirit unites believers with Christ, the Head of the church, and with other believers as members of His body (Rom. 12:5; 1 Cor. 12:12–13; Col. 1:18). Membership in Christ's body gives us some wonderful privileges and some important responsibilities.

Our first responsibility is to submit to Christ as our Head. And through the Spirit's power we can submit to His headship by following His directions.

If we obey Christ's directions, then we can depend on Him as our Head to nurture, sustain, preserve, guide, and empower us (Eph. 5:23–30). And obedience to Christ is essential to minister effectively to other believers, to receive ministry from them, and to grow together in Christ (4:11–16).

Responsibility Based on Our Interdependency in Christ's Body

Many people highly value independence and self-sufficiency, and deplore slackers and freeloaders. However, we can overdo independence and behave as loners even though we are members of Christ's body and of one another. The words from a song, "No man is an island; no man stands alone," are relevant to the members of Christ's body. Human interdependency is firmly grounded in Scripture. As Richards observes, "From early Genesis we learn that humans cannot live isolated lives. People were not intended to live alone."[4] And in the case of Christians, "We are linked by

God's Spirit to Jesus and to each other, and our life is intended to be lived in supportive, caring community."[5] Isolationism contradicts our membership in the body of Christ and our responsibility for interpersonal ministry in the body (1 Cor. 12:12–27).

Rather, Christians should function like Velcro which has tiny hooks that reach out and interlock with each other so that two items are held together. Christians must reach out and interact with each other to maintain unity and attain spiritual maturity.

Believers may know that Christ expects interpersonal relationships and reciprocal ministry among the members in His body and yet practice a covert isolationism and protectionism in the body. They believe that close fellowship is not worth the hassle because it creates too many relational problems. The Lord knew about these risks of close human interaction when He united believers as a body. Still, He commands believers to practice togetherness and to function as interdependent members (Rom. 12:5–8; 1 Cor. 12–14; Eph. 4:3; Phil. 2:1–2). Trying to bond together with other Christians may seem like a group of porcupines huddling together on a cold night. Closeness with Christians from diverse backgrounds can become "sticky business." But keeping our distance from other believers to escape relational headaches is not justifiable except in the case of a professed believer who is living in flagrant sin (1 Cor. 5:11; 2 Thess. 3:6, 14–15).

Some believers have tried to have interpersonal relationships and ministry with their fellow believers, but they have stopped trying because they have been severely hurt. They react to their negative experience with a "never again" attitude and consequently keep aloof from spiritual intimacy with other believers. But believers with a protectionist attitude hinder their own spiritual growth and that of others. Trying to help others grow does not work well from long distance or when relational barriers have been erected.

Christ our Head planned for His bodily members to grow through loving service to each other. And we grow most when we resolve conflicts and hurts with other believers rather than denying or avoiding these relational barriers. Withdrawing from others without biblical justification, giving the silent treatment, or denying differences between persons does not build either a healthy marriage or a healthy relationship between believers. However, in both marriage and relating to other believers, we can strengthen our love, unity, and appreciation by working through our differences.

If we have an attitude of independency and aloofness from other members in the body of Christ, we need to repent and be humble before God and replace it with an attitude of interdependency with other believers. Then we can fulfill our biblical roles and responsibilities in the body of Christ so that we edify other members (Rom. 14:19), we ourselves are edified, and we glorify God.

I think of Ernest who willingly served in a local church but suffered burnout from the overload of "Christian work" that others unwisely foisted on him. Ernest left his local church with a bitter attitude and remained detached from Christian fellowship. He should have worked with his Christian brothers and sisters and they with him to find a better approach—a biblical approach that could lighten his load, help him mature spiritually, and strengthen his fellowship with other believers.

Susan presents a different scenario. She considers her local church her second family, and she readily receives love, care, and counsel from other Christians. Through her Christian faith and the support of other believers, Susan has overcome personal addictions, and she seeks to respond to her addictive and cysfunctional husband according to biblical principles. Her dynamic faith and growth encourage other Christians so that she contributes significantly to the body of Christ.

Follow Ernest's choices and you will become bitter, spiritually stunted, and alienated from other believers. Follow Susan's example and you will become more spiritual, fruitful, and united with other believers.

RECIPROCAL MINISTRY TO HELP EACH OTHER GROW

The apostle Paul taught and practiced reciprocal ministry with other believers. One reason he wanted to see the Christians at Rome was so *he* could "be encouraged together with you while among you, each of us by the other's faith, both yours and mine" (Rom. 1:12). Think of that! The great apostle desired ministry from other Christians to help him grow spiritually, and his words were not just to patronize and flatter his hearers. Paul knew he had not attained spiritual perfection and that other Christians could help him become more Christlike.

Paul's example teaches us that even the most mature Christians can receive spiritual ministry from other Christians. A new convert may share with a veteran Christian his newly discovered blessing from John 3:16 or some other familiar passage. Then suppose the veteran Christian tells the enthusiastic convert, "Don't even bother to mention John 3:16. I learned that verse when I was hardly out of the crib. You're not teaching me anything. I've already covered that ground." This new believer's spiritual zeal would be squelched instead of stimulated, and it could be a long time before he tries to express any more spiritual exuberance. Even if we have known that wonderful verse for over a half-century, we can always appreciate God's love even more and rejoice to see its transforming power in a new convert.

How different when a mature believer patiently listens to a new Christian share familiar truth with such zeal and joy that he revives the older Christian's passion for Christ. Young Christians have the potential to grow up to be mature Christians and profitable servants. Mature Christians should see this potential and nurture spiritual infants. Besides seeing people come to faith in Christ, another great joy is seeing them grow in Christ (1 Thess. 1:2–10; 2 John 4). We need to see the growth potential of new believers and to stimulate their spiritual growth rather than squelch it. As Hebrews 10:24 says, "Let us consider how to stimulate one another to love and good deeds."

Unlike Paul, we may balk at letting either new converts or even mature Christians minister to us. Pride and self-sufficiency make us resist and decline help from others. After all, rugged individuals, we think, should not receive help from others; they should be able to make it on their own. Highly individualistic believers with this "go it alone" attitude disobey God and miss His blessing to them through others. We need the support of other Christian brothers and sisters in our spiritual journey as "aliens and strangers" on earth (1 Pet. 2:11). As Sharon Parks remarks, "The pilgrimage of faith must be made in the company of others."[6]

Guides find that one of their greatest problems is dealing with mavericks in a group of people whom they lead. Wanting to be on their own, these mavericks have little concern for the welfare of themselves and others. A conscientious guide wants to lead people who will work together as a team for enhancement of each individual and of the group as a whole. Likewise, Christ our Head wants to guide us so that all the members of His body will serve together harmoniously, grow personally, and help each other grow.

Jesus taught His disciples to minister freely to others and to be ministered to by others. Some Christians struggle to receive spiritual or material help from other believers. They need to exchange their aloofness for a humble and joyous acceptance of fellow believers with equal standing ("fellow citizens," "fellow heirs," "fellow members," and "fellow partakers," Eph. 2:19; 3:6) and to begin receiving ministry from others eagerly. Are we willing to give and receive spiritual ministry to enhance each other's growth in Christ's body?

BIBLICAL MEANS TO HELP EACH OTHER GROW

God has instituted the human family (including both nuclear and extended forms of the family), the local church, and the spiritual body of Christ as primary corporate contexts for mutual ministry among believers. Believers can also help each other grow through mutual ministry with their Christian friends, in their Christian community (including but extending beyond their local church), in various Christian groups (within and outside their local church), and wherever they come in contact with other believers.

A one-on-one relationship is obviously the smallest corporate context for spiritual growth. Christian training in discipleship or mentoring may involve a one-on-one relationship in which the trainer or mentor helps another believer develop spiritually. Evidently this type of relationship existed between Jesus and Peter (Luke 22:31–32; 24:34) and between Paul and Timothy (Acts 16:1–3; 1 Tim.; 2 Tim.), though both Jesus and Paul also led disciples in groups.

Thought the words *mentor* and *mentoring* do not appear in the Bible, they may be considered a more specific form of discipleship. Mentoring emphasizes a closer relationship between a mentor as model, guide, teacher, coach, and counselor and his trainee than a leader might have with a disciple or circle of disciples. Both Timothy and Titus exemplify a mentoring relationship with Paul (1 Tim. 1:2; 2 Tim. 3:10–11; Titus 1:4), though they were also in a group of other disciples or team members that Paul led (2 Tim. 2:2; Titus 3:12–13; see Acts 9:25). Barnabas was a mentor for Paul (9:27; 11:22–26, 29–30; 13:1–12) and for John Mark (15:39; Col. 4:10; 2 Tim. 4:11).

While the focus of discipleship training and mentoring is on the development of the trainee, discipleship leaders or mentors can also receive ministry and spiritual benefit from their followers (Rom. 1:12; 2 Cor. 7:6; 2 Tim. 1:4; 4:9, 11–12, 21). So discipleship training and mentoring can be one of the most effective relationships for believers to help each other grow, and this is the way our Lord trained His twelve disciples.[7]

Have Spiritual Fellowship with Other Believers

True fellowship with other Christians depends on one's fellowship with God.[8] "What we have seen and heard we proclaim to you also, that you also may have fellowship with us; and indeed our fellowship is with the Father, and with His Son Jesus Christ" (1 John 1:3). Biblical fellowship begins with a vital relationship to God through Christ (1:1–2; 2 John 9). Since Christ is the indispensable and common factor in spiritual fellowship, we can have Christian fellowship only with those who share Him in common with us. Thus genuine fellowship with God and with other believers differs from just socializing around coffee, punch, chips, and dip.

The quality of fellowship we experience with other believers depends on our growth in fellowship with the triune God (1 Cor. 1:9; 1 John 1:3). We grow in fellowship with Him as we walk in the light of His holiness, His Son, and His Word (1:4–7). Our growth in fellowship with God enriches our fellowship with other believers (1:7), and we can help them grow in their fellowship with God by our example and ministry to them (1:3, 7).

Practice the New Testament "One Another" Exhortations

"Again and again, New Testament writers exhorted believers to engage in specific activities that would enable the body of Christ to function effectively and to grow spiritually."[9] Believers are to practice these specific activities with "one another" so that reciprocal ministry takes place. For instance, believers are to "love one another" (John 13:34–35), "serve one another" (Gal. 5:13), "bear one another's burdens" (6:2), and "be hospitable to one another" (1 Pet. 4:9).

Gene Getz believes that love is the greatest of the "one another" exhortations[10] and that "the additional 'one another' exhortations in the New Testament actually demonstrate love in action."[11] He suggests that these additional "one another" exhortations "can be reduced to approximately 12 significant actions Christians are to take toward 'one another' to help build up the body of Christ."[12] The following enumeration is adapted from Getz's list, with biblical references added.[13]

- Recognize all believers as members of one another (Rom. 12:5)

- Be devoted to one another (12:10)

- Honor one another (12:10)

- Be of the same mind with one another (15:5)

- Accept one another (15:7)

- Admonish one another (15:14)

- Greet one another (16:16)

- Serve one another (Gal. 5:13)

- Bear one another's burdens (6:2)

- Bear with one another (Eph. 4:2, NKJV)

- Submit to one another (5:21, NIV)

- Encourage one another (1 Thess. 5:11)

Practicing these exhortations obviously requires reciprocal ministry between believers to produce mutual spiritual benefit. Furthermore, successful mutual ministry between believers requires personal involvement with them, and such involvement always takes time, energy, and other personal sacrifices. How can we obey the "one another" exhortations with the right motivation and still carry out our own responsibilities? And how can we help other people with their problems when we can hardly handle our own?

First, we can regard these "one another" exhortations as a blessing and not a burden if we obey them from Spirit-produced love. God does not overload our schedule; we do. And His command to "bear one another's burdens" (Gal. 6:2)[14] should be seen in light of His promises to help us with our burdens so that we can help others with their burdens. True, Christians cannot bear everyone else's burdens. But by depending on the Lord, we can discern those whose burdens God wants us to bear.[15] Believers who use their heavy schedule of activities as an excuse to avoid practicing the "one another" exhortations need to reorder their priorities and begin to fulfill these "one another" responsibilities. When Christians are fully committed to God, He always gives them the time, energy, finances, material goods, preparation, and other requirements to fulfill His will.

Second, we can rely on God's Spirit for power to obey the "one another" requirements. The Spirit infuses God's love into His people (Rom. 5:5) so that they can love and obey Christ (John 14:21) and help care for the members of His body (1 Cor. 12:25). Spirit-produced love will motivate us to pray, visit, teach, counsel, perform menial tasks, and meet other needs in our care for each other (Rom. 13:8–10).

Third, we can be encouraged that faithful ministry to "one another" produces some wonderful results. (a) We demonstrate genuine love for the Lord. (b) We show people we are truly Christ's disciples, especially by our love for one another (John 13:34–35). (c) We use God's methods rather than pressure tactics to minister to others. (d) We serve other Christians out of love (Gal. 5:13; 1 Pet. 4:10–11). (e) We help other Christians grow so that the body of Christ matures. (f) We receive ministry from other Christians who help us grow. (g) We will be remembered and rewarded by the Lord for faithful service to His people (Heb. 6:10).

Exercise Your Spiritual Gift(s)

The "one another" exhortations cover a variety of ministries to other believers, yet each believer's spiritual giftedness determines his or her specific emphasis of ministry to other believers (Rom. 12:6–8). So another way we can help other Christians grow is by exercising our spiritual gifts (Eph. 4:11–16; 1 Cor. 12–14).[16]

Spiritual gifts are supernatural abilities Christ gives His people to serve one another in different ways for the edifying of His body (Eph. 4: 16; Rom. 12:6–8; 1 Cor. 12:7; 1 Pet. 4:10). Each Christian has at least one spiritual gift (1 Cor. 12:11), though evidently no one has all the spiritual gifts (Rom. 12:6). We are responsible to God and fellow believers to exercise our spiritual gifts "as good stewards of the manifold grace of God" (1 Pet. 4:10).

The church body is always prominent in key passages on spiritual gifts because the local church is the main context for believers to discover, develop, and exercise their spiritual gifts. The best individual effort alone cannot substitute for believers ministering to each other. So I wholeheartedly agree that "the faith community provides a context for growth in maturity."[17]

Why are we to exercise spiritual gifts? To equip believers for the work of service (Eph. 4:11–12), to serve each other (1 Pet. 4:10), to help each other grow spiritually (1 Cor. 14:12, 26), and above all, to glorify God through Jesus Christ.

The first two goals for spiritual gifts converge on the third goal—for believers to grow spiritually. This truth is based on the teaching of Ephesians 4:7–16 that "Christ's giving of gifts to the Church is to enable the Church to move toward its goals, and that movement is seen in terms of believers' growth toward Christ."[18] Thus believers help each other grow by exercising their spiritual gifts, and the more Christlike we become, the more we glorify God.

The ministry of Christians to each other through interpersonal relationships sharply contrasts with the inability of many people today "to sustain deep and enduring personal relationships."[19] Believers are responsible to sustain deep and enduring personal relationships with God and with each other. "Let each of us please his neighbor for his good, to his edification" (Rom. 15:2).

As believers progress in sanctification and help other believers grow through interpersonal ministry in the nuclear family, in the local church, in the body of Christ, and in various other Christian groups, they promote "the growth of the body for the building up of itself in love" (Eph. 4:16).

CHAPTER SIXTEEN

Maximizing Spiritual Growth:
A Lifetime Plan for Sanctification

GEORGE MUELLER SERVED GOD with great success. He and his wife, Mary, established Christian orphanages in Bristol, England in the 1830s. By the 1880s Mueller had received the equivalent of several million dollars for the orphanages and other Christian projects. Through many remarkable answers to Mueller's prayers, the orphans were always provided for, though often at the last minute.

Did Mueller just exercise his remarkable faith in God and watch Christian work automatically happen? No, he planned his orphanage work and other Christian endeavors with definite aims. Thus Mueller succeeded in Christian service because he planned as well as prayed with great faith in God.

Just as George Mueller planned for his Christian service, so we must plan for our Christian sanctification if we expect to succeed as he did. This chapter discusses how to develop and practice a successful lifetime plan for sanctification based on the teaching of this book.

COMMIT TO LIFETIME SANCTIFICATION

Many start well in the Christian race, but not all finish well (1 Cor. 9:24–27). Failure to finish well is especially prevalent among Christian leaders.[1] When we fail in the race of sanctification we can recover (1 John 1:9), but this race has no reruns.

Believers should commit to pursue sanctification zealously and consistently. They should also count the full cost of their commitment as Jesus taught His followers to do (Luke 14:28–33). Initial salvation comes as a free gift received by faith. Sanctification also operates by faith, but pursuing holiness and conquering sin may cost us blood, sweat, and tears. This cost can be literal, as Hebrews 12:4 suggests: "You have not yet resisted to the point of shedding blood in your striving against sin." As stated earlier, the pursuit of sanctification involves obeying the Scriptures (John 14:21), perseverance (Phil. 3:12–14), trials (James 1:2–4), and even persecution (2 Tim. 3:12). We are to "press on to maturity" (Heb. 6:1).

Christians should state their lifetime commitment to sanctification in their own words. I suggest this sample: "I commit to pursue sanctification toward Christlike maturity for my lifetime by relying on the Holy Spirit and obeying Scripture. I will practice God's means of sanctification with my fullest intensity and persistence. I will make biblically appropriate changes in my lifetime plan for sanctification in order to maximize my spiritual progress."

DEVELOP A LIFETIME PLAN FOR SANCTIFICATION

Christians need both lifetime commitment to sanctification and also a lifetime plan for their sanctification so that their commitment is channeled in the right direction. Recently a woman entertainer was paying tribute to her deceased former husband. She commended his ability to attract people to follow him. And then she indicated that this man did not really know where he was going, but that everybody wanted to be there with him and follow him. The audience broke out in laughter at the ridiculous idea of committing oneself to follow a man who does not know where he is going. And it is just as ridiculous to try to pursue sanctification if we do not have a clear plan of action that we can follow to a holier life.

A lifetime plan for sanctification should include both a daily devotional time and special occasions for spiritual nurture.

Daily Devotional Time

Daily devotional time is a regularly scheduled period in each twenty-four-hour cycle for undistracted personal response to the Lord and nurture of our spiritual relationship to Him. This practice is also known as a *daily quiet time* or simply *daily devotions.*

Two or more persons may have devotions together, such as Christian parents leading their children in devotions or a gathering of several Christians for a devotional time. However, here the emphasis is on *personal* daily devotions as a private time of fellowship with God.

The personal devotional time is not primarily academic Bible study or preparation of spiritual truths to share with others. Instead it is a special time focused on intimate fellowship with the Lord.

Our personal response to the Lord and nurture of our spiritual life during devotions should be empowered by the Spirit and directed by Scripture so that our devotional time is dynamic, spontaneous, and properly controlled rather than dull and rigid. Hence Christians should not take a legalistic approach to their daily devotions. Neither should they try to impose a daily devotional time on others or require a strict format for personal devotions. Legalism makes a daily devotional time dead and discouraging rather than attractive, vital, and spiritually uplifting. Furthermore, legalism can mislead people by causing them to measure and compare each other's spirituality by the length or other characteristics of their devotions.

We should also avoid judging others' preferences concerning the best time, place, length, and contents for personal devotions so long as one's devotional practices are within biblical bounds. Our daily devotional time must be handled within a context of grace.

Nor should we call just any type of Christian practice a successful daily devotional time. One of the worst excuses for a devotional time I ever heard was this: "I have my devotions by reading the Christian bumper stickers during my daily driving." Many so-called Christian bumper stickers are biblically inaccurate, and the rest hardly give the reader even a spoonful of spiritual skim milk.

Others claim that since they "pray without ceasing" (1 Thess. 5:17) they do not need a specific devotional time. To commune constantly with God and to send a continual stream of prayer requests to heaven is wonderful. But this does not substitute for a daily devotional time. Believers can pray without ceasing while driving a vehicle, doing housework, or tending their lawn. But they cannot give undistracted attention to the Lord while doing these other activities. Suppose I tell my wife I am going to spend some quality time with her by thinking pleasant thoughts of her and saying endearing things to her while I mow the lawn. She may appreciate my pleasant thoughts and endearing words, but she will hardly think this practice can replace quality time when I focus just on her and our relationship. Likewise, a quality devotional time with the Lord must include our undistracted personal response to Him.

Why should Christians have a daily devotional time? Scripture does not explicitly say we must practice daily devotions, but the Scriptures suggest the wisdom and value of this practice.

By spending special times of undistracted attention in God's presence, we hear Him and fellowship with Him (Pss. 27:8; 46:10). We cannot love God and develop our relationship to Him more than we know Him. And we can get to know Him more through focused attention in a daily devotional time.

The broadest and most basic reason why we should have daily devotions is because God seeks fellowship with believers, and this truth starts in the early chapters of Genesis and continues in Scripture through the Book of Revelation (for example, Gen. 3:8; Pss. 27:8; 42:1–2; 63:1–8; John 1:14; 4:23–24; 1 Cor. 1:9; Rev. 3:20). It is understandable that human creatures should seek fellowship with their Creator. But that the holy Creator should seek reconciliation and fellowship with human beings is amazing, particularly after the fall of the human race.

Two more specific reasons why we need daily devotions relate to communication between God and His people.

(a) We need a scheduled time each day to study, memorize, meditate on, and apply Scripture. God has spoken to us in Scripture, and if we want to know what He has said, we must search Scripture with receptive and expectant hearts. Believers should respond to the Bible as a dry sponge responds when it contacts liquid. We should passionately soak up Scripture and let it saturate our souls. Passages such as Joshua 1:8; Job 23:12; Psalms 19:7–14; 119:97–104; Matthew 4:4 Hebrews 5:12–14; and 1 Peter 2:2 show the vital necessity of God's Word. Thus daily devotions should include a time for serious intake and application of Scripture. Paul exhorted Christians, "Let the word of Christ richly dwell within you" (Col. 3:16).

(b) We need a scheduled time each day for worship, prayer, and fellowship with God.

God speaks to us through His Word, and He desires us to respond to Him through prayer. Scripture reveals many godly persons whose prayers were a vital part of their daily practice. David mentioned the practice of praying to the Lord three times a day (Ps. 55:16–17), and this was also Daniel's practice (Dan. 6:10–11). Daniel's times of prayer were more important to him than life itself (6:12). Christ evidently prayed frequently and also practiced continual and perfect communion with the Father (Mark 1:35; John 8:29). Paul repeatedly prayed, especially for believers in various churches (for example, Phil. 1:3–4; Col. 1:3; 1 Thess. 1:2–3), and his times of prayer must have occurred at least daily.

When is the best time to have a daily devotional time? Before answering this question, we are wise to examine some relevant biblical data.

Scripture records that Jesus prayed early in the morning on at least one occasion (Mark 1:35), and it may have been His regular habit. Acts 10:9 mentions a situation in which Peter prayed at about noon. "Toward evening" Isaac went out in the field "to meditate" (Gen. 24:63).[2] Before Christ chose the twelve apostles, He "went off to a mountain to pray, and He spent the whole night in prayer to God" (Luke 6:12). Again, Daniel, like David, prayed three times a day (Dan. 6:10–11). Therefore Scripture does not indicate a best time for devotions in the twenty-four-hour cycle. And some of these instances may not refer to a daily prayer practice. For example, Jesus did not spend every night in. So God gives us freedom—and we should give other people the same freedom—to choose the best time for daily devotions.

Differences in individual biological clocks may also influence one's choice of time for daily devotions. Some Christians are "morning persons"; they are wide awake when they first arise and they function well in early morning hours. Others are like owls; they are more energetic and alert in the evening than during the day. Wise Christians will choose the time of day for devotions when they are most alert, undistracted, and free from their work schedule. Therefore you should give God the best time feasible in your daily schedule for your daily devotions. If you try to squeeze devotions into your leftover time, you probably will have little or no time at all, or it will be a poor time.

Biblical examples also give believers the option to have two or more special times with the Lord each day. These more frequent times would normally be briefer periods than a single period for a daily devotional. Meeting with the Lord several times each day could be the best arrangement for a person with a heavy administrative schedule such as Daniel evidently had. A busy executive might desire to seek the Lord several times a day about decisions, problems, and difficult relationships. These special times with the Lord can recharge a person spiritually, mentally, emotionally, and physically, resulting in more effective Christian living and growth.

Christians who do not have their devotional time early in the morning should still take time to commit themselves, their family, and their daily activities to the Lord before they begin the day. I also use an early morning period to review Bible memory verses and to meditate on the truths reviewed. Then in the late afternoon or early evening I have my Bible reading, prayer, and other devotional activities. My wife and I have a brief time of prayer together each morning to acknowledge the Lord in praise and worship, to take our major concerns to Him, and to seek His blessing on our lives and activities for the day.

Each Christian needs to determine the best time to set aside each day for devotions and then follow that schedule. Emergency adjustments in the schedule for devotions are understandable. We should not consider lapses in our devotional practice as final failures since God can restore us and our devotional time to even greater success. Nevertheless we should aim for consistency, which tends to produce more consistency, while inconsistency in daily devotions tends to reinforce the habit of inconsistency. A sporadic approach to devotions usually produces sporadic results just as sporadic eating and working are not generally healthy and productive approaches. Serious athletes seldom use an irregular training schedule for their special sport if they hope to attain excellence and keep improving their athletic skills. And pursuing sanctification is like an athletic contest that demands our utmost effort (1 Cor. 9:24–27; Phil. 3:13–14; Heb. 12:1–3). So we can be encouraged that our devotional time can constantly improve so that it becomes the high point of our day and not an irksome task to endure.

Where is the best place to have a daily devotional time? Believers need a place for their devotions where they can obey the command, "Be still and know that I am God" (Ps. 46:10, NKJV). Modern technological societies with their performance-oriented people usually equate activity with accomplishment. The mind, the mouth, and the body operate at a rapid rate while the spirit shrivels for lack of attention. Christians need a place where they can be still, silent, relaxed, and relieved from the rapidity and racket of intense living. That place should also be free from disturbing noise, distraction, and interruption.

Jesus sought out such a place for His prayer time. "And in the early morning, while it was still dark, He arose and went out and departed to a lonely place, and was praying there" (Mark 1:35, NASB). Both the "inner room" where Jesus taught us to go for prayer (Matt. 6:5) and the "secluded place" where Jesus went for prayer (Mark 1:35) show the importance of selecting a location where the world is temporarily shut out from our lives, and we are shut in alone with God for intimacy with Him.

We have also seen several instances where biblical characters spent time with God outdoors. During several years of my seminary training in Dallas, Texas, my wife and I lived near White Rock Lake. I felt the heavy pressures of family responsibilities, academic demands, church ministries, and a part-time job. I would walk along the shore of this lake and worship the Lord and commit myself, my family, my responsibilities and cares, and other persons to God in prayer. God used this practice to give me relief from worries, peace, and renewed strength as His Word promised. Moreover, the walking helped alleviate nervous tension and invigorate me for prayer. The lake and its surroundings buoyed my spirit and turned my focus away from my problems and toward the refreshing presence of the Lord. You may not live by beautiful mountains, the seashore, a majestic forest, or even a lake.

But I hope you have a place where you can walk and talk with the Lord, even if it's your own neighborhood, backyard, or inside your home. Walking physically and talking with the Lord can help us walk closer to Him spiritually so that we become like Enoch who "walked with God" (Gen. 5:22, 24) and "was pleasing to God" (Heb. 11:5).

How long should a daily devotional time last? Some people claim that they never have time for daily devotions. These same people may schedule three meals a day and snacks between the meals. Obviously it is difficult to find legitimate excuses for not having a daily devotional time. So taking time for daily devotions is an issue of priorities. We take time or make time to do the things that are really important to us. The priority we give to our daily devotions helps show how much our relationship to God means to us.

The quality and depth of a devotional time is more important than its quantity and length. Nevertheless you can hardly have a successful devotional time by rushing in and out of the presence of God for a spiritual lift as you would operate a vending machine for a soda. Therefore you should not hurry your devotional time but should plan for sufficient time to focus on the Lord and communicate meaningfully with Him. Then you will strengthen your relationship to God and see your devotional time develop rather than decline.

The length of personal devotions may be limited by your schedule for sleeping, eating, working, family time, and other responsibilities. Exceptions to these factors are days off work, periods of fasting, or special occasions planned for time with the Lord. However, we usually find time for the activities we really desire to do. And we should be willing to miss a meal or some sleep if necessary in order to spend time with the Lord.

On occasions such as a trip to the mountains, we may be free from our routine schedule to have a longer devotional time. Before major decisions Christians might extend their prayer time throughout the night (Luke 6:12–13). Again, shorter and more frequent devotional times often best fit a daily schedule filled with decisions, meetings, advising, and numerous intense activities that call for renewed wisdom and strength from the Lord.

What practices we can use to have an effective daily devotional time? The practices listed below include the biblical means of sanctification, and also some practices that may be helpful but are not essential for personal daily devotions. This list is not exhaustive, so you may know of other helpful devotional practices. You can indicate in the blank to the left of each item the practices you now use regularly and also those you want to add to your daily devotional activities. One can have excellent devotions and yet follow only a few of the items on this list. So you should not overload and hinder your devotions with too many different practices.

_____ Brief opening prayer to God

_____ Some form of worship, praise, or adoration

_____ Acknowledgment of God and some of His attributes

_____ Reference to God as Father

_____ Reference to Jesus Christ specifically

_____ Reference to the Holy Spirit specifically

_____ Direct or indirect reference to God's will

_____ Reference to specific promises in God's Word

_____ Confession of sin

_____ Thanksgiving in general or for specific things from God

_____ Personal requests

_____ Reference to relationships with other people

_____ Intercessory prayer (prayer for other persons)

_____ Use of the Bible (perhaps noting the different ways you use the Bible)

_____ Memorization of Scripture

_____ Meditation on the Lord, His Word, and His works

_____ Period of quietness and inactivity (waiting before the Lord)

_____ Expression of personal feelings to God

_____ Singing, use of a musical instrument, or both

_____ Reading of hymns or songs

_____ Listening to recorded music or messages

_____ Use of devotional aids or commentaries

_____ Use of other types of literary aids

_____ Notation of key thoughts

_____ Use of a devotional diary or journal

Christians usually start a daily devotional time with high expectations, but many soon experience discouragement and disappointment with their daily devotions. Some even give up trying to have daily devotions, convinced that their likelihood of success with a daily devotional time is about as good as trying to throw a watermelon across the Mississippi River. This warning is not to discourage you but to help you prepare for a major struggle to keep your daily devotional practice consistent, vital, and meaningful. Christians need to have a daily devotional time to learn biblical truth and to respond to the Lord in biblical worship, prayer, and fellowship. That is the best way to build a more intimate relationship to God, leading to spiritual growth and fruitfulness (John 15:1–8). Also, by following some suggestions in the preceding list you can put more variety and creativity into your devotions to make them fresh and exciting rather than stale and monotonous.[3]

What results can we expect from a daily devotional time? Our main motivation in having daily devotions should not be our personal gain but God's glory (1 Cor. 10:31). Love should motivate Christians to seek God for worship, prayer, and fellowship because of who He is and what He has done for them.

However, when we do seek intimacy with God and deepen our relationship with Him, He provides wonderful spiritual results for us. No human list can encompass all these results because in these focused times of intimacy with God we experience innumerable changes that will impact our lives throughout eternity. Only God can recount all that transpires as we commune in His presence. Here we will highlight seven beneficial results of successful devotional time with God.

- We become better acquainted with the Father, the Son, and the Spirit through Scripture and through communion with them. This experience goes beyond increased biblical knowledge about God and includes a more intimate relationship to the triune God.

- We love God more as we grow in awareness and appreciation of His love for us (1 John 4:19). And our love for God is really His love infusing our hearts and returning to Him (Rom. 5:5).

- We develop a closer fellowship with the triune God (1 John 1:3). Christians have been called into a position of fellowship with Christ (1 Cor. 1:9). Still, we are responsible to practice that fellowship and to develop an increasingly intimate fellowship with all three Persons of the Trinity (1 John 1:3, 5–7).

- We abide in Christ more. The life of abiding in Christ is a life cleansed from sin, obedient to Christ's commandments, and shared with Christ. These requirements of abiding in Christ are enhanced by an effective daily devotional time. And as we develop a stronger abiding relationship with Christ, we become more fruitful (John 15:5, 8), prayerful (15:7), and joyful (15:11).

- We develop godly virtues such as the fruit of the Spirit in Gal. 5:22–23 and the list of virtues in 2 Peter 1:5–7, "faith . . . moral excellence . . . knowledge . . . self-control . . . perseverance . . . godliness . . . brotherly kindness . . . love." And through daily devotions each of these virtues can continue to grow and profoundly influence our Christian life and service as 2 Peter 1:8 teaches: "For if these qualities are yours and are increasing, they render you neither useless nor unfruitful in the true knowledge of our Lord Jesus Christ."

- We can expect God to give us wisdom for decisions, help with problems, grace through trials, and peace in place of fears and worries. God's provision for us depends on a right relationship to Him (Matt. 6:33; 1 John 3:22), and a successful daily devotional time is the major way we can develop and improve our relationship to God.

- We become more like Christ. The greatest result and goal of our daily devotional time is to become more like Christ for God's glory. A daily devotional time is a primary way to fulfill God's command to "grow in the grace and knowledge of our Lord and Savior Jesus Christ" (2 Pet. 3:18). So our growth in Christlike maturity is the ultimate test of how effective our daily devotions are.

People can tell when a Christian consistently spends time with the

Lord. When we spend time in Christ's presence, we are "transformed" more into His character (2 Cor. 3:18), and other people can detect our Christlike character as if it were a fragrant aroma. Paul had a similar thought in mind when he wrote, "But thanks be to God, who always leads us in His triumph in Christ, and manifests through us the sweet aroma of the knowledge of Him in every place" (2:14).

Special Occasions for Spiritual Nurture

An ideal lifetime plan for sanctification will include special occasions to focus on Bible study, prayer, devotions, Christian fellowship, family life, church life, interpersonal ministry, or other topics relevant to Christian living, or a combination of these. And these special occasions may be scheduled weekly, monthly, quarterly, yearly, at some other interval, or as needed and in no regular pattern. Christians should continue their daily devotions during these special occasions.

Christian retreats, camps, conferences, and other meetings can give us an extra boost in our spiritual walk with the Lord. However, we should not depend totally or even mainly on such events for our spiritual growth. These special occasions for building up our lives can be like major tune-ups along the Christian journey, but they alone are not enough to sustain us spiritually. For instance, believers can attend a weekend Christian conference and enjoy good food, good fellowship, and fun along with spiritual enrichment. But then Sunday evening they return home and by the next day they have reentered their normal routine. When they face blue Monday they wonder where their spirituality and Christian joy have gone. The time away helped build their spiritual lives, but how effectively they practice Christian living when they are back in their routine schedule depends on the spirituality already built into their lives.

The New Testament emphasizes the *daily* character of Christian living such as praying for daily food (Matt. 6:11), taking up one's cross daily (Luke 9:23), searching the Scriptures daily (Acts 17:11), and having daily concern for other Christians and Christian ministries (2 Cor. 11:28). Therefore our lifetime plan for sanctification must be based primarily on daily practices to promote continual and substantial spiritual growth. The special times and events for spiritual enhancement can contribute greatly to our Christian life. But we must have a plan for daily spiritual nutrition and exercises and then practice that plan in order to achieve significant spiritual growth.

Interpersonal Relationships and Ministry with Other Believers

Sanctification is fundamentally a personal experience, but believers optimize their personal sanctification by helping each other grow in the body of Christ.

Daily Christian Service

Some may wonder how they can perform Christian service *daily*. Christian service can encompass everything that we do, because everything we do can be service to God and for His glory (1 Cor. 10:31).

Christians who have a lifetime plan for sanctification and who put that plan into practice will become better prepared for Christian. Likewise, daily Christian service is one way to express our sanctification and to keep our spiritual lives healthy, vigorous, and growing. Also the rigor of daily Christian service shows us our need for receiving more of God's enabling. And God's greater grace by which we serve is also the grace by which we grow more in Christ.

ADJUST YOUR LIFETIME PLAN FOR SANCTIFICATION

Christians should keep fine-tuning their lifetime plan so that they maximize their progress in sanctification. This requires that we make improvements in our lifetime plan for sanctification and adapt our plan to our personal changes.

Developing and practicing our lifetime plan for sanctification is a learning process that may show the need for changes in our plan, for example, switching to an updated translation of the Scriptures. Or we may add biblical meditation to other practices in our plan in order to boost our sanctification. We can continually improve our lifetime plan for sanctification by using God's Word to evaluate our plan and by learning significant lessons about sanctification from others Christians.

Change is another certainty about earthly life. Wise Christians accept change and adjust their plans to change, including their lifetime plan for sanctification. For example, the housewife who finds midmorning the best devotional time might switch to early morning once her children have left home. Likewise, a man who has an extremely busy schedule may have several special times with the Lord during the day, but after he retires he may find one longer daily devotional time more effective. As Christians move through the various ages and stages of development from adolescence to young adulthood and then to middle and older adulthood, they will need to adapt their lifetime plan of sanctification to their age and stage of life as well as to their other personal changes. However, we will always need such practices as reliance on the Holy Spirit, intake of God's Word, and prayer, though we may change how we do them.

PRACTICE YOUR LIFETIME PLAN FOR SANCTIFICATION

We can formulate a great lifetime plan for sanctification, but the best plan will not help us grow unless we practice that plan consistently and diligently. Like Paul, we should "press on toward the goal for the prize of the upward call of God in Christ Jesus" (Phil. 3:14). A football coach can have the best playbook and players in their league, but if the players do not execute the plays, they probably will not win many games. We can execute our lifetime plan for sanctification successfully if we are motivated by love for God, empowered by the Holy Spirit, guided by Scripture, and focused on Christlike maturity.

Practicing your plan can be adynamic, and creative experience if you use it to build your relationship to God. Nothing succeeds like success, and nothing can motivate you to grow more than the joy of knowing the Lord is conforming you to the image of His Son (Rom. 8:29; 2 Cor. 3:18).

And that is what sanctification is all about—making us more like Christ in every aspect of our lives! Don't let sanctification be a forgotten blessing.

 ENDNOTES

CHAPTER 1—LEARNING ABOUT SANCTIFICATION

1. "Even after regeneration . . . there is need for continuing progressive growth, which we usually call sanctification" (Millard Erickson, *Christian Theology* [Grand Rapids: Baker, 1985], 256).

2. For the meaning of the Old Testament verb for sanctify, see Thomas E. McComiskey, *"qādash,"* in *Theological Wordbook of the Old Testament,* ed. R. Laird Harris, Gleason L. Archer, Jr., and Bruce K. Waltke (Chicago: Moody, 1980), 2:786. The New Testament verb for sanctify *(hagiazō)* can specifically mean "to make holy, consecrate, sanctify," depending on the context (see Walter Bauer, William F. Arndt, and F. Wilbur Gingrich, *A Greek-English Lexicon of the New Testament and Other Early Christian Literature,* 2d ed., rev. F. Wilbur Gingrich and Frederick W. Danker [Chicago: University of Chicago Press, 1979], 8).

3. Likewise, to "sanctify," is equivalent to "declare holy" or "make holy," and "sanctification" is equivalent to "holiness."

4. The following examples show that Scripture applies

sanctification to animals, places, things, periods of time, and actions as well as to people. "Every firstborn" of men and male animals in Israel was sanctified (Num. 8:17; Deut. 15:19). Sanctification was also used of the seventh day (Gen. 2:3), Mount Sinai (Exod. 19:23), gifts for the Lord (28:38), parts of animal sacrifices (29:27), the altar of sacrifice (29:36), Israel's tabernacle and its furnishings (40:9), the temple (2 Chron. 36:14), the fiftieth or jubilee year (Lev. 25:10), a house (27:14), a field (27:17), the head of a Nazirite (Num. 6:11–12), ceremonial bread (1 Sam. 21:4, 6; Matt. 12:4), the fixed festivals of the Lord (Ezra 3:5), a gate (Neh. 3:1), heathen nations as God's instruments of judgment on other nations (Isa. 13:3, 5; Jer. 51:27–29), an appointed prophet (1:5), a fast (Joel 1:14), the gold of the temple (Matt. 23:17), and food "sanctified by means of the word of God and prayer" (1 Tim. 4:5).

5. Though the common Old Testament word for sanctify does not occur in Judges 17:5, 12 and in Ezekiel 14:7, the concept of sanctification is seen in the human action of separation from God and for idolatry.

6. Three other types of biblical sanctification appear less frequently than positional, progressive, and perfective sanctification.

First, "primary sanctification" means that the Spirit sets apart God's chosen persons for saving faith in Christ (2 Thess. 2:13; 1 Pet. 1:2). God performs His sovereign choice through primary sanctification and assures us that He will reap a harvest of saved people (John 4:25; Acts 18:9–10).

Second, "prebirth sanctification" means that God sets apart certain persons before their physical birth for special divine service. Paul is the clearest Christian example of prebirth sanctification (Gal. 1:15); Jeremiah and John the Baptist are other examples (Jer. 1:5; Luke 1:15).

Third, "privileged sanctification" means that certain unbelievers are set apart to special privileges through their particular relationships. Paul noted that an unbelieving spouse is sanctified by marriage to a believing spouse and that the children in such a mixed union are also sanctified (1 Cor. 7:12–16). Their sanctification is clearly not equivalent to their salvation, but they are privileged to live in a family with at least one saved person.

Hebrews 10:29 refers to a person who "has trampled underfoot the Son of God, and has regarded as unclean the blood of the covenant by which he was sanctified, and has insulted the Spirit of grace." Even though such a person is "sanctified" or "set apart" to the privilege of knowing about this covenant and its saving provision through the Spirit's ministry, his response shows that he is an unbeliever since he rejects rather than receives this provision of salvation. Other interpreters believe that Hebrews 10:29 refers to believers who do not confess sin in their lives and thus treat the blood of Christ as a light thing. In this view "sanctified" in verse 29 refers to positional sanctification.

7. God alone initiates and performs primary, positional, and perfective sanctification. He uses primary sanctification to bring people to saving faith in Christ, which immediately provides positional sanctification and ultimately provides perfective sanctification when Christ returns (Acts 16:18; 2 Thess. 2:13; 1 John 3:2).

8. According to Walvoord, "A new believer may be immature and quite ignorant of God and His truth but even so can have a measure of spirituality and can experience thef illing of the Spirit, as illustrated by the conversion of Cornelius (Acts 10) and the conversion of John's disciples (Acts 19)" (John F. Walvoord, "The Augustinian-Dispensational Perspective," in Melvin E. Dieter, ed., *Five Views of Sanctification,* [Grand Rapids: Zondervan, 1987], 215).

9. The term "spiritual" (Greek, *pneumatikos)* is applied to persons in four New Testament passages (1 Cor. 2:15; 3:1; 14:37; Gal. 6:1), and evidence from these passages leads to three significant conclusions. First, the "spiritual" Christian (1 Cor. 2:15) is sharply contrasted with the unsaved person. The latter is a "natural man" who "does not accept the things of the Spirit of God" (1 Cor. 2:14) because he is "devoid of the Spirit" (Jude 19).

Second, spiritual Christians are in a special class of believers described as "mature" (1 Cor. 2:6; 14:20; Phil. 3:15; Col. 1:28; Heb. 5:14; 6:1). For further development of this point, see Henry W. Holloman, "The Relation between Spirituality and Spiritual Maturity: Is the Spiritual Christian the Mature Christian?" (paper presented to the 44th

Evangelical Theological Society Meeting, San Francisco, 20 November 1992), 2-7.

Third, spiritual Christians are distinct from other believers who are called "infants in Christ" (1 Cor. 3:1; cf. Heb. 5:13), "fleshly" (1 Cor. 3:3 [twice]), and those who walk "like mere men" (3:3). See J. D. G. Dunn, "Spirit, Holy Spirit," In *New International Dictionary of New Testament Theology,* ed. Colin Brown (Grand Rapids: Zondervan, 1978), 3:707.

Christians will not attain *perfect* Christlike maturity in this earthly life. Yet they can grow enough through sanctification to become characterized as "spiritual" or "mature in Christ." Even the mature Christian can continue to grow (1 Cor. 2:15; Phil. 3:12-15; Col. 1:28; Heb. 5:12–6:2). The apostle Paul denied that he was perfect, but he was certainly mature and was aggressively pursuing further growth in Christ (Phil. 3:12–14). For the Wesleyan perspective on "sanctification" and "perfection" and for responses to this viewpoint, see Melvin E. Dieter, "The Wesleyan Perspective," in *Five Views of Sanctification,* 11–57.

10. Four basic steps can help us study and interpret the Bible correctly. First, observe the significant features of the biblical passage to determine its contextual meaning. Second, interpret the biblical passage based on observed cultural, grammatical, literary, and contextual evidence. Hermeneutics is the technical name for studying principles of correct interpretation. A readable and useful book on hermeneutics is Roy B. Zuck's *Basic Bible Interpretation* (Wheaton, Ill.: Victor, 1994). For practical help on personal Bible study, consult the work by Howard G. Hendricks and William D. Hendricks, *Living by the Book* (Chicago: Moody, 1991). Third, use the inductive method to discover biblical teaching. With this method we base our doctrinal conclusions on all relevant biblical evidence about a biblical topic or passage. This approach helps avoid wrong teaching based on biased or partial selection of biblical evidence. Fourth, apply biblical teaching to real life needs. Biblical teachings are God's solutions that we must match with human problems. In this final step of biblical study, you should ask, "What is the practical significance of this biblical truth in my relation to God, to myself, and to others in my family, my church life, and

society?" This step should take us from biblical information to personal action. Jesus emphasized this "action" step in John 13:17, "If you know these things, you are blessed if you do them."

The Holy Spirit has a crucial role in Bible study. Rely on the Spirit to teach you the spiritual content of Scripture (John 16:12-15; 1 John 2:20, 27), to apply Scripture (John 13:17; James 1:22–25), to empower you to obey biblical truth (Rom. 8:4, 13), and to enable you to communicate biblical truth effectively and boldly (Acts 4:31; 1 Thess. 1:5). For a fully developed study on the teaching ministry of the Spirit, see Roy B. Zuck, *Spirit-Filled Teaching: The Power of the Holy Spirit in Your Ministry,* Swindoll Leadership Library (Nashville: Word, 1998).

CHAPTER 2—REFLECTING GOD'S CHARACTER: GOD'S PURPOSE THROUGH SANCTIFICATION

1. Genesis 9:6 and James 3:9 refer simply to humanity's creation in the image and likeness of God. Yet these passages would have no real significance in their contexts unless humankind still bears the image of God in some sense. Also 1 Corinthians 11:7 refers to the image of God in man in the present tense.

2. James I. Packer, *Knowing God* (Downers Grove, Ill.: InterVarsity , 1993).

3. Ibid., 21–23

4. Ibid., 17.

5. Erickson, *Christian Theology,* 267.

6. For further enumeration and explanation of the attributes of God, see ibid., 263–300; Wayne Grudem, *Systematic Theology* (Grand Rapids: Zondervan, 1994), 156–225; and A. W. Tozer, *The Knowledge of the Holy* (San Fancisco: Harper & Row, 1961).

7. Tozer, *Knowledge of the Holy,* 2–3.

8. God's moral holiness is usually distinguished from His transcendent or majestic holiness which indicates His distinction as infinite Creator from His finite creation. "For thus says the high and exalted One Who lives forever, whose name is Holy, 'I dwell on a high and holy place'" (Isa. 57:15; see also Exod. 15:11; Ps. 113:5–6; Isa. 55:8–9; John 8:23).

9. Erickson, *Christian Theology,* 285.

10. Christians will be made perfect at Christ's return for He will transform them into the likeness of His glorified humanity (Phil. 3:20–21); 1 John 3:1–2). Glorified saints will have *perfect* holiness, love, righteousness, and so forth, but not *infinite* holiness, love, righteousness, and so forth, as the triune God does. Though we are finite human creatures, we will have perfect moral character as Christ does in His glorified human nature.

     For example, God's holiness is infinite and inherent whereas glorified Christians will have holiness that is perfect but still finite and derived. Scripture makes this same distinction between God's immortality which is inherent and unique (1 Tim. 6:10) and the immortality of glorified Christians and of good angels which is derived from God (1 Cor. 15:51-57; see also Luke 20:25–36).

11. When we talk about the work of God in our sanctification, do we mean the Godhead consisting of Father, Son, and Spirit as the triune God, or do we mean a particular person of the Trinity? In some cases biblical references to God do indicate the Godhead. For example, "God" in Philippians 2:13—"It is God who is at work in you, both to will and to work for His good pleasure"—probably refers to the triune Godhead, since Father, Son, and Spirit are all at work in sanctifying the believer.

     Biblical references to the Son, or to the Spirit, or to their other respective titles clearly indicate which person of the Trinity is meant. Even where "God" is used of the Son (John 1:1), or the Spirit (Acts 5:3–4), the respective context clarifies which person of the Trinity is meant. However, in some occurrences of the word "God" it is more difficult to determine whether the reference is to the full Godhead or to God the Father.

     In some cases the language indicates that God the Father is specifically referred to. In Romans 1:7 "God our Father" is distinguished from the "Lord Jesus Christ." In other contexts evidence indicates that God the Father is in view (for example, Rom. 1:8, "I thank my God through Jesus Christ").

12. J. I. Packer, *Rediscovering Holiness* (Ann Arbor, Mich.: Servant, 1992), 61.

13. Bauer, Arndt, and Gingrich, *A Greek-English Lexicon of the New Testament and Other Early Christian Literature,* 603 (italics theirs).
14. Ibid. (italics theirs).

CHAPTER 3—DISCOVERING THE NEW YOU IN CHRIST: UNITED WITH CHRIST IN SANCTIFICATION

1. Neil T. Anderson, *Victory over the Darkness* (Ventura, Calif.: Regal, 1990), 13.
2. Evidently the Father, the Son, and the Spirit each indwell the believer in a real and distinct sense (John 14:20, 23; 1 Cor. 6:19–20; 2 Cor. 13:5; Eph. 4:6; Col. 1:27). However, it is possible that the indwelling of the Father and the Son is only through the Holy Spirit rather than through a direct, distinctive indwelling, just as revelation from the Father and the Son is communicated to the believer by the Spirit (John 16:12–15; 1 Cor. 2:9–16). If so, then the full reality of their indwelling presence is maintained because the Spirit perfectly represents and reveals the Father and the Son.
3. Henry Clarence Thiessen, *Lectures in Systematic Theology,* rev. Vernon D. Doerksen (Grand Rapids: Eerdmans, 1979), 279.
4. A more technical feature of our union with Christ is its biblical designation as a "mystery." Believers are individually united with Christ and corporately united with Him to form His body (1 Cor. 12:12–13). This corporate union between Christ and His church (based on individual union) is called a "mystery" by Paul. "This mystery is great; but I am speaking with reference to Christ and the church" (Eph. 5:32). This spiritual union of believers with Christ goes beyond human comprehension and is mysterious to some extent because it involves union with Christ who is infinite deity as well as perfect man. However, "myster" (Greek, *mystērion*) in this passage and in certain other contexts does not emphasize the "mysterious" element. Rather, "mystery" here emphasizes that the truth of Christ's spiritual union with Jewish and Gentile believers to form the church body was not clearly revealed until Christ came to inaugurate the New Covenant and to establish the New Testament church (John 14:20; 16:12–15;

1 Cor. 12:13; Eph. 3:1–12; Col. 1:24–27). The truth of the spiritual union between Christ and His church is a mystery to spiritually immature believers because of their limitation in discerning spiritual truth in the Word (1 Cor. 3:1–3; Heb. 5:12–14). It is a mystery to unbelievers because they lack the Spirit to teach them the spiritual content of Scripture (1 Cor. 2:14; Jude 19). But mature believers can understand this mystery (1 Cor. 2:6–7).

5. Some of the Christian's spiritual blessings are associated with the technical expression "in Christ," as in Ephesians 1:3 and 2:6. Other spiritual blessings are based on the Christian's relationship to Christ, though the exact expression "in Christ" is not used (for example, Eph. 2:18, "*through* Him [Christ] we both have our access in one Spirit to the Father" [italics added]).

6. Packer, *Rediscovering Holiness,* 25.

7. Ibid.

8. Do we rely on God in general, the Father, Christ, or the Spirit for power? Basically we rely on the triune God. However a particular biblical context may emphasize reliance on one of the persons of the Trinity (see Matt. 22:29; Rom. 1:4; 15:13, 19). This does not exclude the other two persons since the persons of the Trinity work together in perfect harmony. In their functional roles, Scripture emphasizes the Father as the Source of power (that is, power *from* the Father; 1 Cor. 8:6), the Son as the Mediator or intermediate Agent of power (that is, power *through* the Son; Phil. 4:13), and the Spirit as the direct Agent of power (that is, power *by* the Spirit; Zech. 4:6; Rom. 8:13). So there are not three different powers of God, but three divine persons who share the same omnipotent nature and function in different ways to administer that power in relation to creation, especially to believers.

9. Lewis Sperry Chafer, *Systematic Theology,* ed. John F. Walvoord (Wheaton, Ill.: Victor, 1988), 2:135–48.

10. Neil T. Anderson and Robert L. Saucy, *The Common Made Holy* (Eugene, Oreg.: Harvest, 1997), 177–79.

11. John R. W. Stott, *Christ the Liberator* (Downers Gorve, Ill.: InterVarsity, 1971), 38.

CHAPTER 4—CONQUERING SIN AND THE FLESH THROUGH CHRIST'S VICTORY:
INTERNAL OPPOSITION TO SANCTIFICATION

1. People who die in unbelief must still face God's judgment as the consequence of their sin (John 3:36; Rom. 2:5–7; Rev. 20:11–15).
2. *Orange County Register,* 11 July 1998.
3. Inherent sin is the predisposition and tendency to sin that all people receive immediately through natural generation and ultimately from Adam (John 25:4; Ps. 51:5; Rom. 5:12–21). Inherent sin is sometimes called original sin.
4. E. K. Simpson and F. F. Bruce, *Commentary on the Epistles to the Ephesians and the Colossians,* New International Commentary on the New Testament (Grand Rapids: Eerdmans, 1957), 236.
5. In Romans 6:3–4 the verbs are passive (for example, v. 3, "have been baptized [*ebaptisthēmen*] into His death"), and so is the verb in Galatians 2:20, "have been crucified with [*synestaurōmai*] Christ." These and other references show that Christians are identified with Christ in His death, burial, and resurrection, not by what they do but by what God has already done for them when they trusted Christ (1 Cor. 12:12–13; Eph. 1:13–14).
6. Donald K. Campbell, "Galatians," in *The Bible Knowledge Commentary, New Testament,* ed. John F. Walvoord and Roy B. Zuck (Wheaton, Ill.: Victor, 1983), 609.
7. This conclusion is based on the perfect passive Greek verb *synestaurōmai* ("I have been crucified"), which indicates that we died through crucifixion in the past and the results of that crucifixion continue.
8. I believe that Romans 7:14–25 has in view the struggle of a true believer. The present tenses in these verses (in contrast to the imperfict and aorist tenses Paul had used) imply the present experience of a believer who tries to keep the Law and defeat the flesh by his own power. The Spirit is conspicuously absent from this passage compared to the verses surrounding it (see 7:6; 8:2–13).

   The statements, "I joyfully concur with the law of God in the inner man," (7:22), and "I myself with my mind am serving the law of God" (7:25), are characteristic of believers.

The attitude and conflict expressed in Romans 7:14_25 are in sharp contrast to the self-righteous attitude that Paul evidently maintained in his preconversion condition (see Phil. 3:4–7).

For further support of this view, see Anderson and Saucy, *The Common Made Holy*, 95–99; and C. E. B. Cranfield, *A Critical and Exegetical Commentary on the Epistle to the Romans*, International Critical Commentary (Edinburgh: Clark, 1975), 1:355–70, esp. 356.

CHAPTER 5—
OVERCOMING THE WORLD THROUGH CHRIST'S VICTORY: EXTERNAL OPPOSITION TO SANCTIFICATION

1. In addition to its ethical sense as the evil world system, the word *world* (Greek, *kosmos*) is used in two other ways in Scripture: the created earth or univers (for example, Matt. 13:35; Acts 17:24; Rom. 1:20) and the human race of manking (for example, Matt. 5:14; John 3:16–17).
   The occurrence of *world* in the most famous verse of Scripture, John 3:16 ("God so loved the world"), does not mean the evil world system but the world's people. God loves the people of the world; Christ died for them; and we are to love them, to do them good, and to evangelize them (Matt. 22:39; 28:19–20; Gal. 6:10).

2. Jesus taught the general principle that inner character determines outward communication and conduct, just as the root of a tree determines the fruit of a tree (Matt. 12:33–35; Mark 7:21–23). Jesus also recognized that people can "outwardly appear righteous to men" but inwardly be "full of hypocrisy and lawlessness" (Matt. 23:28). Because Christians retain the sinful flesh, they still manifest fleshly characteristics such as refraining from worldly actions externally while tolerating worldly thoughts and attitudes internally.

3. Lewis Sperry Chafer, *He That Is Spiritual* (1918; reprint, Grand Rapids: Zondervan, 1964), 61.

4. Anderson and Saucy, *The Common Made Holy*, 42.

5. This is a main theme in Viktor E. Frankl's book, *Man's Search for Meaning*, trans. Ilse Lasch, rev. ed (Boston: Beacon, 1962).

6. Perhaps the intermediate state should be considered stage one and a half.

7. W. Phillip Keller, "Otto C. Keller," in *Chosen Vessels*, ed. Charles Turner (Ann Arbor, Mich.: Servant, 1985), 106.

CHAPTER 6—GETTING TO KNOW THE DIVINE HELPER: THE SPIRIT'S ROLE IN SANCTIFICATION

1. The sovereign Spirit also executes certain ministries apart from human response. He convicts unbelievers (John 16:7–11), fills God's people for special tasks (Exod. 31:2–3; Acts 2:4; 8:29, 39; 2 Pet. 1:19–21), and distributes spiritual gifts to members of Christ's body (1 Cor. 12:4–11). Still Scripture indicates that certain ministries of the Spirit depend on the believer's response to Him (Gal. 5:16; Eph. 4:30; 5:18).

2. The Spirit has the characteristics of personality (Rom. 8:27; 1 Cor. 12:11; Eph. 4:30); the Spirit acts, communicates, and responds as a person (Ps. 104:30; John 15:26; 16:13–15; Rom. 8:16–17; 2 Cor. 13:14; Eph. 4:30); and the Spirit is considered a person by Christ and others (Matt. 28:19; Mark 3:29; John 14:16-17; Acts 5:3–4; Rom. 8:26–27; Eph. 6:18; Heb. 10:29).

   Scripture also teaches the deity of the Spirit. He is identified as God (Acts 5:3–4). He is associated with the Father and the Son as an equal, divine person (Matt. 28:19; John 14:16–17; 2 Cor. 13:14; 1 Pet. 1:2); He has the characteristics of God (Ps. 139:7; 1 Cor. 2:11; Heb. 9:14); and He does the works of God (Gen. 1:2; Ps. 104:30; John 3:5; Rom. 8:11; 2 Pet. 1:20–21).

3. The disciples definitely knew the Spirit when Christ stated, "But you know Him [the Spirit] because He abides with you, and will be in you" (John 14:17). They came to a deeper knowledge of the Spirit when Christ's promise that the Spirit would be in them was fulfilled at Pentecost (14:17; see Acts 1:5; 2:1–4).

4. In 2 Corinthians 13:14 (v. 13 in Greek) the phrase *hagiou pneumatos* ("of the Holy Spirit") may mean, "fellowship brought about by the Holy Spirit"; and the same is true of the Greek form *pneumatos* ("of the Spirit") in Philippians 2:1 (Bauer, Arndt, and Gingrich, *A Greek-English Lexicon of the New Testament and Other Early Christian Literature*, 439).

Even apart from these two references, the abundant New Testament evidence for a close relationship between the believer and the Spirit strongly implies fellowship between them, just as the believer has fellowship with the Father and with the Son (1 John 1:3).

5. Ibid., 438.

6. Paul's use of the present tense, "I am pressing on" (*diōkō*), in Philippians 3:12, 14 further emphasizes that his sanctification was still in progress.

7. As much as three to four years had elapsed between the conversion of the Corinthian believers and Paul's communication to them in 1 Corinthians. By this time Paul expected them to be "spiritual men" (that is, spiritually mature persons) instead of still "infants in Christ" (3:1) and "fleshly" Christians (3:3).

   Likewise, the Christians addressed in the Book of Hebrews probably already had several years to progress from being taught the Word to being teachers of the Word, from needing the milk of the Word to needing the solid food of the Word, and from spiritual infancy to spiritual maturity (Heb. 5:12–16). In spite of having had sufficient "time" to attain spiritual maturity (5:12), they were still spiritual infants (5:12–6:1).

8. Dallas Willard, *The Spirit of the Disciplines* (San Francisco: Harper & Row, 1988), 70.

9. Even after Christians have initially dedicated themselves to God (Rom. 12:1–2), their dedication can become more intense and extend to more areas of their lives through increased spiritual knowledge and growth (2 Cor. 8:7; 10:5; Phil. 3:10–14; 2 Pet. 3:18).

10. This viewpoint is examined and rejected by H. A. Ironside in his book, *Holiness: The False and the True* (New York: Loizeaux Brothers, 1955).

11. The goal of perfect Christlikeness for Christian sanctification is developed in chapter 8, "Aiming for Christlikeness."

12. See Charles Hodge, *An Exposition of the Second Epistle to the Corinthians* (reprint, London: Banner of Truth Trust, 1959), 77, for his explanation that the believer's vision in 2 Corinthians 3:18 is "that manifestation of his [the Lord's] glory which is made in his Word and by His Spirit, whose office it is to glorify Christ by revealing him to us."

13. Helpful discussion about the Spirit's working through inner promptings is presented in Packer's *Rediscovering Holiness,* 1036; and in Charles R. Swindoll's chapter 7, "Those Unidentified Inner Promptings," of his *Flying Closer to the Flame* (Dallas: Word, 1993), 129–50.

CHAPTER 7—RESPONDING BIBLICALLY TO THE SPIRIT: THE SPIRIT'S ROLE IN SANCTIFICATION (CONTINUED)

1. Swindoll, *Flying Closer to the Flame,* 151–74.
2. Chafer, *He That Is Spiritual,* 86.
3. Friedrich Lang, in *Theological Dictionary of the New Testament,* ed. Gerhard Friedrich and Gerhard Kittel, trans. Geoffrey W. Bromiley (Grand Rapids: Eerdmans), 1971, 7:165–68.
4. C. F. Hogg and W. E. Vine, *The Epistles to the Thessalonians,* rev. ed. (1914; reprint, Grand Rapids: Kregel, 1959), 194.
5. The Greek verb *plērousthe* is a present-passive form from *plēroō.*
6. Walvoord also believes that filling with the Spirit means "control of a believer's life by the Holy Spirit" (Walvoord, "The Augustinian-Dispensational Perspective," 215).
7. Forms of the Greek verb *pimplēmi* ("to fill") are used with the Spirit in Luke 1:15, 41, 67; Acts 2:4; 4:8, 31; 9:17; 13:9; and with other things in Luke 4:28–29; 6:11; Acts 5:17–18; 13:45. Forms of the Greek verb *plēroō* ("to fill") are used with the Spirit in Acts 13:52; Ephesians 5:18.
8. Forms of the Greek adjective *plērēs* are used with the Spirit in Luke 4:1; Acts 6:3; 5; 7:55; 11:24; and with other things in Acts 13:10; 19:28.
9. Walvoord, "The Augstinian-Dispensational Perspective," 216.
10. Bauer, Arndt,, and Gingrich, *A Greek-English Lexicon of the New Testament and Other Early Christian Literature,* 633.
11. See also John 14:15, 21, 23; 15:1–11; 21:15–17; Romans 8:37; Galatians 6:14; Ephesians 3:17; Philippians 1:20–21; 3:10–14; Colossians 1:18; 2:9–10; 3:4; Titus 2:13–14; Hebrews 12:2; 1 Peter 2:21.
12. "Speaking to one another in psalms and hymns and spiritual songs, singing and making melody with your heart to the Lord; always giving

thanks for all things in the name of our Lord Jesus Christ to God, even the Father" (Eph. 5:19–20).

"Let the word of Christ richly dwell within you, with all wisdom teaching and admonishing one another with psalms and hymns and spiritual songs, singing with thankfulness in your hearts to God. Whatever you do in word or deed, do all in the name of the Lord Jesus, giving thanks through Him to God the Father" (Col. 3:16–17).

13. The normal Christian life is the Spirit-filled life, which accords with God's command to be filled with the Spirit (Eph. 5:18). However, at certain stages or points in the Christian life, believers may be so immature or fleshly or both that they are not living under the control of the Spirit (1 Cor. 3:1–3; Heb. 5:12–6:1). They may be "walking like mere men" and in a "fleshly" manner (1 Cor. 3:3) instead of walking under the Spirit's control (Gal. 5:16). Christians disobey biblical commandments when they are not Spirit-filled, walking under the Spirit's control, and growing in Christ.

Every Christian is Spirit-filled or Spirit controlled to some extent, but for some Christians the Spirit's control of their lives is not sufficient for them to be characterized as "Spirit filled." Even Christians characterized as "Spirit-filled" can become more Spirit-filled. This does not mean that they can get more of the Spirit but that the Spirit gets more control of them.

No Christian perfectly obeys Scripture, and the more we obey Scripture the more the Spirit fills or controls us. Paul was certainly a Spirit-filled Christian, yet he obediently progressed in sanctification toward perfect Christlikeness (Phil. 3:10–14). The more Paul progressed in obedience, the more Spirit-filled he became. And all Christians can and should do likewise.

14. Walvoord, "The Augustinian-Dispensational Perspective," 215.

CHAPTER 8—
AIMING FOR CHRISTLIKENESS:
GOD'S GOAL FOR SANCTIFICATION

1. J. Oswald Sanders discusses the difference between unworthy and worthy ambition for Christians in *Spiritual Leadership*, rev. ed. (Chicago: Moody, 1989), 17–21.

2. T. K. Abbott, *Epistles to the Ephesians and to the Colossians*, International Critical Commentary (Edinburgh: Clark, 1897), 124.

3. Harold W. Hoehner, "Ephesians," in *The Bible Knowledge Commentary, New Testament*, 635.

4. For an excellent development of this theme, see Michael J. Wilkins, *Following the Master: Discipleship in the Steps of Jesus* (Grand Rapids: Zondervan, 1992).

5. Packer, *Knowing God*, 108.

6. Larry Crabb emphasizes that God changes Christians from the inside out, and he mentions three means by which believers can examine their inner selves. "When we're serious about taking an inside look, God provides three sources of light: 1. the Spirit of God, 2. the Word of God, 3. the people of God. Each resource can be used to replace the blindness of self-deceit with the clear vision of integrity" (Larry Crabb, *Inside Out* [Colorado Springs: NavPress, 1988] 156).

   Some may wonder why discipleship and tactics for victory in spiritual warfare are not included as means of spiritual transofrmation.

   "In its broadest sense discipleship is the metaphor most descriptive of the doctrine of 'progressive sanctification'" (Wilkins, *Following the Master*, 343). Discipleship and sanctification both emphasize progress through proper response to God's Word, and both have Christlikeness as their goal.

   Spiritual warfare emphasizes the opposition of the devil and his demons to the spiritual life, growth, and service of christians. Thus spiritual warfare is not primarily a means to sanctification but an activity that accompanies sanctification. The general means for victory in spiritual warfare overlap the general means for sanctification, and therefore spiritual victory and progress in sanctification enhance each other. Even the more specific means for victory in spiritual warfare (Eph. 6:10–17; 2 Cor. 10:3–5) also promote sanctification. Winning in spiritual warfare is so crucial to sanctification that we devote a whole chapter to it (chapter 14).

7. For practical help in how to reflect Christ's likeness in modern living, see Michael J. Wilkins, *In His Image: Reflecting Christ in Everyday Life* (Colorado Springs: NavPress, 1997).

8. These nine virtues do not include all the moral characteristics of Christ (for example, holiness; see Heb. 7:26), but through the Spirit, Christians can produce any other Christlike virtues (see Isa. 11:1–5, esp. v. 2; John 16:14) as well as the nine virtues called "the fruit of the Spirit."

9. Christ showed in three ways that He did not compromise in His personal life with the sinners' sin or sinful lifestyle: (a) by His own moral separation from all sin because He was "holy, innocent, undefiled, separated from sinners and exalted above the heavens" (Heb. 7:26; see John 8:29), (b) by His forgiveness of the sins of repentant sinners, which showed that their sins were offensive to Him as the Son of God and that their sins needed divine forgiveness (Luke 7:47–50), and (c) by His warning to sinners whom He forgave that they should not continue in sin (John 5:14; 8:11, 34).

10. All true Christians have done the Father's initial will for them by trusting Christ as their personal Savior (John 6:28–29; 1 John 3:23). Also, doing the Father's will is a general characteristic of the overall life of believers (Matt. 7:23–23; 1 John 2:17). However, Christians are still urged to offer themselves to God so that they can more fully experience His will as "good and acceptable and perfect" (Rom. 12:1–2).

11. Christ's determination to accomplish God's purpose is seen in the messianic prophecy of Isaiah 50:7, "Therefore, I have set My face like flint, and I know that I will not be ashamed," and also in the statement of Luke 9:51, "When the days were approaching for His ascension, He resolutely set His face to go to Jerusalem."

12. Edwin A. Blum, "1 Peter," in *The Expositor's Bible Commentary* (Grand Rapids: Zondervan, 1981), 12:251.

13. For practical instruction on how Christ made disciples and how Christians can follow His model as a disciple-maker, see Bill Hull, *Jesus Christ, Disciple Maker* (Colorado Springs: NavPress, 1984).

CHAPTER 9—GROWING IN GRACE:
GOD'S SUFFICIENCY FOR SANCTIFICATION

1. Several popular books on divine grace have appeared in recent years, and three of the better-known ones are Max Lucado, *In The Grip of Grace* (Dallas: Word, 1996); Charles R. Swindoll, *The Grace Awakening* (Dallas: Word, 1990); and Philip Yancey, *What's So Amazing About Grace?* (Grand Rapids: Zondervan, 1997). Others published in earlier years include Lewis Sperry Chafer, *Grace* (1922; reprint, Grand Rapids: Dunham, 1967), and Charles C. Ryrie, *The Grace of God* (Chicago: Moody, 1963).

2. The words *grace* or *favor* in the Old Testament are most frequently translated from forms of the Hebrew word *ḥēn*, and the words *grace* or *favor* in the New Testament are most frequently translated from forms of the Greek word *charis*.

3. W. E. Vine, *Vine's Expository Dictionary of Old and New Testament Words* (Old Tappan, N. J.: Revell, 1981), 170.

4. The *charismata* ("grace-gifts"; 1 Cor. 12:4, 9, 30–31) are functionally the same as the *pneumatika* ("spiritual gifts"; 12:1; 14:1, 12). The latter Greek word emphasizes that these gifts are spiritual in nature and are related to the Spirit in origin, function, and purpose (12:4, 7–9, 11; 14:1, 12).

5. A more detailed discussion of the believer's relationship to God's law is provided by Anderson and Saucy, *The Common Made Holy,* 235–55.

6. Richard Henry Dara, *Two Years before the Mast* (Pleasantville, N.Y.: Reader's Digest, 1995).

7. This is an actual case but with the woman's real name changed to protect her identity.

CHAPTER 10—LIVING BY THE WORD:
SCRIPTURE'S ROLE IN SANCTIFICATION

1. Mortimer J. Adler and Charles van Doren, *How to Read a Book,* rev. ed. (New York: Simon & Schuster, 1972).

2. Howard G. Hendricks and William Hendricks, *Living by the Book* (Chicago: Moody, 1991).

3. Committee translations are produced by a council of scholars who consult with each other and review each other's work. These translations are usually superior to those produced by a single translator.

4. One program is "The Topical Memory System," available from The Navigators, P. O. Box 6000, Colorado Springs, Co 80934.

5. For example, Matthew 7:24; 28:19–20; Luke 11:28; John 13:17; 14:15, 21, 23; Romans 6:17; James 1:22; Revelation 1:3.

6. "These things" in John 13:17 refer to Christ's teachings in the preceding verses (13:1–16), especially His teaching about humble service exemplified when He washed the disciples' feet (13:14–15). Biblical evidence warrants the application of 13:17 to all Scripture (see Matt. 4:4; 2 Tim. 3:16–17), and therefore God's blessing accompanies all biblical teaching that Christians know and do.

7. This Greek grammatical form is called a first-class condition (H. E. Dana and Julius R. Mantey, *A Manual Grammar of the Greek New Testament* [New York: Macmillan, 1955], 289). People can coincidentally follow Christian truth without knowing it. But believers can never be certain that they are practicing Christian truth unless they do know it.

8. Matthew 5:29–30 does not teach that rejection of sin in itself can keep a person out of hell. However, all who receive an inward change of heart or regeneration through faith in the Lord will escape hell (John 1:12-13; 3:18; 5:24). Regenerate people have a built-in repulsion toward both inward sin such as lust and outward sin such as adultery (Matt. 5:28; 2 Cor. 5:17; 1 John 3:9). Therefore one must be regenerate and rely on the Spirit in order to follow Jesus' teaching in dealing with sin (Matt. 5:29–30; Rom. 8:13; 1 John 3:9).

9. The two actions commanded in James 1:21, "Therefore putting aside all filthiness and all that remains of wickedness, in humility receive the word implanted, which is able to save your souls," are similar to 1 Peter 2:1–2, "Therefore, putting aside all malice and all guile and hypocrisy and envy and all slander, like newborn babes, long for the pure milk of the word, that by it you may grow in respect to salvation." The negative command to reject sin is in 2:1, and the positive command to receive the Word, just as physical babes receive literal milk, is in 2:2.

CHAPTER 11—TRAINING FOR GODLINESS:
DISCIPLESHIP AND DISCIPLINES FOR SANCTIFICATION

1. The Greek verb *diōkō* ("press on") in Philippians 3:14 ("I press on toward the goal for the prize of the upward call of God in Christ Jesus") is the same basic Greek verb *diōkete* ("pursue") that occurs in Hebrews 12:14 ("Pursue peace with all men, and the sanctification without which no one will see the Lord"). The use of this verb in these two verses reinforces the idea that pressing on toward the goal of Christlikeness and pursuing sanctification are the same process.

2. Some believe that the church should not use Jesus' discipleship process in training believers because the church is a community of equality between brothers and sisters, and this contrasts with discipleship in which a master leads followers as Jesus did while on earth (for example, Lawrence O. Richards, *A Practical Theology of Spirituality* [Grand Rapids: Zondervan, 1987] 228–29). For the opposite view that Jesus' discipleship process does have relevance for the church, see Wilkins, *Following the Master,* 278–80, 308–10. Based on the evidence Wilkins presents, we believe that the practice of discipleship applies to the church.

3. Richard D. Calenberg, "The New Testament Doctrine of Discipleship" (Th.D. diss., Grace Theological Seminary, 1981), 245–46.

4. Wilkins, *Following the Master,* 40.

5. Merrill C. Tenney, "Luke," in *The Wycliffe Bible Commentary,* ed. Charles F. Pfeiffer and Everett F. Harrison (Chicago: Moody, 1962), 1044.

6. For an excellent detailed study of fruit in the Christian life, see James E. Rosscup, *Abiding in Christ* (Grand Rapids: Zondervan, 1973), 78–90.

7. In Hebrew thought a lesser love for someone might be represented as hate, and this principle is seen in Genesis 29:30–33. A literal translation of 29:31 is, "Now the LORD saw that Leah was hated." However, 29:30 indicates that Jacob "loved Rachel more than Leah."

8. This principle pervades Willard's book, *The Spirit of the Disciplines.*

9. Suggested books are Richard Foster, *Celebration of Discipline* (New York: Harper & Row, 1978); Donald S. Whitney, *Spiritual Disciplines for the Christian Life* (Colorado Springs: NavPress, 1991); and Willard, *The Spirit of the Disciplines.*

10. For example, Willard includes and discusses disciplines of abstinence (solitude, silence, fasting, frugality, chastity, secrecy, sacrifice) and disciplines of engagement (study, worship, celebration, service, prayer, fellowship, confession, submission) (Willard, *The Spirit of the Disciplines,* 158).

11. Here we are not entering the debate about whether fasting in itself has value for one's physical health. However, medical experts suggest that anyone considering the practice of fasting should first have a physical examination to be sure that fasting will not harm his or her physical health.

12. Maxine Hancock, *Living on Less and Enjoying It More* (Chicago: Moody, 1976), and Richard J. Foster, *Freedom of Simplicity* (San Francisco: Harper, 1981).

CHAPTER 12—COMMUNICATING WITH GOD: HOW PRAYER PROMOTES SANCTIFICATION

1. Hoehner, "Ephesians," 644.

2. The model prayer Jesus taught His disciples (Matt. 6:5–13; Luke 11:2–4) was addressed to them and was not altogether applicable to Him: "When *you* pray . . ." (Luke 11:2, italics added). He prayed as a sinless person and they prayed as imperfect humans. So the request "forgive us our debts [that is, sins]" (Matt. 6:12) was applicable to them but not to Him.

3. Stott, *Christ the Liberator,* 57.

4. For a helpful treatment of several of Paul's prayers, see D. A. Carson, *A Call to Spiritual Reformation: Priorities from Paul and His Prayers* (Grand Rapids: Baker, 1992). Also see A. W. Pink, *Gleanings from Paul* (Chicago: Moody, 1967).

5. W. Bingham Hunter, *The God Who Hears* (Downers Grove, Ill.: InterVarsity, 1986), 138–40.

CHAPTER 13—HANDLING OUR CIRCUMSTANCES: HOW GOD'S PROVIDENCE WORKS IN SANCTIFICATION

1. For an excellent treatment of the Christian's proper response to poverty and riches, see Willard, *The Spirit of the Disciplines,* 193–219.
2. *The World Book Dictionary,* 1972 ed., s. v. "adversity."
3. Larry Crabb, *Inside Out* (Colorado Springs: Colo.: NavPress, 1988), 13.
4. Ibid., 14.
5. Les L. Steele, *On the Way: A Practical Theology of Christian Formation* (Grand Rapids: Baker, 1990), 27.
6. Willard, *The Spirit of the Disciplines,* 2.
7. *The World Book Dictionary,* s.v. "adversity."

CHAPTER 14—WINNING IN SPIRITUAL WARFARE: SATAN'S OPPOSITION TO SANCTIFICATION

1. For two standard biblical studies on Satan and demons as well as good angels, see C. Fred Dickason, *Angels: Elect and Evil,* rev. ed. (Chicago: Moody, 1995); and Robert P. Lightner, *Angels, Satan, and Demons: Invisible Beings That Inhabit the Spiritual World,* Swindoll Leadership Library (Nashville: Word, 1998).
2. Three other major judgments will be executed against Satan: (1) He will be cast down from heaven and onto the earth at the middle of the seven-year Tribulation (Rev. 12:7–9, 13). (2) He will be imprisoned in the bottomless pit at the beginning of the Millennium (20:1-3). (3) After his release and rebellion at the end of the Millennium, he will be cast into the lake of fire, where he will be tormented forever (20:7–10).
3. "Do not lead us into temptation" (Matt. 6:13) may be understood as a petition that God will not allow any temptation beyond one's ability to endure it. This petition takes the form of a promise from God in 1 Corinthians 10:13.

CHAPTER 15—HELPING OTHER CHRISTIANS GROW:
INTERPERSONAL MINISTRY FOR SANCTIFICATION

1. Steele, *On the Way: A Practical Theology of Christian Formation,* 112.

2. Daniel Jenkins, *Christian Maturity and Christian Success* (Philadelphia: Fortress, 1982), 4.

3. Richards, *A Practical Theology of Spirituality,* 28–29.

4. Ibid., 85.

5. Ibid., 88–89.

6. Sharon Parks, "Love Tenderly," in Sharon Parks, Walter Brueggemann, and Thomas Groome, *To Act Justly, Love Tenderly, Walk Humbly* (Mahwah, N.J.: Paulist, 1986), 33.

7. For detailed information on mentoring and discipleship training, see J. Robert Clinton and Richard W. Clinton, *The Mentor Handbook* (Altadena, Calif.: Barnabas, 1991).

8. The Greek word for "fellowship" (*koinōnia*) also means "association, communion, . . . close relationship" (Bauer, Arndt, and Gingrich, *A Greek-English Lexicon of the New Testament and Other Early Christian Literature,* 438). In some passages (for example, 1 Cor. 10:16; 2 Cor. 8:4) the word *koinōnia* means "participation" (ibid., 439). In extrabiblical literature *koinōnia* is "a favorite expression for the marital relationship as the most intimate between human beings" (ibid., 438). Thus biblical "fellowship" may also indicate the intimate relationship of believers to their God and to other believers.

9. Gene A. Getz, *Building Up One Another* (Wheaton, Ill.: Victor, 1973), 4.

10. Ibid., 5.

11. Ibid., 6.

12. Ibid., 5.

13. Ibid., 3. Getz explains and applies these twelve "one another" exhortations in his book, *Building Up One Another.*

14. The command, "bear one another's burdens (Greek, *barē*], and thus fulfill the law of Christ" (Gal. 6:2), shows that we can share certain burdens with others and also bear certain burdens for others. Galatians 6:5; "For each one shall bear his own load [Greek, *phortion*]," teaches

that each believer has certain responsibilities that cannot be transferred to others. Thus God expects us to distinguish between burdens
transferable to and from others, such as prayer requests (1 Thess. 5:25;
James 5:16), and untransferable responsibilities, such as love for God
and our neighbor (Matt. 22:37–40) and personal giving (2 Cor. 9:7).

15. One way we can "bear one another's burdens" is through intercessory
    prayer, and we should "put feet to our prayers" so that our prayers are
    accompanied by appropriate action. In chapter 12, "Communicating
    with God," we discussed how we can help other believers grow through
    intercessory praying.

16. For a biblical and practical guide to the spiritual gifts, see William J.
    McRae, *The Dynamics of Spiritual Gifts* (Grand Rapids: Zondervan,
    1976).

17. Steele, *On the Way: A Practical Theology of Christian Formation,* 113.

18. Andrew T. Lincoln, *Ephesians,* Word Biblical Commentary (Dallas:
    Word, 1990), 261.

19. Willard, *The Spirit of the Disciplines,* viii.

CHAPTER 16—MAXIMIZING SPIRITUAL GROWTH: A LIFETIME PLAN FOR SANCTIFICATION

1. Clinton and Clinton, *The Mentor Handbook,* 17–18.

2. The NASB, NIV, NKJV, and NLT all agree on the translation "meditate," for
   this difficult word.

3. For creative ways to keep your daily devotions vital and interesting,
   see Pam Farrel, "Twenty Ways to Wak Up Your Quiet Time," *Discipleship Journal* 18 (January–February 1998): 33–35. See also Paul Cedar,
   A Life of Prayer: Cultivating the Inner Life of the Christian Leader,
   Swindoll Leadership Library (Nashville: Word, 1998).

BIBLIOGRAPHY

Alexander, Donald L., ed. *Christian Spirituality: Five Views of Sanctification.* Downers Grove, Ill.: InterVarsity Press, 1988.

Anders, Max. *Thirty Days to Understanding the Christian Life.* Brentwood, Tenn.: Wolgemuth and Hyatt Publishers, 1990.

Anderson, Neil T., and Robert L. Saucy. *The Common Made Holy.* Eugene, Oreg.: Harvest House Publishers, 1997.

Bailey, Mark. *To Follow Him: The Seven Marks of a Disciple.* Sisters, Oreg.: Multnomah Press, 1997.

Boa, Kenneth. *That I May Know God: Pathways to Spiritual Formation.* Sisters, Oreg.: Multnomah Publishers, 1998.

Bonar, Horatius. *God's Way of Holiness.* Chicago: Moody Press, n.d.

Bridges, Jerry. *The Pursuit of Holiness.* Colorado Springs: NavPress, 1978.

Bruce, A. B. *The Training of the Twelve.* 5th ed. Grand Rapids: Zondervan Publishing House, 1963.

Calvin, John. *Golden Booklet of the True Christian Life.* Grand Rapids: Baker Book House, 1952.

Cedar, Paul. *A Life of Prayer: Cultivating the Inner Life of the*

Christian Leader. Swindoll Leadership Library. Nashville: Word Publishing, 1998.

Chafer, Lewis Sperry. *He That Is Spiritual* 1918. Reprint, Grand Rapids: Zondervan Publishing House, 1967.

Crabb Larry. *Inside Out.* Colorado Springs: NavPress, 1988.

Deison, Peter V. *The Priority of Knowing God.* Grand Rapids: Discovery House Publishers, 1990.

Dieter, Melvin E., ed. *Five Views of Sanctification.* Grand Rapids: Zondervan, 1987.

Downs, Perry G. *Teaching for Spiritual Growth.* Grand Rapids: Zondervan Publishing House, 1994.

Foster, Richard. *Celebration of Discipline.* New York: Harper & Row, 1978.

_____. *Freedom of Simplicity.* New York: Harper & Row, 1981.

Gangel, Kenneth O., and James C. Wilhoit, eds. *The Christian Educator's Handbook on Spiritual Formation.* Wheaton, Ill.: Victor Books, 1994.

Hughes, R. Kent. *Disciplines of a Godly Man.* Wheaton, Ill.: Crossway Books, 1991.

Ironside, H. A. *Holiness: The False and the True.* New York: Loizeaux Brothers, 1955.

Law, William. *A Serious Call to a Devout and Holy Life.* Edited and abridged by John W. meister et al. Philadelphia: Westminster Press, 1955.

Mayhue, Richard. *Spiritual Intimacy.* Wheaton, Ill.: Victor Books, 1993.

Packer, James I. *Rediscovering Holiness.* Ann Arbor, Mich.: Servant Publications, 1992.

_____. *Knowing God.* Downers Grove, Ill.: InterVarsity Press, 1993.

Pentecost, J. Dwight. *Pattern for Maturity.* Chicato: Moody Press, 1966.

Richards, Lawrence O. *A Practical Theology of Spirituality.* Grand Rapids: Zondervan Publishing House, 1987.

Ryrie, Charles C. *Balancing the Christian Life.* Chicago: Moody Press, 1969.

Sanders, J. Oswald. *Spiritual Leadership.* Rev. ed. Chicago: Moody Press, 1989.

Schaeffer, Francis A. *True Spirituality.* Wheaton, Ill.: Tyndale House Publishers, 1971.

Stanley, Charles. *The Wonderful Spirit-Filled Life*. Nashville: Thomas Nelson Publishers, 1995.

Steele, Les. L. *On the Way: A Practical Theology of Christian Formation*. Grand Rapids: Baker Book House, 1990.

Swindoll, Charles R. *The Grace Awakening*. Dallas: Word Publishing, 1990.

_____. *Flying Closer to the Flame*. Dallas: Word Publishing, 1993.

Tozer, A. W. *The Knowledge of the Holy*. San Francisco: Harper & Row, 1969.

Tryon, Howard A., Jr. *Praying for You: A Workbook for Reaching Others through Prayer*. Grand Rapids: Kregel Publications, 1996.

Wiersbe, Warren W. *Being a Child of God*. Nashville: Thomas Nelson Publishers, 1996.

Whitney, Donald S. *Spiritual Disciplines for the Christian Life*. Colorado Springs: NavPress, 1991.

Wilkins, Micahel, J. *Following the Master: Discipleship in the Steps of Jesus*. Grand Rapids: Zondervan Publishing House, 1992.

Willard, Dallas. *The Spirit of the Disciplines*. San Francisco: Harper & Row, 1988.

Zuck, Roy B. *Spirit-Filled Teaching: The Power of the Holy Spirit in Your Ministry*. Swindoll Leadership Library. Nashville: Word Publishing, 1998.

_____, ed. *Vital Christian Living Issues: Examining Crucial Concerns in the Spiritual Life*. Grand Rapids: Kregel Publications, 1997.

SCRIPTURE INDEX

❧ SUBJECT INDEX